REDRESSING THE EMPEROR

**Recent Titles in
Contemporary Psychology**

REDRESSING THE EMPEROR

Improving Our Children's Public Mental Health System

John S. Lyons

Contemporary Psychology
Chris E. Stout, Series Editor

Westport, Connecticut
London

Library of Congress Cataloging-in-Publication Data

Lyons, John (John S.)
   Redressing the emperor : improving our children's public mental health
system / John S. Lyons.
      p. cm. — (Contemporary psychology, ISSN 1546–668X)
   Includes bibliographical references.
   ISBN 0–275–98143–6 (alk. paper)
   1. Child mental health. 2. Child mental health services. 3.
Children—Mental health. 4. Public health. I. Title. II. Contemporary
psychology (Praeger Publishers)
RJ111.L96 2004
362.2'083'0973—dc22   2004000481

British Library Cataloguing in Publication Data is available.

Library of Congress Catalog Card Number: 2004000481
ISBN: 0–275–98143–6
ISSN: 1546–668X

First published in 2004

Praeger Publishers, 88 Post Road West, Westport, CT 06881
An imprint of Greenwood Publishing Group, Inc.
www.praeger.com

Printed in the United States of America

The paper used in this book complies with the
Permanent Paper Standard issued by the National
Information Standards Organization (Z39.48–1984).

10   9   8   7   6   5   4   3   2   1

To Melanie
My inspiration and my anchor

CONTENTS

FOREWORD

In one of my past professional lives, I worked as a psychiatric technician for an inpatient psychiatric children's unit, on my way to becoming a clinical psychologist with a specialty in children and families. I have also worked as a child psychologist (and later as executive clinical director) in a therapeutic day school where metal detectors and confiscated weapons were the norm. I have worked in public systems for youth as well as private practice, managed-care settings. Thus, I have been spit on, cursed at, lied to—you name it. I have conducted and published a moderate amount of research on the diagnosis and treatment of differing disorders in children. Thus, with a modicum of clinical, scientific, and administrative experiences in public, educational, and private settings, it was with a great deal of anticipation that I read the early draft of this work.

I can tell you, I was not disappointed.

Although it may be easy for some critics to take potshots at the magnificently flawed, faltering, and fragmented approaches to providing care for children in need, John Lyons avoids the easy temptation of joining in with the howls of dinosaurs, and instead delivers an inspired vision supported with pragmatic solutions and principles—but without now familiar bromides.

Lyons devotes much of this work to providing the reader with the concepts for understanding the historic nature of the current circumstances. In addition, half of this work pragmatically offers a tool-supported vision for the next phase of development that wisely includes prevention and community development (inclusive of all aspects), and he offers up this ratchet of progress in what he terms Total Clinical Outcomes Management. This informed approach is not some new nostrum, but I believe it can serve as a galvanizing totem of real inspiration. His approach provides readers with a unique, but genuine, alchemy of ideas and method.

His frank examination of national trends and circumstances provides a cohesive and coherent contextual understanding in the context of a rich and enlightening texture, without being a tedious read. He does not avoid the additionally complicating factors of racial disparities, cultural competency, or stigma. Limitations of model generalizations and naive expectations of transportability or magical scalability are called into question. Disappointing, formerly touted magic bullets are exposed to the light of day as duds. Peppered throughout the book are real experiences and situations, with wise examination and critique highlighting the exquisite frustrations involved in working with systems intended to help but that instead, may iatrogenically do more harm.

His edgy and refreshing writing style engenders a true engagement and intimacy among the reader, the author, and the content. Good historic context is established to ground the reader's understanding of the calamity of the contemporary issues we now face, as well as the anemic promise of Evidence-Based Practices (EBPs) in children's mental health service research.

Again, I am not surprised, as I have long known and episodically collaborated with John Lyons, and have always found his work to serve as a lightening rod of systemic change. To paraphrase Walker Percy, I see John as being northwestern smart and southern shrewd. Just read his wonderfully fun and heuristic characterizations of syndromes as examples attesting to this point.

Beneath the author's tousled, low-key approach is a boiling drive to take on the lumpen pip-squeaks, the zealots, the copycats, and the walk-ins. Lyons is a Roman candle of child welfare enthusiasm, unafraid to push back on the gravitational center of popular opinion or currently touted therapy du jour. His approach is to latch onto that occasional shivering truth that flies centrifugally out of its insular, centripetal whirl, and build on contemporary realities with science and psychological horsepower so that ignorance and the sacred cows fall in a hail of pedantry.

It is rare indeed to read in one book of Nobel laureates in economics, Kuhn, child welfare, mental health, family, stigma, racism, management theory, psychopharmacology, DRGs, Individual Education Programs, community, faith, and poverty—to just name a few of what may have previously seemed to be divergent topics, finely articulated thanks to John Lyons's expert weaving of them into the beautiful tapestry that is this volume.

This work has the potential to unleash a Niagra of new work, if not improved thought for avoiding the traditional Pyrrhic victories so common in this field. This body of work indicates that the future of improving children's mental health systems of care is already here, it's just not evenly distributed. In this book, Lyons says it best in that it is incumbent upon us to "evolve an effective system of care for children." This book gives readers the tools to do so. I encourage you to get started reading.

Chris E. Stout
Series Editor
Contemporary Psychology

ACKNOWLEDGMENTS

There are an enormous number of people who have contributed either directly or indirectly to the experiences contained in these pages. I am sure that I cannot thank everyone whose efforts are reflected in this work, but I will try. I am particularly grateful to Harry Shallcross, who introduced me to working with the children's public system and whose wisdom and vision is reflected in my experiences. Also, I am indebted to Ken Howard, who was a mentor and colleague and inspired my interests in outcomes management approaches. Melanie Lyons has been instrumental in the success of the Child and Adolescent Needs and Strengths (CANS) through her work with the Buddin Praed Foundation, for which I am very grateful.

Purva Rawal and Annie Engberg were exceeding helpful in the preparation of this book, as were Justin Burnholdt, Inger Burnett-Ziegler, Julie Eisengart, Crystal Jackson, and Elyse Hart. I do not know how I would have finished it without them.

I have had the pleasure of working with a number of people in the child service system whom have shared their experiences in ways that influenced my thinking. Among these people, I am particularly grateful to Connie Almedia, Barbara Anderson, Sheila Bell, Brita Bishop, Lise Bisnaire, Dianne Borgesson, Bill Bouska, Julie Caliwan, Allison Campbell, Sharon Carpinello, Kathleen Cassidy, Pat Chesler, Jon Collins, Bill Conlin, Mary Jane England, Marcia Fazio, Chip Felton, Tom Finegan, Susan Furrer, Tim Gaeworin, Joe

Gordon, Stephanie Greenham, Gene Griffin, Grant Grissom, Stacey Hirsch, Ardas Khalsa, Michael Lee, Joe Loftus, Joan Mechlin, Wanda Miles, Peter Neirman, Angelica Oberlightner, Celeste Putman-Tanzy, Candace Putter, Mary Beth Rauktis, Laura Rogers, Linda Rosenberg, Sue Ross, Patricia Tennant Sokol, Ann Stanley, Linda Touche-Manley, Peter Tracy, Gwen White, and Michael Zuber.

Over the past decade, my academic colleagues have had an enormous impact on my thinking. Much thanks to Rachel Anderson, Mary Armstrong, Peter Budetti, Rowland "Bing" Chang, Robert Cohen, Judith Cook, Peter de Jonge, Norin Dollard, Mina Dulcan, Dorothy Dunlop, Elizabeth Durkin, Jane Holl, Frits Huyse, John Lavigne, Tony LoSasso, Zoran Martinovich, Michael O'Mahoney, Frank Reyes, Joris Slaets, and Peter Zeldow.

Many of my students, fellows, and staff over the past decade have all contributed to this effort. I would like to thank Melissa Abraham, Dana Baerger, Julia Cathcart, Nina Christopher, Kya Fawley, Jena Helgerson, Michael Jenuwine, Renanah Kaufman-Lehner, Cassandra Kisiel, Scott Leon, Dan Marson, Adam Naj, Farah Quadri, Michael Scherer, Matthew Shaw, Courtney West, and many others for their help.

And finally, I would like to acknowledge my children, Trevor and Caitlin, and my stepdaughters, Cassie and Hillary, from whom I have learned most of what I think I know about growing up.

CHAPTER 1

THE HISTORY OF CHILDREN'S PUBLIC MENTAL HEALTH SERVICES

The modern history of efforts to address the needs of children can be dated to the Renaissance and the beginnings of the industrial revolution. As cities became larger and the population center of gravity shifted from farms, the problems of children became apparent and a variety of strategies were introduced, initially to contain them and eventually to help them. One of the first approaches tried was to open penal institutions to house children whose behavior had become a burden to society. The first penal institutions for children were developed in 1695 in Halle, Germany, by August Francke and in 1704 by Pope Clement in Rome. Around the same time, orphanages were organized by religious and charitable organizations to serve abandoned and homeless children in large cities. The "treatment" component of these institutions could be described as "moral" in that religious training was a common focus of daytime activities. The first orphanage in the United States was opened by the nuns of the Ursuline Convent in New Orleans in 1745.

Over time, the number and size of these orphanages grew and the philosophies regarding the use of daytime activities began to evolve. In the early nineteenth century, the case of the Wild Boy of Aveyron sparked the introduction of the concept of "milieu therapy." This was the case of a boy who was captured by villagers in rural France. The boy was dirty, moved on all fours, and grunted like a beast. Despite a grim prognosis from the imminent Philippe Pinel and a period of exhibition in a cage, a young physician, Jean Marc Gaspard Itard, took the boy in and over a period of years taught him to read and obey simple commands.

From this case—both the wild origins of the boy and the effects of his education—the notion of the potentially therapeutic effects of the environment were recognized. Milieu therapy is a treatment approach that seeks to foster a therapeutic environment by facilitating the natural interaction of persons with similar or like conditions. In applying this approach, groups of troubled children were brought together so that therapeutic approaches could be applied to all the children as they interact with each other.

Milieu treatment was a powerful force in the early children's mental health system, because it provided a justification for institutionalizing children. What better way to form a milieu than to create long-term placements for children so they could interact among themselves over an extended period of time. Thus, milieu therapy—although at the time seen as a humanistic breakthrough in the treatment of all persons with mental illness, including children—supported the creation of large institutional structures for the children's treatment system. Milieu therapy was just the first example of a theory of treatment supporting the popular approach at that time—in this case the removal of problem children from society. We now understand that the unintended consequence of milieu therapy was that the basic model of care required that children with mental health problems were identified and attempts were made to put them together with other children with mental health problems.

Despite the utility and efficiency of milieu therapy, as it turns out, it might not have been a particularly good idea. As Peter Senge (1990) notes in his book, *The Fifth Discipline: The Art and Practice of the Learning Organization*, most of today's problems are yesterday's solutions. Dishion, Bullock, and Granic (2002) have recently provided a careful integration of existing research findings from randomized clinical trials to demonstrate a contagion effect in group treatments of high-need youth, particularly those involved in delinquency and/ or substance abuse. In other words, aggregating youth with serious problems into a milieu may have disturbing iatrogenic effects of making these youth's problems worse.

In addition to stimulating the creation of milieu therapy, the Wild Boy case also may represent the first time notable public attention was turned toward the idea that troubled children could be helped. Stigma against mental illness is probably as old as civilization;

however, in the past century we have appeared to make progress in reducing the unfairly negative views. In this regard, the Wild Boy of Aveyron might represent a critical event in beginning to turn public opinion toward a less stigmatizing view of mental illness.

Throughout the nineteenth century, institutions that served children continued to evolve. Innovation in children's services began to come more rapidly, as shown in the timeline in Table 1.1. Perhaps the most striking development was a differentiation of the developing child-serving system. At the start of this century there were no distinctions made based on different needs. Children with problems of delinquency, mental illness, or development disabilities were all served at the same institutions. However, during the century, attempts to create different milieus for children with different needs were initiated.

Table 1.1

A Timeline for the History of Children's Mental Health Services in the United States

1824	Society for the Prevention of Pauperism became the Society for the Prevention of Delinquency
1840s	Dorthea Dix began her work founding psychiatric hospitals
1860	Eugenics movement began
1880	National Association for the Protection of the Insane and Prevention of Insanity was formed
1883	G. Stanley Hall published *The Contents of Children's Minds*
1887	Hermann Ebbinghaus published the first systematic view of psychiatry
1890s	John Hopkins began to open institutions for children
1896	Lightner Witmer opened the first clinic for children at the University of Pennsylvania
1899	First juvenile court established in Cook County, Illinois
1905	Freud published *Three Contributions to the Theory of Sex*, which established a conceptual basis for child psychiatry
1908	Clifford Beers published *A Mind that Found Itself*
1909	The first White House Conference on the Care of Dependent Children was held in Washington, D.C.
1910	William Healy established the Psychopathic Institute for Children in Chicago, Illinois
1912	National Committee for Mental Hygiene made mental health a public health issue

1918   New York State Hospital Commission recommended the elimination of poverty as a preventive measure against mental illness

1920   The Child Guidance Movement began

1921   The Monmouth County Demonstration was initiated as the first experimental project of the National Committee for Mental Hygiene on the prevention of delinquency

1922   The National Committee for Mental Hygiene began waging a campaign for the creation of children's clinics

1930   The First International Mental Hygiene Congress was held in Washington, D.C.

1942   Leo Kanner published the first text on child psychiatry in English

1944   Bruno Bettleheim integrated psychoanalytic treatment with milieu therapy at the Orthogenic School

1946   The National Mental Health Act was passed

1947   The World Federation for Mental Health was established

1949   The National Institute of Mental Health was established

1951   John Bowlby published "Maternal Care and Mental Health" in the *Bulletin of the World Health Organization*

1955   The Mental Health Study Act was signed

1963   The Community Mental Health Act was signed

1965   Joint Commission on the Mental Health of Children was established

1974   Public Law 94–142 was passed, which mandated that children with disabilities, including behavioral and emotional disorders, be treated in the least restrictive environment

1975   Passage of the Individuals with Disabilities Act, which established special education rights for school children with emotional and behavioral problems

1978   The President's Commission on Mental Health, Task Force on Infants, Children, and Adolescents issued its report

1980   The Willie M. class action suit was filed

1982   Judith Knitzer published *Unclaimed Children: The Failure of Public Responsibility to Children and Adolescents in Need of Mental Health Services* (1982)

1984   The National Institute of Mental Health initiated the Child and Adolescent Service System Program

1989   The Federation of Families for Children's Mental Health was formed

1996	Costello et al. (1996) published the first community-based epidemiological study of psychiatric disorders in childhood
1999	David Satcher, M.D., released the U.S. Surgeon General's report on mental health
2001	David Satcher, M.D., released the U.S. Surgeon General's report on the Conference on Children's Mental Health
2003	President's New Freedom Commission on Mental Health released its final report

Late in the nineteenth century, the concept of treatment of mental health problems began to evolve. Sigmund Freud is generally credited with the innovation of talking therapies (although in his case, it involved mostly listening). His psychoanalytic treatment was designed initially to treat hysteria, a disorder thought to be relatively common among women at that time. Most of Freud's early patients were wealthy European women. Although the focus of Freud's treatment innovations was on adults, his theory of the development of psychopathology emphasized childhood experiences and developmental stages.

In the United States, the current public mental health system for children received its formal start with the Mental Hygiene Movement of the nineteenth century, which is credited with the creation of our modern concepts of mental health and illness and the origins of a compassionate care system. One component of the movement was the belief that mental illness arose from painful childhood experiences. This causal assumption naturally created interest in understanding the development of psychiatric problems among children. That is, childhood would be the time in which mental illness would first start to manifest itself. Although prevention was not yet a common concept, the value of initiating treatment at the earliest possible time was a commonly held belief. Thus, it was believed that if you could detect mental illness in children, the best time to initiate treatment would be in childhood.

A primary locus of all mental health services during the nineteenth century was the psychiatric hospital. In the early parts of this century, when children were hospitalized, they were placed with adults. This began to change during the 1820s. Around this time, society was beginning to recognize the differences between children and adults that suggested different intervention strategies might be necessary. For example, in 1824, the Society of the Prevention of Pauperism became the Society for the Prevention of Delinquency. This group encouraged the initial steps of separating children who broke the law from adult criminals. The society supported the proposition that children were easier to correct and heal than were adults and that this correction should involve training, not punishment.

About this time, the first efforts to address the mental health needs of youth involved with the criminal justice system were established. In 1909, William Healy, a neurologist, established the Juvenile Psychopathic Institute in order to advise the courts on the psychology of youthful offenders. However, even at the turn of the century, the focus remained on conceptualizing behavioral health problems within a moral framework. For example, hyperactivity was conceptualized as a defect in moral judgment well into the 1900s.

During this period, institutions were the primary locus of treatment. Admission standards to these hospitals were rather vague; there were few legal restrictions placed on decisions to admit a person. Thus, most power in the system was placed with the admitting physician.

Beginning in the middle of the twentieth century, the nature of treatment of children, particularly those in institutional settings, began to change. "Child Psychiatry" was first defined as a distinct focus within psychiatry in the 1930s, although it did not really expand until after World War II. This led to recognition of the need for, and development of, specialized knowledge about children's mental health.

In the most comprehensive initial example of a child-specific treatment approach, Bruno Bettleheim, who became the Director of the Orthogenic School at the University of Chicago in 1944, is credited with combining milieu therapy approaches with psychoanalytic treatment. This innovation represents the first generation of what is now referred to as residential treatment for children. Having experienced the profound effects of Nazi concentration camps on changing personality for the worse, Bettleheim became convinced that one's environment also could change personality for the better. Sadly, his understanding of psychoanalytic theory led him to place a significant amount of blame for children's behavioral problems on their parents, particularly mothers. It was standard practice at the Orthogenic School to forbid parental visits for the first six months of treatment because it was thought to be "countertherapeutic." This theory of the pathogenic nature of parenting, shared by many theorists in the mid-twentieth century, was the origin of the tensions that are still manifest in the system between clinicians and parents of children with serious emotional or behavioral problems.

In the early 1960s, a set of factors worked together to create the Community Mental Health Movement. These factors included an aging and expensive state hospital infrastructure, breakthroughs in psychopharmacology, and recognition of the civil rights of persons with mental illness. Initially, this movement was characterized by deinstitutionalization, which primarily involved adults with severe mental illness. Deinstitutionalization describes the process of relocating long-term residents of state psychiatric hospitals into community settings. However, the formation of community mental health centers (CMHCs) has had a lasting impact on the children's system as well. Within the CMHCs created by the Community Mental Health Acts of 1963 and 1965, each CMHC was developed to serve a specific geographic area, known as a catchment area. (Note: For linguistic buffs the term "catchment area" resulted from the initial use of the sewer maps to define geographical areas. Catchment basins are used to collect sewage within certain geographies. The translation of this term to public mental health only reinforces our field's problems with stigma.) In many areas, CMHCs became the primary community agencies providing outpatient mental health services to children and families.

In 1969, the United States federal government officially recognized the inability of the mental health service system to meet the needs of children through a report issued by the Joint Commission on the Mental Health of Children (1969). One of their major findings was that children often were involved with multiple child-serving agencies simultaneously. The overlap among children served by public mental health, child welfare, juvenile justice, and special education was enormous. This overlap represented both an opportunity and a challenge that continues today. Historically, different child-serving agencies tend to function in a vertical organization within the agency. Thus, child welfare would create an entire system of care for the wards of the state. Juvenile justice would create a different system. Child-serving agencies in this organization structure have been referred to as silos because they are self-contained and there is little opportunity for cross-agency collaborations.

In 1974, United States Public Law 94-142 was passed, which mandated that children with disabilities, including behavioral and emotional problems, receive education in the least restrictive environment. The concept that it is a civil right to have the most personal liberty possible given one's clinical needs is one of the foundational principles of the system of care philosophy.

Although the 1960s and 1970s witnessed the creation of a number of committees and task forces that assembled and reported, it was not until 1982 when Judith Knitzer published her classic book *Unclaimed Children: The Failure of Public Responsibility to Children and Adolescents in Need of Mental Health Services* (1982) that the next stage of evolution occurred in the children's mental health service system. Funded by the Children's Defense Fund, Knitzer combined multiple data sources from all 50 states and focused on three million children with serious emotional disturbances. She found that the majority were either not receiving services or were receiving inappropriate care. Knitzer specifically cited the lack of a federal role in the children's service system. She observed that there was little funding provided, and for what was provided there was little or no follow-through to ensure effective applications of scarce dollars. Knitzer's book led to the renewed interest in children's services and activated a coalition of advocates. In many ways, the development of the current system of care was a direct result of this book.

In 1975, Congress first passed the Individuals with Disabilities Act (IDEA), which mandated special educational opportunities for children with disabilities, including behavioral health problems. This legislation was reauthorized in 1990. IDEA established special education services for children with emotional and behavioral problems. Although IDEA represents an important breakthrough for attending to the unique educational needs of these children, it is largely an unfunded mandate because most school funding comes from local districts. Because the majority of children in special education are poor minorities, they tend to reside in poorly funded school districts (American Institute for Research, 1994).

Although the epidemiology of psychiatric disorders had been studied by the National Institute of Mental Health in the late 1970s and early 1980s (Reiger & Burke, 1987), the extent of mental health problems among children was unknown. This changed in 1996 when Costello et al. published the first community-based study of the epidemiology of psychiatric disorders in childhood. These researchers reported that 25 percent of children had at least one moderate psychiatric disorder and that 5 percent had severe emotional/behavioral disorders marked by significant impairments in functioning. Only one in five children with a diagnosable psychiatric disorder received any specialty behavioral health services. These data clearly established that psychiatric disorders were common among children and adolescents and that the existing service system failed to address many of these children's needs.

System-of-Care Philosophy

Partially in response to Knitzer's work, a group of children service system experts began to reconceptualize what the children's service system should look like in order to better approximate an ideal system. From this work the concept of a system of care has arisen. Stroul and Friedman (1986) are credited with first laying out a system-of-care philosophy to design and implement comprehensive and effective services for children. The philosophy is expressed through a set of care values and guiding principles that can be found in Table 1.2. Essentially, the overarching goals are to keep children at home, in school, and out of trouble (Rosenblatt, 1993). These outcomes and goals come from a belief that the best place to raise a child is with their family living in the community.

Table 1.2
Core Values and Guiding Principles of the Child and Adolescent Support Services Programs (CASSP)

CASSP Core Values

1. The system of care should be child centered, with the needs of the child and family dictating the types and mix of services provided.
2. The system of care should be community based, with the locus of services as well as management and decision-making responsibility resting at the community level.

CASSP Guiding Principles

1. Emotionally disturbed children should have access to a comprehensive array of services that address the child's physical, emotional, social, and educational needs.
2. Emotionally disturbed children should receive individualized services in accordance with the unique needs and potentials of each child, and guided by an individualized service plan.
3. Emotionally disturbed children should receive services within the least restrictive, most normative environment that is clinically appropriate.

4. The families and surrogate families of emotionally disturbed children should be full participants in all aspects of the planning and delivery of services.

5. Emotionally disturbed children should receive services that are integrated, with linkages between child-caring agencies and programs and mechanisms for planning, developing, and coordinating services.

6. Emotionally disturbed children should be provided with case management or similar mechanisms to ensure that multiple services are delivered in a coordinated and therapeutic manner, and that they can move through the system of services in accordance with their changing needs.

7. Early identification and intervention for children with emotional problems should be promoted by the system of care in order to enhance the likelihood of positive outcomes.

8. Emotionally disturbed children should be ensured smooth transitions to the adult services system as they reach maturity.

9. The rights of emotionally disturbed children should be protected, and effective advocacy efforts for emotionally disturbed children and youth should be promoted.

10. Emotionally disturbed children should receive services without regard to race, religion, national origin, sex, physical disability, or other characteristics, and services should be sensitive and responsive to cultural differences and special needs.

Source: Adapted from the Child and Adolescent Support Services Programs guidelines (Stroul, 1993).

A key approach that arises out of the system-of-care philosophy is enhancing the degree to which the partners in a system collaborate to achieve shared goals. As programs and services grow in size, scope, and specialization, the organization and management of these programs and services become more difficult. For instance, it used to be that you could go to your family physician for most medical care. Now, with most insurance plans, you have to go to a primary care doctor to get permission to go to a specialist. In the children's system, a parent might take their child one place for medication management and another place for therapy, all while the child is in a day-treatment program funded through the school system. Although each program might function in the best interests of the children and families it serves, the resultant inefficiency in the overall system can result in less-than-optimal outcomes. For this reason, system-of-care philosophy has emphasized local control and management of service system. Multiple, centralized bureaucracies can be less responsive to individuals and less flexible in addressing different needs with different strategies. Large bureaucracies have a tendency to continually develop polices and procedures (they employ people whose primary job it is to develop these documents). The ever-evolving policies and procedures with their inevitable paperwork serve to make service receipt increasingly complex in these circumstances. When a parent is forced to deal with multiple bureaucracies (e.g., school, court, and child welfare) at the same time, significant barriers to an integrated approach to services are natural by-products.

Among the most important work in the development of systems of care has been the establishment of programs initially funded by the Robert Woods Johnson Foundation (RWJ). These projects were intended to nurture the development of local systems of care for children and families based on the principles laid out by Stroul and Friedman (1986) for the Child and Adolescent Support Services Programs (CASSP). The intervention strategy was the wrap-around process (Burchard, Burchard, Sewell, & VanDenBerg, 1993; VanDenBerg & Grealish, 1998). Following the experiences with the RWJ-funded sites, the federal government became involved in the process through the Center for Mental Health Services of the Substance Abuse Mental Health Services Administration (SAMHSA). SAMHSA has funded more than 100 system-of-care demonstration sites over the past decade. For children and adolescents with mental health challenges, the CASSP principles have become the foundation for system-of-care initiatives around the country. Few would argue with the proposition that services for children and families should be designed with these principles in mind.

In 1999, the United States Surgeon General, David Satcher, M.D., published the first Surgeon General's report on mental health (U.S. Surgeon General, 1999). This groundbreaking document may well be one of the first times an independent health care entity recognized and endorsed the effectiveness of existing behavioral health services. The report points to a number of significant events over the prior decade, including the breakthroughs in our understanding of brain–behavior relationships, the introduction of a wide range of new treatments, the transformation of how behavioral health services are organized and financed, and the emergence of powerful consumer and family movements. This report identified eight goals related to children's mental health that can be found in Table 1.3.

Table 1.3

Goals of the U.S. Surgeon General's 1999 Report on Mental Health

1. Promote public awareness of children's mental health issues and reduce stigma associated with mental illness.

2. Continue to develop, disseminate, and implement scientifically proven prevention and treatment services in the field of children's mental health.

3. Improve the assessment and recognition of mental health needs in children.

4. Eliminate racial/ethnic and socioeconomic disparities in access to mental health care.

5. Improve the infrastructure for children's mental health services, including support for scientifically proven interventions across professions.

6. Increase access to and coordination of quality mental health care services.

7. Train frontline providers to recognize and manage mental health issues, and educate mental health providers in scientifically proven prevention and treatment services.

8. Monitor the access to and coordination of quality mental health care services.

Source: Adapted from U.S. Surgeon General. (1999). *Mental health: A report to the Surgeon General.* Washington, D.C.: Department of Health and Human Services.

In 2001, Dr. Satcher published the results from a conference on children's mental health (U.S. Surgeon General, 2001b). His report set out a vision and specific goals for the U.S. children's mental health service system. The vision had four guiding principles:

1. Promoting the recognition of mental health as an essential part of children's health.

2. Integrating family-, child-, and youth-centered mental health services into all systems that serve children and youth.

3. Engaging families and incorporating the perspectives of children and youth in the development of all mental health care planning.

4. Developing and enhancing a public-private health infrastructure to support these efforts to the fullest extent possible.

The conference members then outlined the following eight goals:

1. Promote public awareness of children's mental health issues and reduce stigma associated with mental illness.

2. Continue to develop, disseminate, and implement scientifically proven prevention and treatment services in the field of children's mental health.

3. Improve the assessment of and recognition of mental health needs in children.

4. Eliminate racial/ethnic and socioeconomic disparities in access to mental health care services.

5. Improve the infrastructure for children's mental health services, including support for scientifically proven interventions across professions.

6. Increase access to and coordination of quality mental health care services.

7. Train frontline providers to recognize and manage mental health issues, and educate mental health care providers about scientifically proven prevention and treatment services.

8. Monitor the access to and coordination of quality mental health care services.

Also in 2001, the U.S. Surgeon General's office (2001a) came out with a supplemental report on race, culture, and ethnicity. In this report, the research demonstrated a significant and disproportionate burden of unmet mental health needs among minority populations. Addressing these racial disparities in service receipt was identified as a national priority.

In early 2001, President George W. Bush announced the formation of his New Freedom Initiative, which was intended to promote increased access to employment and educational opportunities for persons with disabilities. The initiative also had the stated mission of improving access to full community life and to assistive and universal technologies that promote health, well-being, and full access. The vision of the New Freedom Commission on Mental Health (2003, p. 1) was stated as follows:

> We envision a future when everyone with mental illness will recover, a future when mental illnesses can be prevented or cured, a future when mental illnesses are detected early, and a future when everyone with a mental illness at any stage of life has access to effective treatment and supports—essentials for living, working, learning, and participating fully in the community.

Three primary barriers were identified that prevent persons with mental health challenges from obtaining the excellent services they need and deserve:

1. The stigma of mental illness.
2. Unfair treatment limitations and financial restrictions placed on mental health benefits in private insurance.
3. A fragmented mental health service system (New Freedom Commission on Mental Health, 2003).

Thus, both the New Freedom Commission and the previous U.S. Surgeon General agree that standing in the way of progress toward an accessible and effective system of care for children and adolescents are attitudes about mental health, financing strategies with unintended consequences on the quality of care, and a lack of cohesion in the organization and functioning of service components. Success requires overcoming these barriers.

The Current State of System Components

Consistent with the New Freedom Commissions identification of barriers and despite the focus on developing systems-of-care philosophy in the children's public mental health system, in most places the system primarily consists of its component parts and thus is a system in name only. As such, it is useful to review the current status of these public mental health system service components.

Wraparound Process

Although not a formal component in the system of care, the wraparound process has been identified as a critical strategy for developing systems of care through the creative use of existing services and natural supports. Essentially, wraparound refers to a planning process that results in an individualized and, therefore, unique array of community services and natural supports that are selected in a team process directed by the child and family. The focus is on strengths, with attention to flexibility, cultural relevance, and coordination across system partners (Burchard, Bruns, & Burchard, 2002).

The ten principles of the wraparound can be found in Table 1.4. Taken from Goldman and Faw (1999), these principles essentially build a bridge between the CASSP principles and the service planning or case management process. They represent an important link

Table 1.4
Principles of the Wraparound Process

1. Wraparounds must be based in the community.

2. The wraparound approach must be a team-driven process involving the family, child, natural supports, agencies, and community services working together to develop, implement, and evaluate the individualized plan.

3. Families must be full and active partners in every level of the wraparound process.

4. Services and supports must be individualized, built on strengths, and meet the needs of children and families across the life domains to promote success, safety, and permanence in home, school, and community.

5. The process must be culturally competent, building on the unique values, preferences, and strengths of children and families and their communities.

6. Wraparound child and family teams must have flexible approaches and adequate flexible funding.

7. Wraparound plans must include a balance of formal services and informal community and family supports.

8. There must be an unconditional commitment to serve children and families.

9. The plans should be developed and implemented based on an interagency, community-based collaborative process.

10. Outcomes must be determined and measured for the system, for the program, and for the individual child and family.

Source: Adapted from Goldman and Faw, 1999.

between the philosophy and implementation of a system of care. They create a strategy by which the formal services within the system can be managed.

Psychiatric Hospitals

Over the past several decades, many state hospital programs have closed and there has been a substantial decline in the number of psychiatric hospitals for children, the number of beds dedicated to children, and the duration of hospital stays (Blodgett & Molinari, 2001; McFarland, Khorramzadeh, Millius, & Mahler, 2002; Nierman

& Lyons, 2001). However, there has been very little decline in the number of psychiatric hospital admissions for children (Reeder et al. 2002). Psychiatric hospitals function in a complex ecosystem to which they are very sensitive. The community that a hospital serves has a major impact on the nature and functioning of that hospital's care. The existence of alternative approaches to crisis intervention; the availability of intensive community services; and accessible outpatient services, including medication management, can all impact the demand for psychiatric admissions. Poverty and homelessness impact community hospitals as well.

Psychiatric hospitalization has changed dramatically in its approach. Although only 20 years ago it was thought that significant treatment could be accomplished in the hospital environment, the current philosophy is that psychiatric hospitalization cannot provide treatment but can provide differential diagnosis, including drug response, and crisis stabilization. The psychiatric hospital's primary role involves maintaining safety. Children living in situations that are less tolerant of psychopathology (e.g., foster care) or those living in households without sufficient supervision are at greater risk for hospitalization (Leon, Uziel-Miller, Lyons, & Tracy, 1999).

In our study of the New York State public mental health system (Lyons & Shallcross, 2000), we found that psychiatric hospitals served a critical role in the pathway of children into residential treatment. Although less than half of the children in residential treatment had documented history of extended outpatient services, more than 90 percent had documented histories of psychiatric hospital admissions. Often, children would be admitted to the hospital or released without successful linkage to community-based services; readmitted to the hospital (sometimes repeatedly); and, eventually, transferred to a state hospital with a follow-up admission to a residential treatment facility.

Residential Treatment

Currently, the term "residential treatment" covers a range of residential programs from highly structured institutions on campus settings to small group homes and treatment foster care homes located in communities (Wells, 1991). The common theme of residential treatment is that the living environment is designed to support the active treatment of the child's mental health needs. A multidisciplinary team works with the child and family to develop and implement a treatment plan and offer a wide variety of therapeutic interventions. Eligibility criteria for these placements include a serious emotional or behavioral disorder (Stone, 1997).

Currently, the theoretical approaches to residential treatment centers are best described as varied and eclectic. The shift toward shorter lengths of stays and greater accountability has led to a greater emphasis on behavioral approaches that generally have clearer outcomes. However, different programs institute different treatment approaches or bring in outside clinicians with training in various approaches. Whittaker (2000, pp. 20–21) has suggested that the current eclecticism "yields a structure that...lacks coherence as a total milieu."

Residential treatment continues to be a major component of our public mental health service system. At the turn of this century, there were 27,642 children in residential treatment in the United States (Manderscheid, Henderson, Witken, & Atay, 2000), 95 percent of whom were under 18 years of age. About two-thirds of children in residential treatment were between the ages of 13 and 17. The majority of children are in these placements as a result of involvement with either the child welfare system or the juvenile justice system, making the public-funded system the major payment source for these services.

Special Education

Currently about 1 percent of the student populations receives special education services; however, estimates of the students with actual special education needs range as high as 20 percent (American Institute for Research, 1994). The criteria for emotionally disturbed students include the following (Duchnowski, 1994, p. 15):

- An inability to learn that cannot be explained by intellectual, sensory, or health factors.
- An inability to build and maintain satisfactory interpersonal relationships with peers or teachers.
- Inappropriate types of behaviors or feelings under normal circumstances.
- A general or pervasive mood of unhappiness or depression.
- A tendency to develop physical symptoms of fears associated with personal or school problems.

Of the school children classified as emotionally disturbed, estimates are that 75 percent are educated in self-contained classrooms (38.5%), resources rooms (30%), or special centers (13.4%), where they are removed from the mainstream school population for at least one half of the day or more. Duchnowski (1994) has noted that these special environments are generally organized through the use of token economies or other behavioral control strategies that are focused on controlling or limiting inappropriate behavior, but do not appear to foster positive behaviors.

In 1990, in response to the mixed initial findings with regard to special education, the Office of Special Education Programs implemented the National Agenda for Achieving Better Results for Children and Youth with Serious Emotional Disturbance. In the past decade, advances appear to have been made in some settings with regard to improving access to special education services and outcomes from those services. However, Vernberg, Roberts, & Nyre (2002) report that although the needs of children identified for special education services often go well beyond the walls of the school, even the segregated programs often fail to incorporate out-of-school issues in the child's educational plan.

Partial Hospital/Day Treatment

Full-day programming for children with serious emotional and behavioral challenges has emerged as an important component of the existing service system. Typically, these programs function like a school or are located within a school, so that treatment is woven into the educational curriculum. The daytime programming allows children to return home daily to benefit from peer, family, and community involvement (Burns, Hoagwood, & Mrazek, 1999). The goal of these programs is generally to prevent hospitalization (partial hospital) or provide a therapeutic school environment for children with significant behavioral difficulties in the regular classroom.

The first partial hospital program for psychiatric patients was opened in Moscow, Russia, in 1933 (Maxey, 1979; Whitelaw & Perez, 1987). Motivated by a critical shortage of hospital beds, a Russian psychiatrist, Dzhagarov, established a partial hospital as a substitute for inpatient psychiatric hospitalization in response to economic constraints, rather than as a treatment philosophy. About 10 years later, Dr. D. Ewen Cameron founded the first partial hospital program in North America (Maxey, 1979). In 1946, Cameron created the term "day hospital" to describe his program, which served as both an extension of and supplement to inpatient treatment (Whitelaw & Perez, 1987).

Soon, day hospital programs began to appear in the United States and served as transitional treatment facilities (Whitelaw & Perez, 1987). The popularity of partial hospitals grew slowly in the United States; there were just eight reported programs by 1956 (Maxey, 1979). However, during the 1960s and 1970s, the number of programs in the United States increased sharply (National Institute of Mental Health, Survey and Reports Branch, Division of Biometry, 1974). A variety of factors contributed to this rapid increase (Casarino, Wilner, & Maxey, 1982), including the introduction of pharmacotherapy and deinstitutionalization (Maxey, 1979; Whitelaw & Perez, 1987).

Following the increase in programs, problems were noted that were rooted in the diversity of programs that developed rapidly, without communication on standards for content, purpose, structure, or populations served (Maxey, 1979; Whitelaw & Perez, 1987). Literature from this era and beyond reflects these difficulties. Many researchers (e.g., Rosie, 1987) pinpoint divergent definitions of partial hospitals as the primary problem. Labels such as day care, day hospital, day treatment center, and day/night program are used interchangeably in some publications, organizations, and programs (Burns et al., 1999; Maxey, 1979), whereas others distinguish the terms as referring to very different services (Maxey, 1979; Whitelaw & Perez, 1987). The variation in emphases across programs illustrates this diversity (Astrachan, Flynn, Geller, & Harvey, 1971; Maxey, 1979; Whitelaw & Perez, 1987). The following four functions have been identified:

1. An alternative to inpatient hospitalization.
2. A transitional care facility for reintegration into the community.
3. A treatment and rehabilitative facility.
4. A service for a specific population in need, such as adolescents.

In 1975, the Federation of Partial Hospitalization Study Groups, Inc., was established and was renamed the American Association for Partial Hospitalization (AAPH) in 1979. This organization generated the Standards Committee of the AAPH in response to the problems that stemmed from the heterogeneity of programs. The committee agreed on a working definition developed by the Task Force on Partial Hospitalization in 1980:

[A]n ambulatory treatment program which includes the major diagnostic, medical, psychiatric, psychosocial and prevocational modalities designed for those patients suffering from serious mental disorders

such that they require an intensive, comprehensive, coordinated, multidisciplinary treatment which cannot be provided by an outpatient
department or clinic setting. (Whitelaw & Perez, 1987, p. 62)

During the 1980s, assessments of partial hospital programs repeatedly demonstrated their efficacy, financial benefits, and client satisfaction (Herz, Ferman, & Cohen, 1985; Whitelaw & Perez, 1987). Partial
hospitals became a growing mode of care for children and adolescents
with mental health needs (Burns et al., 1999). By 1985, there were
about 350 partial hospital/day treatment programs for youth with
psychiatric needs in the United States (Zimet & Farley, 1985), and, to
date, this number has remained fairly constant (Burns et al., 1999).

Although evidence of the effectiveness of these programs was
available in the 1980s, more recent literature reviews reveal a pau-
city of well-controlled studies for youth (Burns, 1991; Burns et al.,
1999; Grizenko, 1997). In a review of 20 studies, Burns et al. (1999)
noted improvements in both youth behavior and family functioning.
Approximately three-quarters of children and adolescents reinte-
grate into public schools. Further, the authors found that several of
the studies provided evidence that partial hospital/day treatment
prevented more costly placements, such as residential treatment or
inpatient hospitalization.

Despite the fact that both uncontrolled studies and newer con-
trolled studies point to improvements in mental health as well as
cost savings over inpatient hospitalization or residential treatment
centers, partial programs continue to be underutilized (Burns, 1991).
However, recent scandals involving fraudulent practices among for-
profit partial hospitals in Florida has dampened many third-party
payers' enthusiasm for these services.

In summary, intensive day-long programs offer some promise as a
component of the system of care. Obstacles include developing consistent eligibility guidelines, treatment models, and expectations for
length of stay. Understanding how to best integrate the mental health
and education mandates of these programs is particularly important.

Outpatient Services

One of the most common services offered to children and families
in the public mental health system is psychotherapy and counseling.
This can take the form of individual therapy with the child, family

therapy, or group therapy, or some combination of these approaches. Typically, weekly sessions are offered.

The most common types of problems among children presenting to outpatient treatment are attention deficit/hyperactivity disorder, depression, disruptive behavior disorders, and trauma reactions including posttraumatic stress disorder (Burns, Compton, Egger, Farmer, & Robertson, 2002). Burns & Hoagwood (2002) provide a detailed summary of the variety of treatments for which evidence of effectiveness exists. Although there is a growing body of research that indicates the effectiveness of certain psychotherapeutic treatments over others for different indications (e.g., Cohen, Mannarino, & Deblinger, 2002; Saunders, Berliner, & Hanson, 2003; Timmer & Urquiza, 1996; Webster-Stratton, Hollinsworth, & Kolpacoff, 1989; Webster-Stratton, Kolpacoff, & Hollinsworth, 1988), there is still an incredible array of treatment approaches used in practice. In addition, most treatments supported by empirical evidence are for only one diagnosis although many children who present to outpatient treatment have multiple diagnostic indicators (Burns et al., 2002; Lyons & Shallcross, 2000).

Although evidence of the efficacy of specific treatments has grown, other studies question the general effectiveness of psychotherapy with children (Andrade, Lambert, & Bickman, 2000; Weiss, Catron, Harris, & Phung, 1999). Due to training experiences and loyalties of therapists and a considerable amount of skepticism among clinicians regarding the science of treatment research, even therapies for which there is little or no evidence of effectiveness are difficult to eliminate from the system. Thus, despite all the recent innovations in specific treatments, our review of New York State outpatient clinics suggested that most continued to practice supportive or psychodynamic psychotherapy for which little evidence of effectiveness with children exists (Lyons & Shallcross, 2000).

Like adult outpatient services, the majority of service episodes end when the youth and/or family simply stop coming to visits. In the New York planning study, we estimated that this occurs in about two-thirds of all outpatient episodes of care (Lyons & Shallcross, 2000). Only about 10 percent end with mutually agreed on closure based on successful outcomes. Another 10 percent end due to an escalation of behavioral and emotional problems requiring a more intensive type of service. The remaining cases end for a variety of reasons, including moves out of the area, aging out of the program, and so forth.

A Fork in the Road?

So where are we today? After nearly a century of steady evolution from an institutional-based to a community-based system, we find ourselves somewhere in between these two extremes. In many places, much progress has been made in creating intensive community alternatives (Burns & Hoagwood, 2002). Other places have limited, if any, options with regard to community-based services. Some progress has been made in developing collaborative relationships among child-serving partners; however, much room for improvement remains. Thus, despite the observable movement toward a system-of-care philosophy, it remains the case that psychiatric hospitalizations continue to rise, at least in absolute numbers. Placement in residential treatment centers remains relatively common. The majority of expenditures on services for children remain invested in institutional services (U.S. Surgeon General, 1999). Long waiting lists exist in many places for outpatient and intensive community services.

What about the evidence? This is perhaps the most troubling aspect of the entire picture. Although new treatments have been identified that demonstrate efficacy, there is less evidence that many of the commonly used services are particularly effective (Andrade et al., 2000; Bickman, Lambert, Andrade, & Penaloza, 2000). Psychiatric hospitalization may well stabilize crises and prevent very bad outcomes (e.g., suicide, homicide), but there is emerging evidence to suggest that in some situations, hospitalizing a child may be harmful. Children in residential treatment, on average, appear to get better, although we have demonstrated that in some circumstances, they become even worse (Lyons, Terry, Martinovich, Petersen, & Bouska, 2001). In that study, we found evidence that although most residential treatment centers had positive outcomes, some centers actually serve children who become worse with treatment. There is growing evidence to suggest that group treatment approaches, at least for high-need children, may be associated with worse outcomes due to "contagion effects" (Dishion et al., 2002). Supportive psychotherapy does not appear to be effective with disruptive behavior problems (Weiss et al., 1999). There are some evidence-based practices for children and there are other practices that are promising (Burns & Hoagwood, 2002; Hoagwood et al., 2001). However, these evidence-based approaches have not been widely or consistently implemented within the child-serving system.

The existing research on traditional outpatient psychotherapeutic services is quite mixed. Specific treatments for specific types of problems demonstrate efficacy. However, studies of services in the field demonstrate little or no effectiveness (Andrade et al., 2000). It appears overcoming inertia is a significant challenge for evolving the existing service system. Diffusion of innovative treatments is generally slow, if it occurs at all.

Leonard Bickman and his colleagues have found no evidence that system-of-care initiatives are effective (Bickman, 1996; Bickman, Noser, & Summerfelt, 1999; Bickman et al., 2000). However, there is some contention regarding whether this research has actually studied system-of-care initiatives or is merely evaluating the impact of case management on traditional services.

Scott Hennggler and his group have created Multisystemic Treatment (MST; Hennggler et al., 1997). This is an intensive community-based approach to working with children with disruptive behavior disorders, particularly those who are engaged in delinquent behavior. There is substantial evidence that MST is clearly superior to traditional treatment approaches (which are not particularly effective). However, even MST appears to be effective only about 50 percent of the time and is very expensive to implement.

Breakthroughs in pharmacotherapies have been incredible over the past two decades (Burns & Hoagwood, 2002; Kazdin & Weisz, 1998). However, most of the research on the efficacy of psychotropic drug therapies has been with adults. Recruiting youth samples for drug-industry-sponsored clinical trials is very difficult. Thus, few new drug therapies have been developed specifically for children. With the exception of Ritalin, few drugs have noted indications that include use with children and adolescents. This has led to an ongoing natural experiment whereby new drugs are tried in all possible combinations with little formal attention to their possible impact on developing minds and bodies (Geller, 1991; Jensen, 1998; Vitiello & Jensen, 1995). Vast amounts of money ride on the use of these prescription drugs and the potential for abuses is enormous.

Significant racial disparities exist in the public mental health system (U.S. Surgeon General, 2001a). Issues of cultural sensitivity and competence and the stigma of mental illness appear to have a disproportionate effect on access to specialty mental health services for minority children and families.

Given these circumstances, significant work lies ahead if we hope to evolve an effective system of care for children. The president's New Freedom Commission on Mental Health (2003) identified the following six goals that must be met if we are to successfully transform the service system consistent with the commission's vision of access and excellence:

Goal 1: Americans understand that mental health is essential to overall health.

Goal 2: Mental health care is consumer and family driven.

Goal 3: Disparities in mental health services are eliminated.

Goal 4: Early mental health screening, assessment, and referral to services are common practices.

Goal 5: Excellent mental health care is delivered and research is accelerated.

Goal 6: Technology is used to access mental health care and information.

The commission created a set of recommendations of how to achieve these six goals. These recommendations can be found in Table 1.5. Although these recommendations are quite sensible and are a positive contribution to improving the lives of children and families with mental illness, they are broad and, therefore, lack the level of specification required to create a road map to achieve them. For example, recommendation 3.1 seeks to "improve access to quality care that is culturally competent." No one would argue with this very worthwhile recommendation. The problem lies in definitions of "access," "quality," "culture," and "competency." Before we can achieve the vision of this recommendation, we must work through the complexities of developing clearer definitions of what we seek to communicate with such terms.

Table 1.5
Goals and Recommendations of the President's New Freedom Commission on Mental Health

Goal 1: Americans understand that mental health is essential to overall health.

| Recommendations: | 1.1. | Advance and implement a national campaign to reduce the stigma of seeking care and a national strategy for suicide prevention. |
| | 1.2. | Address mental health with the same urgency as physical health. |

Goal 2: Mental health care is consumer and family driven.

Recommendations:

2.1. Develop an individualized plan of care for every adult with serious mental illness and every child with a serious emotional disturbance.

2.2. Involve consumers and families fully in orienting the mental health system toward recovery.

2.3. Align relevant federal programs to improve access and accountability for mental health services.

2.4. Create a Comprehensive State Mental Health Plan.

2.5. Protect and enhance the right of people with mental illness.

Goal 3: Disparities in mental health services are eliminated.

Recommendations:

3.1. Improve access to quality care that is culturally competent.

3.2. Improve access to quality care in rural and geographically remote areas.

Goal 4: Early mental health screening, assessment, and referral to services are common practices.

Recommendations:

4.1. Promote the mental health of young children.

4.2. Improve and expand school mental health programs.

4.3. Screen for co-occurring mental health and substance use disorders and link with integrated treatment strategies.

4.4. Screen for mental disorders in primary health care, across the life span, and connect to treatment and supports.

Goal 5: Excellent mental health care is delivered and research is accelerated.

Recommendations: 5.1.   Accelerate research to promote recovery and resilience, and, ultimately, to cure and prevent mental health illnesses.

5.2.   Advance evidence-based practices using dissemination and demonstration projects and create a public–private partnership to guide their implementation.

5.3.   Improve and expand the workforce providing evidence-based mental health services and supports.

5.4.   Develop the knowledge base in four understudied areas: mental health disparities, long-term effects of medications, trauma, and acute care.

Goal 6: Technology is used to access mental health care and information.

Recommendations: 6.1.   Use health technology and telehealth to improve access and coordination of mental health care, especially for Americans in remote areas or in underserved populations.

6.2.   Develop and implement integrated electronic health record and personal health information systems.

Source: Adapted from the president's New Freedom Commission on Mental Health. (2003). *Achieving the promise: Transforming mental health care in America.* Rockville, MD: Substance Abuse and Mental Health Services Administration, SMA 03-3832.

We stand at a crossroads of three diverging paths. In one direction are new and more effective strategies for providing different youth with different treatments and services that are specifically designed to meet their needs. This is the route toward the full implementation of evidence-based practices (Burns & Hoagwood, 2002). In a second direction are a host of new ideas that are no more effective than the old strategies, but create business opportunities for creative entre-preneurs. On this path, the development and implementation of new practices consumes much of the resources that could be going toward providing treatment to children and families. The third direction is business as usual. We continue with a disjointed and underfunded public mental health system. Clearly, all reasonable people would seek the first path. This is the road that the New Freedom Commission advances. The problems come with distinguishing the first from the second path. A choice between the second and third roads is much more controversial. Many people would prefer the third direction over the second, because it is safer to maintain the status quo. The risk takers and entrepreneurs among us would prefer the second direction over the third. The remainder of this book is designed to inform our choice of which directions to take in our journey to help children and families deal with the challenges of growing up with mental health challenges, with the vision of a society that attempts to eliminate mental health problems when possible, and otherwise treatment them with accessible, effective, and respectful interventions.

CHAPTER 2

PROBLEMS WITH THE CURRENT SYSTEM: TENSIONS AND SYNDROMES

Gnothi suaton.

THE ORACLE AT DELPHI, SOPHOCLES, *Oedipus Rex*

The Oracle's admonition to know yourself followed by George Santana's analysis that those who fail to understand history are condemned to repeat it are different roads to the same essential truth. Self-awareness and understanding are significant components of any change process. Although histories often are presented as a series of facts, sometimes the lessons of history are generally best understood as processes—the way things happen in sequence or together in time. Single events can be best understood within the context in which they occurred. Pressures that arise at a particular time lead to changes in policies and approaches. A failure to understand the complications that have arisen in the patchwork development of current public mental health systems of care may make it impossible to direct a positive evolution of this system. Despite the widespread acceptance of the basic tenets of the system-of-care philosophy, the progress toward the implementation of this philosophy has been slow; in some areas, no progress has been observable.

As discussed in chapter 1, the current system has arisen from a variety of both parallel and intersecting processes. This has led to a system that is neither comprehensive nor integrated. The present chapter discusses the status of the current system in terms of two related phenomena—tensions and syndromes.

The current system can be understood in terms of pressures that pull the system in competing ways. I refer to these pressures as "tensions" in the system. Tensions are defined as competing pressures arising from incompatible or opposing goals and objectives that push or pull the system in opposite directions. For instance, there is a tension between the use of outcomes for accountability and their use in quality improvement. The first use demands evidence of positive effects of a treatment or service, whereas the second use demands identifying problems that can be fixed. These two uses compete with each other, thus creating a tension. There are conceptual and structural aspects of the existing children's mental health service system that create these tensions between contrasting and competing objectives. In most cases, tensions cannot be resolved; they can only be managed. To effectively manage tensions, the system partners must agree on where to balance the system, relative to the competing poles that create the tension.

In contrast, by syndromes, I mean habitual maladaptive patterns of behavior that have developed as a result of the historical, philosophical, and contextual environment in which the children's public mental health has developed. Often, syndromes develop in response to tensions. For example, state personnel in position of authority can become imperial in their approach to community providers. A decision is made with regard to a new policy, a procedure is made, and notification is sent out with a start date. Syndromes work at cross-purposes with the purported goals and objectives of the service system and result in the system functioning in a different, and often opposite, direction from the original intent. Unlike tensions, syndromes can be eliminated. Once a balance is found for tensions, the bad habits that arise from these tensions can be eliminated.

This chapter presents and discusses some of the critical tensions and syndromes that currently affect the design and function of the public mental health system for children. Both tensions and syndromes can develop within three levels of the service system—the system, the program, and the individual child and family. System-level tensions and syndromes impact how the various partners in a system of care interact with each other. These involve problems of interaction among the partners in the system. Program-level syndromes and tensions impact how individual agencies and/or programs function within the larger system. These involve problems that exist within organizations or programs. Finally, child- and family-level syndromes and tensions affect services one family at a time. These are problems that affect how individual children and families interact with the service-delivery system and individual providers.

Tensions

Often, relationships in public mental health are akin to a tug-of-war—two sides pulling from opposite ends of the same rope. The stronger each side pulls, the greater the tension on the rope. In these contests, usually one side eventually wins or the rope breaks. In the children's public mental health system, the struggle usually lasts much longer. Tensions can be quite complicated. They are structural aspects of the system that cannot be eliminated, but must be understood and managed. An active decision must be made as to where in the balance between the sides of a tension a system must be directed. With most tensions, it is likely that the best path is somewhere in the middle of the two extremes. Often there is no "right" answer, just opportunities and dangers that come with shifting the emphasis from one side of a tension to another. A review of some of the most salient tensions in the current children's system reveals some of this complexity.

System-Level Tensions

Cottage Industry versus Systems of Care

Earlier, we discussed the development of mental health services in the community. Often this was done in a fashion that resulted in a number of small agencies, or individual providers, springing up to offer services that were certainly not planfully integrated (see the "Political Dog Walk" section later in this chapter). In many cases, various small providers would be completely ignorant of the existence of other small providers.

Over time, some of these small providers developed into big agencies that now provide a range of services. However, more often than not, a variety of factors conspire to limit the size and reach of individual agencies. These factors include geographical boundaries that define recipient eligibility and funding decisions designed to spread out dollars. As a symptom of this tension, many agencies seek to develop resource directories to help guide their recipients to other available services. This can be a surprisingly difficult task, given the number and range of providers and the different pathways through which referrals occur for each. Often, by the time a resource directory is compiled, it is out of date.

There are some large multistate agencies that specialize in providing certain types of services—some examples include Pressley Ridge Schools and Devereux, who provide congregate care or residentially based services, and Charter, which has operated a chain of psychiatric hospitals. There are also large agencies within states that provide close to a full array of services (e.g., Hillside in upstate New York and Metropolitan Family Services in Chicago).

As discussed in chapter 1, one factor that has influenced the development of the cottage industry model of mental health service delivery has been the use of catchment areas. By giving different agencies responsibilities in different catchment areas, two things are accomplished. First, no agency can readily grow past its allocated geographic boundaries; and second, competition among agencies for improved quality, accessibility, or cost is eliminated. Limiting the size of an agency to its geographic region has both advantages and disadvantages. In many ways, this strategy keeps the agency close to its community. Cultural sensitivity and competence should be enhanced. In addition, if a particular agency is powerful but not particularly good, its limited growth potential helps to keep its ineffectiveness also limited. On the other hand, there is very little economy of scale. Generally, no individual agency has a large enough group of recipients to assume much risk. The assumption of risk—a major financial component in most models of accountability—requires a sufficient pool of recipients so that risk can be spread over a large number of people. This is how private insurance works. By insuring millions of people, when tragedy befalls a few, the entire system is not brought down. When you are covering only one or two hundred individuals, one horrific case can easily bankrupt the entire system. To put it succinctly, ten million dollars is not much money to the federal government; however, this amount would bankrupt almost any individual agency and most counties.

Multiple Models

For much of this century, there has been ongoing tension and controversy among various models of mental health, many of which were given legitimacy by significant segments within the mental health community. Perhaps the two most commonly cited models are the medical and the social model. The tension between these models creates an atmosphere in which professionals are encouraged to "take sides." This is both counterintuitive and, in the long run, destructive to the mental health field.

The medical model's primary assumption is that mental health challenges are illnesses or disorders. The concept of both an illness and disorder implies a common set of symptoms and a common etiology and prognosis/course. Generally, illness models have a concept of a pathogen. In mental health, putative pathogens that have been identified include such things as neurotransmitters, intrapsychic conflicts, and negative thoughts. The goal of treatment is to remove the pathogen. Thus, treatments such as serotonin-reuptake inhibitors, insight-oriented psychotherapy, and thought replacement through cognitive–behavioral interventions are given scientific credibility through their linkage to proposed pathogens. The implication of these approaches is that the individual is the locus of the mental illness and the treatment of that individual then is the goal of mental health intervention.

The social model's primary assumption is that mental health challenges result from normal responses to abnormal situations. In this model, the environment is the source of mental health difficulties. There is a wide range of philosophies and theories that can fall under the general rubric of a social model. Erving Goffman's (1961) and Thomas Szasz's (1974) notions of the social origins of labeling different people as mentally ill would represent one perspective within this framework, as would the ideas of other theorists who talk of the social construction of mental illness. However, this model is a big tent. Family theorists emphasize the family system's role in creating harmful behavior among family members through unhealthy relationships. Sociologists who emphasize poverty, hopelessness, and deprivation represent a third perspective. What binds these perspectives to a single theme is that they all share the basic assumption that mental health challenges reside outside of the individual. The individual's behaviors and problems are really only a symptom of a social or environmental system that is not functioning effectively. Thus, intervention with the individual is not even necessary in order to address the problem. Interventions must be directed either to that individual's social system or to the larger community, or, in the extreme, society (e.g., eliminate poverty).

It is quite likely that both perspectives have something to offer toward the understanding of mental health, illness, and well-being. The artificial dichotomy between the individual and his or her social system is an unneeded relic of abandoned philosophies. In fact, the individual and the environment, although clearly divisible, are inseparable in a comprehensive theory of behavior as they should be in our approaches to treatment. Understanding the complex interactions between people and their environments is a critical component to treatment planning. Several models have been advanced that emphasize this greater level of complexity. The Person-in-Environment System (Williams, Karls, & Wandrei, 1989) emphasizes the importance of assessment across social roles, environmental problems, psychiatric symptoms, and the individual's physical condition. The Biopsychosocial Model (e.g., Nurcombe & Gallagher, 1986) emphasizes the complex interactions among biology and psychological and social factors. Although these models have been resources for quite some time, they have not yet been integrated into service system design and management policies and procedures. For instance, insurance models completely ignore social and environmental factors that can influence a child's health.

Central versus Local Control

A long-standing tension in government-funded services is the relationship between central and local authority. On the one hand, central authority can oversee widespread development of a particular model. It provides opportunities for savings based on the magnitude of scale and can mandate sweeping changes more readily than can ever be accomplished at the local level. As was learned during the civil rights movement, central authority also can intervene to ensure equality and respect for the rights of individuals in situations in which local authority is unable or unwilling to do so.

On the other hand, as demonstrated through the failed experiment of communism, central control can be exceptionally bureaucratic, slow moving, and corrupt. It is generally not responsive to variations in needs at the local level. Central authorities often expect everyone to attempt to do the same thing, whether or not it makes sense in relation to local circumstances. Given the vast diversity of our country, this can pose an enormous challenge. New York City and Chicago are quite different from rural Mississippi or the suburbs of Tucson. Expecting the same model to work equivalently in all settings is, at best, naive. As a result, it is not uncommon for the sweeping changes mandated by central authorities to be met with hostility or indifference at the local level. Local authorities shake their proverbial heads and wonder what on earth the people in Washington were thinking.

In the children's public mental health system, there are at least five distinct levels of the system that must be considered when devolving or centralizing authority. The highest three levels are governmental entities; the lowest two levels are not. The highest level is the federal government. The U.S. government has impact on the system primarily through Medicaid regulations and the activities of the Substance Abuse Mental Health Service Administration (SAMHSA). Although Medicaid is managed through the states, the 50 percent federal match and the regulations that come with these dollars have a significant impact on the public mental health system. Although all Medicaid systems are state run (unlike Medicare, which is centrally managed by the federal government), the dollars coming from Washington provide some leverage for the federal government in this system. Different administrations have tightened or loosened these regulations over the years. In the past decade, for example, relaxing the requirements for obtaining waivers from basic Medicaid has resulted in a variety of innovative state experiments with system-of-care developments.

The federal role is fairly contained, consisting of funding Medicaid, demonstration projects through SAMHSA, and research though the National Institute of Mental Health, the National Institute on Drug Abuse, and the National Institute on Alcohol Abuse and Alcoholism. A number of other cabinet-level agencies (e.g., the Department of Education and the Department of Justice) have small roles in funding research and service demonstration projects that intersect with children's mental health. The federal government also can exert influence through the passage of laws (e.g., Individuals with Disabilities Act, Americans with Disability Act, and parity legislation).

The primary governmental partner in the children's pubic mental health system is the state, which is the second level of authority. Most public mental health services are funded either through the state Departments of Health (Medicaid) or Departments of Mental Health. The level of central authority taken by these state agencies is a key decision within the system. States vary widely in the degree of central control exercised. Some states have powerful central authorities, whereas other states have weak authorities that are generally trumped by large providers in the state. Some states have delegated most of their authority to contracted managed behavioral health corporations.

The third level of authority is the local level—usually a county, but sometimes a city. Medicaid has a local match and counties, sometimes through mental health boards, exercise some control. Often the level of local governmental control is determined by how much authority the state is willing to devolve to its local government partners.

The fourth level of authority in the system is the provider. Historically, because the public mental health system was evolved from the medical model of service delivery, the provider exercised enormous authority in deciding whether an individual child or family was eligible for services, what services to provide, and how long these services should be received. The dramatic impact of managed behavioral health care and related technologies has primarily been the erosion of provider-held power over decision making.

The fifth and final level of authority—and, in many ways, the ultimate arbiter of all decisions—is the individual child and family. Historically, this power has manifested itself through the families' decision making about seeking services and adhering to recommended service plans. One of the primary foci of the consumer movement in public mental health generally, and the family movement in the children's system specifically, has been an effort to increase the authority that the family can exercise over decision making in the children's system of care. Essentially, the belief is that if families are given greater input into the system management, they will have broader options than simply staying in or dropping out of a prescribed treatment.

The degree to which power is shifted across these five levels of authority can have a dramatic influence on the nature and function of a public mental health system of care. Central authority leads to consistency of policy and procedures, but risks insensitivity. Local control leads to flexibility and responsiveness to local needs, but risks unfairness and can increase redundancy in development processes. Family control leads to empowerment, but may risk overspending.

Budget Silos versus Blended Funding

As mentioned in chapter 1, a silo refers to a vertically organized, child-serving agency that does not encourage collaboration with other similarly organized agencies. Blended funding, on the other hand, refers to pooling resources to approach the development and management of the child-serving system from a uniform financing perspective.

A colleague told me a story of being in a meeting about juvenile justice services in a state that had just opened a big new facility to house incarcerated juveniles. In a discussion of community-based alternatives to incarceration, the director of the facility stated something to the effect of "We just opened this place. I'll be damned if I'll support anything that might make it obsolete." This administrator resisted the development of community-based interventions to address the complex needs of youth with juvenile justice involvement in order to maintain census in his newly built facility.

The relationship of child welfare to residential treatment is another example. In a number of states, parents must give up custody of their children to the state in order for them to be placed in a residential treatment facility. A child with serious emotional and/or behavioral needs can be pretty difficult to manage at home. Without options for intensive community services or in situations in which the child's, family's, or community's safety is a concern, use of residential treatment is an important option. However, a family with limited insurance generally cannot afford this level of treatment. In order to obtain the type of service these parents believe their child requires, they are forced to give up guardianship. One can only imagine how demeaning and humiliating this process could be for many parents. Still worse, these parents then have absolutely no control over when they get guardianship of their children back. It is entirely up to the state's child welfare agency. Successful completion of residential treatment may not necessarily result in a return home. If parents believe that their decision regarding placement was a mistake, they have limited recourse to bring their child home. Residential treatment providers are, quite likely, less accountable and responsive to state agencies than to individual parents. Because of the lack of options in the mental health silo, parents are forced to transfer their children to the child welfare silo with no assurances about the actual long-term value of this terrible choice to give up custody of their child in order to obtain services.

A third example of the silo versus blended funding tension comes from the relationship of schools to intensive treatment. Federal law requires schools to address any and all needs of children that interfere with that child's learning. This is accomplished through an Individual Education Plan (IEP), which is the foundation for special education interventions. Schools have to pay for any needs that are identified in the IEP. This can be a major problem for small or poor school districts, if a particular child has complex needs. For obvious reasons, schools are much more comfortable if some other system has financial responsibility for funding mental health treatment. A tension arises between having an IEP and not identifying emotional and behavioral needs in the IEP for fear of taking on a budget-busting commitment for a particularly challenging child. Some school districts are quite

responsible in this regard; others are not. A lot of a school's responsiveness has to do with parental advocacy. The knowledgeable and
assertive parents get services for their children, whereas those who
are less informed or involved have children whose needs are not met.
In two states where we've studied access to intensive community
and residential treatment, we found that parental involvement and
advocacy was one of the best predictors for which children received
services funded by their school district. This creates enormous disparities for less-educated, less-knowledgeable, or less-political parents. This can be a particular problem for children in state custody.
Many of these children (perhaps one-third or more by our estimates
in New York City) might be eligible for special education services due
to diagnosable psychiatric disorders. Many, if not most, never receive
an IEP.

Blended funding as a financing option has gained favor over the
past several decades. The basic idea of this model is that you combine
all the resources of the children's system into a single funding pool
and then allocate services to individual children and families based
on identified needs. Although blended funding is an appealing concept, its operationalization is quite difficult and its implementation
is complex. When money is pooled, there must be some centralized
management of those resources. Competition among perspectives or
system partners remains, the tension just moves "downstream" from
the system level to the program or provider level.

School Districts and Service-Delivery Boundaries

School systems are one of the fundamental institutions in a child's
life. It is the core experience shared by all children 5 to 16 years old in
the United States. Any successful system-of-care approach to children's
services requires the active collaboration of the schools. However, in
the United States, schools are organized by school district, whereas
no other service system is organized using the same geographic limitations. Most mental health services are organized either by county
or by catchment area. School districts are funded primarily through
property tax revenues. Most school districts are neighborhood or city
based, and most counties contain a large number of school districts.
Because each district has its own politics and leadership, coordination
between schools and service system can be extremely difficult. For
example, a single, community-based, mental health program might
serve children who are enrolled across five or more school districts.
County-level programs can have even more school districts. Because

effective systems of care are based, in large part, on the relationships among the representatives of the system partners, developing and maintaining the many associations is daunting.

The service-boundary tension also has implications for cultural sensitivity and competence. In many large urban areas, where the greatest cultural diversity is generally found, the mental health service system is organized by catchment areas. This term refers to the geographic boundaries of the community mental health center. The center is required to serve residents of their catchment area. Other individuals residing outside of these geographic boundaries may or may not be eligible for services, depending on a variety of factors. As mentioned previously, catchment areas often have little to do with the organization of neighborhoods. Neighborhoods are often shaped around shared cultural or ethnic experiences and backgrounds. If catchment-area boundaries are not inclusive of a neighborhood, then potential opportunities are lost for making services responsive to the culture of that neighborhood. Understanding cultural factors is critical to high-quality services; when geographic boundaries cross or ignore neighborhoods, unnecessary limitations are imposed on the creation of localized, culturally sensitive services.

Insurance Model versus Biopsychosocial Model

The notion of health insurance has evolved from a risk-pooling strategy for providing a nontaxable benefit in lieu of salary into the primary means of financing health care in the United States. Much has changed over the past 50 years, including the notion that health insurance is a nontaxable benefit. In addition, the federal government has entered the health insurance industry through its participation in Medicaid and Medicare. However, despite these significant changes, several critical things have remained the same. For the most part, health insurance pays for health care in the presence of a diagnosed medical condition. The payment goes for the medical intervention intended to treat or eliminate the symptoms of that condition. Thus, health insurance has a pretty narrow definition of who gets services and which services are covered. The insurance model is quite consistent with the medical model of mental health.

Over the past several decades, it has become increasingly apparent that mental health problems are complex and have a variety of relevant psychological and social cofactors that either facilitate or impede treatment and recovery. As mentioned previously, it is now accepted that the individual and his or her environment are inseparable in understanding the origins of psychiatric problems. Successful intervention requires a broader way of thinking about an individual's need than simply the presence or absence of specific diagnoses. This is particularly true for children who reside in a complex family environment. To understand and effectively treat the child, it is necessary to understand the entire family. The foundation of family systems approaches to treatment is that you can treat an individual in any family by working with other members of his or her family (e.g., Green & Framo, 1981). Many evidence-based practices for children include things that are not traditionally thought of as treatments. For example, flexible funding to allow for the purchase of music lessons or some other strength-building intervention is a standard aspect of the wraparound model (Burchard, Bruns, & Burchard, 2002). Thus, what is known about what works can be at odds with how the health insurance system has been designed and implemented.

Eligibility versus Prevention

Most services are reserved for people who meet eligibility criteria. For mental health, this eligibility often includes criteria of a sufficient level of need (e.g., a psychiatric disorder, a serious emotional/ behavioral disorder, or risk of hospitalization). In situations in which resources are limited, eligibility criteria are an important strategy for allocating resources by targeting those with the greatest need. There are many examples of eligibility criteria that are used to allocate limited resources. Public welfare is reserved for those living in poverty. Welfare reform in the late 1990s limited entitlements further, to five years for those living in poverty unless a disability limited the individual's ability to work. Entrance to many universities is limited to those with a sufficient academic record of achievement that suggests success in higher education.

Public mental health services for children generally use eligibility criteria. To receive Medicaid coverage for treatment, a psychiatric diagnosis is required. For some services, additional eligibility requirements are created to further target a particular population. Many programs require the diagnosis of a serious emotional or behavioral disorder (Narrow et al., 1998), which is a somewhat more stringent criterion than simply the presence of any psychiatric diagnosis according to the *Diagnostic and Statistical Manual of Mental Disorders*, 4th edition (American Psychiatric Association, 1994). In addition, some intensive community services have the rather ambiguous additional criteria that the child would "otherwise be placed out of community" or "hospitalized" or some other statement implying that if not for the child's enrollment in the community services, the child would be in a much more expensive service environment.

The advantages of eligibility criteria are clear. First, eligibility criteria provide a mechanism to ration services based on need. This is generally perceived to be the fairest way to allocate limited resources. Only children who need a particular service should receive it, and providing services to children with no need (and who, therefore, are implicitly unable to benefit from that service) is wasteful. Second, it allows for the institutionalization of matching the needs of youth with the goals and objectives of the program. If a program or service is designed for children with specific needs and/or characteristics, then making these needs and/or characteristics into eligibility criteria is really quite rational.

On the other side of this tension is prevention. One of the greatest disadvantages of eligibility criteria is that they require a certain degree of "failure to prevent" before services are initiated. In other words, a child has to get to a certain degree of need before services are made available. There is a metaphor that captures the problem. If you have pollution in a river, you have at least two choices: You can treat the river in an effort to remove the pollution or you can go up river, find the source of the pollution, and stop it. Most people would argue that it makes the most sense to go up river and prevent the pollution in the first place. Most of the structure of the existing mental health system takes the former approach: it treats the river.

Program-Level Tensions

Business Model versus Clinical Model

One of the most challenging tensions facing public mental health services for children is the disconnection between the business model under which the service is financed and/or reimbursed and the clinical model under which care is provided. There is often considerable tension between these two perspectives. Perhaps a few examples will help to clarify the complex issues embedded in this tension.

I recently was interviewing a case manager who complained about the lack of availability of respite workers for their agency. Respite workers are a critical component of intensive community services for children because they essentially "baby-sit" challenging children and youth to give primary caregivers a break to relax or take care of other matters. The case manager went on to state that it was no wonder the agency couldn't find enough respite workers because they could only pay them $2.50 an hour. The director of the statewide program also was present for this discussion. Following the meeting, he informed me that the agency was actually paid $10 an hour for respite services. They decided only to provide them if they could make a 300 percent profit on the actual cost of the respite worker. Thus, the agency's business decision regarding how much they could afford to pay a respite worker had the direct impact of rendering this service unavailable for most children and families.

More than a decade ago, New York State developed a comprehensive emergency program (CPEP) that has crisis assessments, mobile crisis, extended observation beds, and crisis housing as components. Although sites have been funded all over the state, only a few sites have successfully implemented the crisis-housing component. In interviews with CPEP directors, two significant barriers were identified. First, the crisis-housing model in the program only provided for up to three days of housing. No semipermanent housing arrangements could be made within that time frame; thus, crisis housing could not be used for homeless individuals with serious mental illness. Once admitted, these individuals would always overstay the arbitrary program limit. Second, the money was given to the hospital that ran the CPEP. It was then expected that the hospital would pay a crisis-housing provider when this service was needed. As one program director stated to me, "My hospital would not be very happy if I had an open bed in the hospital and rather than filling that bed, I decided to actually spend money to purchase crisis housing." Not only would the hospital have the opportunity cost of the open bed, but it would actually lose money that it was not contractually required to spend. The only locations in which the crisis-housing component worked were in places with a nearby state-operated hospital campus that had converted some closed inpatient unit beds into a continuum of housing options for persons with serious mental illness. In these situations, some of the beds could be used for crisis placements at no cost to the hospital.

Another example of shifting a business model to be consistent with the clinical model occurred when the Illinois's Department of Children and Family Services (DCFS) recognized that psychiatric hospitals were being used as transitional placements. Residential treatment centers and foster homes would hospitalize a child that they felt they could no longer manage and then a new placement would have to be found while the child was in the hospital. This use of the hospital as a placement transition created a great deal of place-ment instability in the system. In this circumstance, I referred to the psychiatric hospitals as the "flippers in the pinball of state wards' lives." Foster parents and congregate care providers would hospital-ize difficult kids and then not accept them back at discharge. This was an enormous problem for hospitals that then had hard-to-place chil-dren on their units who, although initially needing hospitalization, stayed well beyond medical necessity because there was no place for them to go. Medicaid would deny payment and the hospitals would be stuck holding the bill for the failure of the child welfare system. To solve this problem, DCFS made two basic policy changes. First, they required any placement from which a child was hospitalized to accept the return of that child upon discharge from the hospital. In other words, the psychiatric hospital could not be used as a placement transition. Second, DCFS agreed to take over payment to the hospi-tals for extended stays when placement problems couldn't be solved. Thus, there was no longer any financial advantage for DCFS to leave a child in the hospital because they were no longer attempting to shift costs to Medicaid. In fact, there was the potential for an enormous expense. These two policy changes had a dramatic impact on both the likelihood that a child returned to placement upon discharge and on the average hospital stay for wards of the state.

Accountability versus Quality Improvement

As outcomes management strategies become more common in pub-lic mental health settings, they introduce an interesting and complex tension for providers. On the one hand, outcomes are used to enhance accountability. States and third-party payers working in the public sector increasingly demand evidence of positive outcomes associated with service use. There is even movement toward performance-based contracting, whereby a provider is paid to obtain certain outcomes. In these circumstances, it is incumbent on providers to document the effectiveness of their interventions.

However, outcomes data are often best used to improve ongoing service delivery through quality-improvement approaches. There is an essential tension between accountability and quality-improvement strategies. Accountability stresses demonstrable effectiveness. The pressure is on programs/providers to prove that their services are working. Evidence of effectiveness is a part of marketing programs and maintaining funding. Quality improvement *requires* the identifica-tion of areas of weakness. There is no point in attempting to improve an intervention that is working well. Rather, the focus of quality improvement is on identifying problems with services, attempting to fix those problems, and reassessing the impact of the improvement initiative.

Leadership Salaries versus Line-Staff Salaries

The problem of high salaries for leadership and low salaries for entry-level employees is not just a problem in the business world. With many community agencies, the problems associated with salary disparities can be nearly as acute as with Fortune 500 companies. Of course, the payment options are not as flexible because, at least in most cases, stock options are not available.

Salary discrepancies are a difficult problem. Working with challenging children is the work of angels, and anybody who attempts to engage in this work should be compensated fairly. Experienced, competent leadership is required in the public mental health system. Because higher salaries are available in other fields and in the private sector, keeping the best and the brightest requires investments in salaries for leadership.

Recently, in New York, provider organizations identified low staff salaries as a primary problem for workforce recruitment and retention. However, when a state agency opened positions for social workers at $62,000 a year, these same organizations went into an uproar. They felt that the agency would draw away their best talent with a higher salary. Thus, instead of applauding an increase in wages for social workers, the provider organizations attempted to block this increase.

Liability versus a Learning Culture Environment

More than any culture, Americans use the legal system to work out grievances; it is well documented that we live in a litigious society. Beginning about 20 years ago, it became common practice for some companies to simply settle out of court any claims brought against them. This strategy has furthered our litigiousness, by increasing the likelihood of a payout regardless of the strength of the case.

For obvious reasons, programs and private practitioners are nervous about lawsuits. Defending oneself in court is an expensive proposition; losing a lawsuit is even more expensive. Although mental health malpractice insurance is substantially less than in other areas of health care, it continues to be a significant operating expense.

Fear of litigation oftentimes can be translated into a fear of documentation. Although this fear is often quite unrealistic, it can feel very real. Many times during an implementation process of an outcomes management initiative, I have been asked about the legal ramifications of documenting success or failure. Although I am unaware of any lawsuits that use outcomes management data on the plaintiff's side, this fact does not always assuage the lawsuit-phobic administrator. It is not uncommon for some programs to focus their documentation practices and policies around what keeps them safe from lawsuits and other legal actions, while still meeting accreditation standards.

This focus on using documentation to avoid trouble can work at cross-purposes to using information to learn about how to best serve children and families. Successful outcomes management strategies require consistent reliable information about clinically relevant issues, so that the system and program can remain focused on the shared vision of helping children and families. If the agency is focused on immunity from lawsuits, this information sometimes is simply unavailable.

Clinician versus Administrator Tension

I sometimes tell the graduate students in my program that in preparing for their careers, they need to consider that there really are only four things Ph.D. clinical psychologists can do: clinical practice, research, administration, or teaching. Anyone can teach, but the other three options are quite limited. If you are a doctoral-level psychologist and working in an organized setting, it is unlikely that you will provide much direct service; you are just too expensive. Thus, to justify your salary, you become an administrator. The program director can be paid more than program staff. In programs and settings that have evolved from a medical model, psychiatrists are nearly always the administrators—different degree, but the same problem. They do not teach administration in either medical school or graduate clinical psychology programs. Not coincidentally, they do not teach business management and administration in many Psy.D. or M.S.W. programs either.

We learned the lesson in hospital management, but haven't yet gotten around to understanding this problem in mental health. Somehow, we have come to believe that people who operate even complex service-delivery systems must come from a background where they were originally trained to provide services. However, training in

administration is generally only experiential. Perhaps it's like working your way up from the mailroom in a corporation—you've got to
pay your dues as a direct-service staff in order to have credibility as a
director. That makes sense in terms of the political culture of a mental
health service delivery organization; however, it has several untoward
consequences. First, by the time the program directors have worked
their way into a leadership position, their clinical training may be
outdated. Second, the lessons learned in direct service can serve to
"institutionalize" an individual into thinking that the way things are
currently done is the right way to do things. In these circumstances,
change becomes more difficult. For example, in our current community mental health system, some of the greatest opponents to change
come from the leaders of the past generation. People created their
programs, carved out a home in the system, and became the status
quo. Metaphorically, the only politicians who are in favor of term limits are the ones who are not in office.

Child- and Family-Level Tensions

The Unequal Information Tension

Recent (2001) Nobel Prize winners in economics, Akerloff (1970)
and Spence (1973), won the prestigious award for their work on the
impact of unequal information on market economies. These economists presented the argument that free market economies do not
function in their usual effective and self-corrective ways in situations
in which the buyer and the seller have dramatically unequal levels of
information about the product. The example they used was that of
used car sales. In a used car transaction, the seller of the automobile
is generally far more knowledgeable about the automobile's history
than is the buyer. This places the seller at a significant advantage
(e.g., he or she can lie). Of course, a knowledgeable buyer can equal-
ize this somewhat through his or her ability to assess the current
condition of the automobile. In general, however, the seller maintains
a distinct advantage. In economics, this is called market asymmetry.
According to Akerloff (1970), the rules of a free market economy do
not describe the behavior of the used car marketplace. It is not difficult to determine that this type of information imbalance very likely
affects a number of other markets as well, including health care and,
specifically, behavioral health care.

Although there are many differences between selling used cars
and providing behavioral health care, the issue of unequal informa-

tion clearly can be a tension in this system. Professionals have a great advantage in terms of the use of language, the understanding of possible causes and effect of behaviors and ways of thinking, and the probable impact and side effects of psychotropic medications. Service recipients—particularly those who are newly entering the system—can have very limited information about the nature and possible causes of psychiatric disorders, the choices for treatment, and the expected durations and outcomes from these various treatments. They may have idealistic expectations about the knowledge of the professional. As recipients become savvier, they begin to learn "how things work." Over time, this shifting information balance can be a very potent tension between the provider and recipient.

To illustrate an extreme example of this tension's potential impact, an experience suffered by a very dear friend comes to mind. She and her husband entered therapy because they were struggling with their marriage. Their therapist split them apart and met with them separately, often two or three times a week with each. The therapist developed boundary problems with her, often describing in detail his wife's problems, her underwear, their sexual behavior, and so forth. He repeatedly pushed the wife to develop and describe sexual fantasies about him. He would tell her one thing and her husband something entirely different to keep them both in therapy, but apart emotionally. Over several years, they had paid more than $100,000 for this therapy. It was not until she decided to go to graduate school to become a psychologist that she caught on to his game. As soon as she became aware of the manipulation, she sat down with her husband and compared experiences. They were both astounded at each other's stories. The final result was a lawsuit with a six-figure settlement and professional censure for the psychologist. Sadly, it was too late for their marriage; the damage had already been done. However, if she had not gone to graduate school and "leveled the playing field" in terms of information available, it is impossible to know how long this unhealthy charade of pseudotherapy would have continued. Further, one could easily imagine that if this couple had been knowledgeable about the appropriate therapeutic process at the outset, this therapist would never have had the ability (or the chutzpah) to attempt his manipulations.

Of course, the vast majority of therapeutic encounters do not have such dire consequences. Most therapists have more character and professional ethics than that unethical therapist. However, the point remains, when buyers of behavioral health services are insufficiently informed about what they are purchasing, the seller—in behavioral health, the therapist, psychiatrist, or case manager—is in an exceptionally strong position to provide whatever he or she sees fit to provide. This tension contributes to initiation of the unethical behavior that can occur in therapeutic relationships.

Provider Convenience versus Recipient Convenience

As described in chapter 1, mental health services derive originally from treatment designed for wealthy European women. The concept of treatment was about having an expert apply a specific and complex treatment to cure a disease or disorder. In this situation, the marketplace problem becomes maximizing the ability of these experts to be able to treat as many individuals as possible. The priority is to ensure that the expert is available and, with a limited pool of experts, their convenience is the supreme consideration. Thus, the system's primary intent is to make it as easy as possible for providers to reach as many individuals in need of treatment as possible. That requires the system to make things easy for the providers.

I had a conversation with a recently trained Master's-level clinician. She was at a training forum for residential treatment providers in Illinois. At a break, I asked her how she had decided to work in residential treatment. Her response was instructive. During her graduate training, and immediately after, she had worked in an outpatient clinic. She stated that she found that very frustrating because the families and children often "wouldn't show up" for treatment appointments. She really liked residential treatment because she "knew the kids would be there so that [she] could treat them." She did not seem to consider the fact that when given a choice, a lot of children and families do not want what we are offering them. When they have no choice, they'll at least attend.

The powerful reality is that all institutions function at the convenience of the institution. It is true of all organizations; it is the nature of making a business model work as effectively as possible. By establishing policies and procedures that make providing services as efficient as possible, providers are more productive and/or profitable. This focus on institutional convenience is influenced by the fact that most decision making, with regard to policy and procedures, is an internal process—informed primarily by voices within the organization that advocate for improvements in their work conditions.

Provider convenience issues can take a turn toward the absurd when financing overlaps with convenience. Often community providers who have contracts for comprehensive, individualized services are hesitant to subcontract to other local agencies for services that they do not offer. In the worst case, agencies would rather deny the person in need of the service than pass what they consider to be their money to a competitor. One example comes from a friend and colleague of mine who is also the mother of a teenage son with serious emotional problems. Her son was enrolled in an intensive community-service program and she was seeking respite services. The agency that was providing this wraparound-type program was unable to maintain respite staff, despite the fact that respite services were one of the four required core services of the statewide program. Instead of facilitating this mother in finding respite elsewhere, the agency simply stonewalled her until the mother could point to the program regulations allowing her to select her own respite provider. If she had not read the fine print and learned how to effectively advocate for her child's respite services, she would not have received the necessary services.

Another example of provider convenience comes with scheduling appointments. It is not uncommon for outpatient clinics to offer most appointments during normal business hours. Evening or Saturday appointment slots can be rare. This means that it is often required that the child miss school and/or the parent miss work in order to attend the session. Most children with emotional or behavior problems have difficulties in school. Removing them from school for a half a day each week so that they can attend a treatment session seems less than optimal. Further, it is not uncommon for single parents of children with serious emotional and behavioral disorders to find it impossible to work, due to the demands of ensuring that the child's needs are met. When the child has problems at school, the school calls and expects the parent to come; treatment visits are scheduled when the clinic has an opening, and so forth. Given these circumstances, it should not be surprising that the majority of outpatient episodes of care end with the child and/or family simply stopping attendance (Lyons & Shallcross, 2000).

Parents versus Professionals—Who Cares More?

As mentioned in chapter 1, early theories of psychopathology in children emphasized the role of parents, particularly mothers, in the development of these problems. In large part because of the widespread knowledge of these theories, there is a tension between parents and professionals. Sometimes this tension can become manifest as a competition regarding who cares the most, and the most effectively, for our children. You see this problem of competition most acutely in the child welfare setting, where foster parents sometimes see themselves as rescuers of children from their biological parents. Foster parenting is the work of angels. All over the country, selfless individuals step in to try to raise children when these children's parents have failed to provide a minimum of safety and nurturance. It is perhaps natural for at least some of these foster parents to see the biological parents as "not in the best interest of the child." However, when the permanency plan is to return the child to his or her parent as soon as the parent addresses the problems that led to state custody (e.g., drug-abuse problems), this tension can make reunification more difficult and may even hinder the biological parent's best efforts to resume their parenting role.

Similarly, I reviewed a case in Texas of a young child who was placed in a residential program due to his developmental disability. In the notes, it stated that because the child cried whenever his mother left from a visit, the staff recommended suspending these visits because they were obviously "upsetting to the child." What kind of logic is this, where the natural sadness of a goodbye becomes some sort of psychopathology engendered by the parental visit?

In New York State, 27 percent of all placements in residential treatment facilities (RTFs) end due to "noncompliance." In some of these situations, the child runs away from the program and does not return. However, in more than half of these situations, the child is removed from treatment by their parents due to a disagreement with the RTF regarding treatment approach. Generally, parents wanted their children home sooner, whereas RTF staff pushed for longer stays. When parents stood their ground, children were released "against medical advice" and the family was seen as resistant or noncompliant with treatment.

Nobody has cornered the market on caring. Many people can care about the same child. When these multiple caregivers compete, it is never in the best interests of the child.

What Youth Want versus What Others Want for Them

I recently ran a series of focus groups with youth who had substantial experience with the public children's service system, including mental health, child welfare, juvenile justice, and special education. The perspectives of these youth were compelling. What was clear in listening to them is that they did not have much enthusiasm for receiving any more services per se. An inventory of what these youth wanted most would be the following three things:

- Somebody to love them
- Something to do with their time that was fun
- A job

There is very little a public system can do about the first wish. Although therapeutic and program staff can be caring and supportive, paid caregivers generally cannot replace natural loving supports in a child's life. There is a lot we can do about the second two issues; however, recreational and vocational activities very often are not the focus of mental health services.

A second observation these youth made was that the very process of receiving services placed them under a higher level of scrutiny than were their peers. Once identified as someone who had mental health needs, adults tended to expect them to have trouble and kept a close eye out for any such trouble. Small mistakes that all youth make got identified and addressed for these youth, whereas they perceived their peers as able to slide by without getting in trouble. I know that my own children have sometimes engaged in the very behaviors that reportedly resulted in some children in foster care being admitted to the psychiatric hospital. I have overheard my kids threatening to kill each other; however, I interpreted it as a figure of speech (e.g., how many of us have said something like "I could just kill you"). Take this language out of the family environment and add a risk-adverse foster parent and the results can be quite different. This form of stigma creates a powerful deterrent within the youth culture to ever being identified as having needs.

Child Focus versus Family Focus

An additional implication of the insurance model is that medical conditions are known to be resident in individuals. Although contagious disease can spread among families, the family is not thought to have the virus—only individuals can have a disease. In this medical model, the treatment is rightly focused on the person with the disease. The implication of this focus in the children's system is that the majority of program design and financing work has been directed toward the child.

There is a rather large body of research demonstrating that the emotional and, particularly, the behavioral problems of children are often familial. It is not uncommon for siblings to enter the system one at a time. In many programs, each new sibling is a "new case." This seems to be missing an opportunity. Why not engage preventive services for the younger sibling of a high-need child while services are already being provided to the family?

A classic example of the differences between a child focus and a family focus comes from Medicaid regulations in New York. In order to limit the opportunities for fraudulent billing, Medicaid regulations stated that no one could receive multiple outpatient services on the same day. Thus, if a child's circumstances required both individual counseling or medication management and family therapy, these would have to occur on separate days. This regulation meant that the parents would have to bring in their children for services at least twice each week. Perhaps that is one of the reasons for the high drop-out rates.

The expansion of Medicaid to cover a larger proportion of children has resulted in greater coverage of children living just above poverty. However, in these situations, you can have circumstances in which Medicaid will pay for service for the child, but the parent cannot get the treatment that he or she needs. To the extent that the parent's mental health is contributing to the family's struggles, this can be counterproductive.

Parent Responsibility versus Parent Blame

Bruno Bettleheim's Orthogenic School at the University of Chicago was seen for years as the best treatment option for autistic children. In Bettleheim's view, autism was caused by flawed parenting. Thus, to effect good treatment, the school banned contact between children and parents for the initial months of the child's residence at the school. It should be no surprise that many parents found this policy excessively blaming. We now are confident that "bad parenting" is not a risk factor for autism. All those children treated at the Orthogenic School were unnecessarily denied a relationship with their parents. This is one of the greatest tragedies of a misguided theory of psycho-pathology.

The same problem arises from the concept that the mothers are "schizophrenogenic" (i.e., cause schizophrenia in their children), based on the patterns with which they communicate by saying one thing and expecting another (the double-bind hypothesis). When Freud attributed almost all psychological development to the first few years of life, he inadvertently placed the responsibility for almost all psychological ills on parents, particularly mothers. Since then, generations of mental health professionals and theoreticians have created an environment in which parents feel blamed. This perception of blame extends the stigma of emotional and behavioral problems from an individual to that individual's parents. As the U.S. Surgeon General (1999) recently noted, stigma is one of the primary barriers to access to mental health treatment. Parents already feel bad when their children struggle. If they feel that they will be further blamed when seeking treatment, the likelihood of scheduling an appointment is dramatically reduced, particularly for emotionally vulnerable or highly defended parents.

At the other extreme of this tension are the parent groups who at times appear to advocate that "the system" is to blame for all problems of childhood. Whether it is insensitive schools, disrespectful clinicians, dangerous neighborhoods, or the influence of the media, some individuals see the causes of emotional and behavioral problems entirely outside of the family. I hope it is obvious from other sections of this book that I am an enthusiastic advocate of parents' rights and the development of a family-friendly community and service environment. However, I have been to several public meetings in which the role of the parent representative appeared to be only to get up and give an emotional and often eloquent rant about the shortcomings of the current system. Because these parents were not given power to inform the change process, they could only comment on the problems of the current system. Sometimes there is not a dry eye among the meeting attendees, but the complaints have little to do with the work at hand and thus the meeting just proceeds. Although ensuring a voice to parents and their representatives is critical to the system of care, this style of voice actually serves to marginalization parents as only a voice of complaint. The spokesparents had nothing to say regarding suggestions for improvement—that was left up to the "experts." This is not particularly helpful. Advocates, whose stake in the system is to complain about it, actually have no stake in fixing it. More importantly, real voice in a system involves inclusion of parent representatives in all phases of the service system planning, development, and management.

Similarly, there are advocates who call for full choice by parents and families. Family choice is an effective mechanism of empowerment. However, this choice must be informed by accountability to other system partners. The most dramatic example of the limitations of a full-choice policy comes from an intensive community program that was serving a mother and daughter both of whom were severely obese. The mother wanted to use her flexible funds to purchase TV trays, so that she could take all her meals in bed. This, of course, would not be in her best health interests. A balance must be struck between greater choice exercised by parents and families, while supporting healthy lifestyles and development.

Of course, it is likely that the truth lies somewhere in between. Perhaps our notions of causality have blurred our thinking about the separation of responsibility and blame. It makes no sense to blame causes for their effects. It is also true that not all effective interventions are directed toward the original causes of emotional or behavioral problems. I have known many adolescents or young adults struggling with schizophrenia or depression to benefit greatly from a vocational program. This does not mean that the lack of a job was causing the mental illness. Parents are critical partners; they are the experts with regard to their children and families. However, with this expertise comes the ultimate responsibility of identifying the strengths and addressing the needs of their children. It is the professional's responsibility to support the parents in this role, and not to assume that responsibility from the parents unless the safety of the child is at risk.

Psychotherapy as a Product versus Psychotherapy as a Process

The design of psychotherapy is a process of uncovering. Although the specific approaches vary according to the specific theory at work, all psychotherapy agrees on the steps: discovery of what is happening to the affected person, followed by a process of deciding what to do about it, followed by some specific actions. Thus, all models of psychotherapy consider it to be a process.

If you look at the data on the utilization of psychotherapy visits, the most common number of sessions utilized is one (Howard, Moras, Brill, Martinovich, & Lutz, 1986; Lyons & Shallcross, 2000). More than half of all individuals entering psychotherapy drop out by eight sessions. The cumulative frequency distribution of dropouts looks a lot like a marginal utility curve from economics. Marginal utility curves model how many units of a product a person might buy. This suggests that most children and families may not be buying a process; rather, they are purchasing sessions. Only about 20 percent of children who attend therapy become involved in a long-term process (Lyons, Uziel-Miller, Reyes, & Sokol, 2000). It may be that many of the remaining 80 percent attend just enough sessions to feel better about things. They are seeking relief rather than entering the transformational change process that is the fundamental theory of psychotherapy. Thinking through how the psychotherapy process is packaged is an important aspect of ensuring access to the full effectiveness of the approaches.

Syndromes

System-Level Syndromes

The Political Dog Walk Syndrome

Anyone who has a canine for a pet has experienced the essential element of this syndrome. A dog quickly learns that if it is taken for a walk, it should hold its urine and let it out in small doses over the largest area possible. No dog with any intelligence or ambition ever just runs outside and empties its bladder immediately. No, the best strategy is to spread it around. For the dog, this serves two complementary objectives. First, it extends the walk, because it becomes essential to walk further and for a longer period of time so that all are sure that the dog's full "business" has been transacted prior to a return home. Second, because dogs mark their territory with their urine, this maximizes the dog's marked area.

Politicians engage in a pattern of behavior much like a dog walk. From a politician's perspective, it is best to spread contracts out to as many people as possible to ensure that the politician's territory is marked and that as many constituents as possible are made happy by receiving money. Any politician will tell you there is very little political benefit in rewarding one contract when you can award two. The Political Dog Walk Syndrome is one of the biggest contributors to the cottage industry development of the current public mental health service system.

The Field of Dreams Syndrome

"If you build it, they will come," was the repeated thought that motivated Kevin Costner to build a baseball field on his farmland in the movie *Field of Dreams*. The parallel problem in mental health services that has resulted from a focus on programs rather than on people is the notion that if you create a service, then people will seek it out, regardless of their levels of need.

For example, the Illinois Department of Children and Family Services went through a process of institutionalization in the early 1990s. In a few short years, the number of children and adolescents placed in out-of-community residential treatment centers went from about 2,000 to around 8,000. This expansion was driven by several factors. First, there was an increase in the number of wards of the state, which created pressure for placements on a strained system. A lawsuit forced the rapid hiring of caseworkers—some very good, others not very skilled or motivated. Second, residential treatment was already an established service. The added benefit of residential treatment is that for about 15 months, the caseworker (if they were still that child's caseworker) wouldn't have to worry about that case. Residential providers had beds and those beds needed to be filled, so close relationships with caseworkers were formed. (Note: This reflects the child welfare equivalent to the marketing of services.) It didn't really matter whether the child or youth needed that type of treatment. One could argue that this process also describes the original use of state hospitals and reflects current processes in juvenile justice.

The Can't Fix Anything Unless You Fix Everything Syndrome

The perfect is the enemy of the possible. When people stop change because it is imperfect, it may be from a passionate concern for perfection. In my experience, however, it more often comes from a passionate wish to do nothing. When people want to obstruct progress in any form, one standard maneuver is to point out all the other problems that need to be addressed. There are always problems, and no change is able to address all problems simultaneously. Changing anything, including mental health services, requires the agents of change to convince large numbers of people with vested interest in the status quo to begin to behave differently. This is no small task.

Every system evolution has complications and problems and, thus, any change is subject to the threat of this syndrome. It is quite powerful, particularly when only the potential problems are communicated to policy makers in the governor's office or the state legislature. Public reforms are easily derailed by the involvement of powerful politicians.

The What's Mine Is Mine and What's Your's...Well, That's Negotiable Syndrome

I was recently at a planning meeting in which partners from mental health, substance abuse, child welfare, and juvenile justice agencies in a large metropolitan area were discussing developing a partnership approach to addressing the complex needs of youth in juvenile justice. One partner stated, "I'm happy to try to work together so long as you don't try to spend my money."

There has been much talk about blended funding mechanisms, in which all paying partners in a system of care essentially place their money in the same pot so that the pooled resources can be used in a more integrated and coordinated fashion. The silos versus blended funded tension is described earlier in this chapter; the What's Mine Is Mine Syndrome arises from this tension, and is a major barrier to achieving blended funding. Ironically, community agencies often do not favor blended funding at the state-expenditure level because they have mastered it at the service-delivery level. These agencies are in a better position to play different state agencies off of each other if funding streams remain independent. In other words, the provider who obtains multiple contracts to provide overlapping services may be in a better negotiating position than is the provider who obtains a single contract to provide coordinated services.

The Imperialism Syndrome

In a centralized service system, staff in the central authority sometimes act in an imperial manner toward other partners in the system. By this, I mean that they make decisions without including others in the system and hand down as edicts new policies and procedures. Acting in an imperial manner nearly always guarantees resistance to any new idea. Sometimes this imperialism comes from the arrogance of leadership—central authorities can come to believe too much in their own infallibility and righteousness. However, sometimes it can occur because the nature of central authority involves crisis management, and it is easier to decide something and pass it down than to complete an inclusive process before implementing a new policy or procedure. Democracy and voice are slow and messy processes. Sometimes people in power simply forget the importance of these processes toward effective implementation. Even the illusion of inclusion is better than no inclusion at all; that is, empirical research indicates that people who are allowed a voice feel better about their involvement in processes, even if nothing changes based on what they say (Tyler, Rasinski, & Spodick, 1985). The field of procedural justice has much to offer central authorities in managing the involvement of system partners (Blader & Tyler, 2003).

Program-Level Syndromes

The Colonel Sanders Syndrome

Beginning a number of years ago, Kentucky Fried Chicken (KFC) advertised its focus on fried chicken by saying, "We do chicken right." The message of this campaign was to emphasize that by focusing on one thing and doing it well, KFC offered a superior product, provided you wanted chicken. The parallel of this in mental health has been specialization, particularly in terms of theoretical approach. Bennet Leventhal, M.D., at the University of Chicago refers to this syndrome as "chronic undifferentiated treatment." For example, for years at the Institute of Psychiatry at Northwestern, all that was provided in the outpatient program was long-term psychoanalytically oriented psychotherapy. If someone came to the clinic, he or she was evaluated in terms of this model. Trainees were often berated for "treatment dropouts" after five months of therapy.

Program models for intervention often suffer this syndrome. Program development emphasizes the development of a treatment approach that is standard, and service plans tend to follow this packaged treatment. One of the criticisms of some versions of partial hospital programs is that they are essentially designed as inpatient hospital programming without the overnight stay. As such, they have a series of groups and activities that are the same for all participants. The question becomes whether every individual served by the program needs the same package of interventions.

The Therapist Illusion Syndrome

The prevailing concept of most mental health treatments is one of an ongoing process of care, whether it is the development of insight into one's own behavior or management of serotonin levels in the brain. Despite the fact that most mental health providers fully believe that what they are providing is a process (often long term), it appears that service recipients are buying something rather different. As mentioned among the tensions, there is evidence to suggest that consumers are buying units of service, not a process of treatment.

As shown in Figure 2.1, the proportion of people participating in sessions of psychotherapy drops rapidly at the start and levels off, with about 20 percent of recipients receiving long-term treatment. This suggests that the majority of recipients do not choose to purchase long-term services. Combine this standard observation with

Figure 2.1
Percent of Children and Families Remaining in Outpatient Treatment by Session

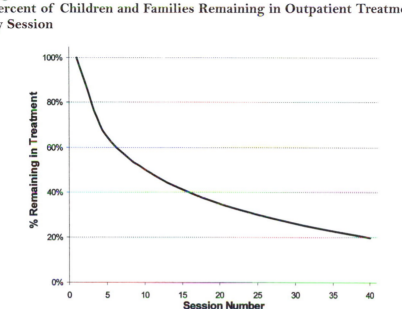

the other observation that about 80 percent of all outpatient service recipients terminate treatment by "dropping out" (from the provider's perspective). These data are very consistent with the hypothesis that buyers of psychotherapy are purchasing the marginal benefits of additional sessions rather than some treatment process.

An interesting secondary effect of this tension is a syndrome that has been referred to as the Therapist Illusion (Vessey, Howard, Leuger, & Kaechele, 1994). If you ask nearly any therapist what they do, they will probably tell you that they provide long-term therapy. However, as can be seen from Figure 2.1, only about 20 percent of any given therapist's cases are long term. What happens is that over a fairly short period of time, this one-fifth of presenting clients fills up the therapist's schedule so that nearly all of that therapist's time is spent serving this subset of patients. Thus, it is seldom the case that a therapist serves *more people* receiving long-term therapy, and more often the case that the therapist spends much *more time* providing long-term therapy.

The primary implication of the Therapist Illusion Syndrome is that in terms of training and continuing education, therapists can come to believe that their primary commitment is to the 20 percent of cases that venture into long-term relationships with them. From a child and family perspective, the majority of cases are given less attention.

The Rose Reversal Syndrome

In Shakespeare's Romeo and Juliet, "A rose by any other name, still smells as sweet" is a classic line. Wise and true, but not so the opposite. Calling a dandelion a rose does not make it so. What we call things can be arbitrary and what they are is more important than what they are named.

In the past several decades of working in the field, I have witnessed innovations and new "best practices" come and go. I've also seen a trend whereby what is seen as the desirable approach is what some people say that they are doing regardless of whether they've changed their service or program. Currently, "wraparound services" fall into this category. I've heard programs based in residential treatment centers and even juvenile justice facilities claim to be providing "wraparound services." That may be true in certain respects (e.g., individualization of services), but it cannot be true with regard to other aspects (e.g., family involvement, least restrictive environment) of the original definition of the wraparound treatment philosophy. After a time, the words simply lose their meaning.

The Rose Reversal Syndrome also has implications for the strengths-based movement. This important approach of emphasizing the strengths of children sometimes gets derailed by attempts to merely relabel problems in positive terms. Calling oppositional behavior toward a parent "asserting one's feeling" doesn't necessarily make it any easier for parents to work effectively with their child, whereas finding actual strengths can. For example, if parents understand that despite their child's behavior toward them, he or she has close peer friends or has notable athletic or artistic talent, these perceptions help them to get through the difficult times with their child and see him or her in a more complete light.

This syndrome is even partially played out in the measurements of strengths. One of the more commonly used tools that was designed to measure strengths is the Behavioral and Emotional Rating Scale (BERS; Epstein, Ryser, & Pearson, 2002). The BERS was created by generating a large number of positive statements and then selecting those statements that best distinguished children with serious emotional/behavioral disorders (SEBDs) from those without. This strategy makes the explicit assumption that children with SEBDs have fewer strengths than do other children. This is likely true with regard to some strengths (e.g., psychological strengths), but untrue with regard to others (e.g., creativity). As a result of the psychometric process of its development, the BERS is likely not a comprehensive measure of strengths and, in fact, may actually function as a positively worded measure of psychopathology. This measurement is still a contribution to the field, because positive ways to identify needs are valuable; however, caution is indicated in interpreting findings as relevant to children's positive assets or strengths.

The Public Funding as an Entitlement Syndrome

I was visiting a European city several years ago and was admiring a hand-laid, crushed, stone sidewalk. I commented on how much work must have gone into this effort, and asked whether this was a traditional approach, thinking the choice of sidewalk style was a matter of history. My colleague who was showing me around stated that the type of sidewalk was actually selected precisely because it was so labor intensive. The primary goal of laying the sidewalk was not really the sidewalk; it was employing the people who laid the sidewalk. Thus, sometimes governments initiate programs more for the sake of the program and its employees than for the product or service generated by the program. On the upside, the political nature of public services keeps these services responsive to the people. However, there is a notable downside to the impact of politics on public mental health. A sad consequence of the political aspects involves public funding as a result of the political process rather than as a purchase of a specific service, program, or set of services. In other words, the agency gets the contract not because they are an outstanding provider of services, but because the agency's leadership is politically connected. In these situations, the funded agency can view its funding as an entitlement rather than a responsibility.

Stories of these types of problems are legion in the proverbial hallways and water coolers of the public mental health service system. However, these stories seldom reach the public. Granted, rumors of political influence are probably substantially more common than is the actual political influence, but that fact notwithstanding, there is a clear and present involvement of political and personal connections in the public mental health system. Of course, it is not the case that all politically connected agencies are corrupt. In fact, some agency leaders become politically connected primarily because their agencies offer superior services. In these circumstances, the political connections actually ease the development and management of an effective service system. If a commissioner has a "go-to agency" that he or she can count on to deliver high-quality or innovative services, and this agency is well established politically, then children, families, and the system all win. The only losers are competing agencies that either do or can provide equally good or better services. However, in circumstances in which the politically connected agency provides subquality services, the connections institutionalize the reduced quality of the system. In these circumstances, it is clear that children and families lose, as do competing agencies and service providers.

Child- and Family-Level Syndromes

Although each of the system- and program-level syndromes can have an impact on how individual children and families are served, there is a set of syndromes that directly affects service delivery at the individual case level that may not have much import at other levels of understanding the system of care.

The Expert Syndrome

After at least 18 years of education, and at least 21 years for Ph.D. doctors or 23 years for M.D. psychiatrists, it is extremely tempting to view education as a basis for an expertise in mental health. There is little doubt that the vast majority of specialty-trained mental health service providers know much more about mental health than do untrained individuals, but there are several problems with this belief in expertise. First, nearly everyone considers himself or herself to have some expertise in psychology and interpersonal relations. Unlike almost all other specializations, absolutely everyone has a great deal of relevant life experiences, whereas most people do not get the opportunity to observe the endocrine system at work or understand the nuances of the functioning of the hypothalamus. Everybody experiences sadness, joy, anger, good and bad relationships, and most of the other foci of mental health. This does not lessen the expertise of training, but just makes the training a bit less credible to people outside of the profession.

A second problem of the Expert Syndrome is more universal to all helping professions. Life is a highly individualized experience. Although we can make powerful generalizations about human experience and human behavior, no matter how skilled the clinicians may be, they cannot compete with the personal expertise of the service recipients. Their minds, bodies, memories, and history are the material of mental health service treatment. Except in cases of involuntary commitment, it is their experience of treatment response that dictates decisions about continued involvement in treatment. As such, the recipient is always inherently more knowledgeable about *his or her own life* than is the mental health provider. It cannot be any other way.

The Hammer–Nail Syndrome

The Hammer–Nail Syndrome is the child- and family-level syndrome that is related to the program-level Colonel Sanders Syndrome. It is the syndrome in which clinicians in a program begin to treat all recipients as the same. This stimulates a problem that has been described with the warning that if the only tool you have is a hammer, then every problem begins to look like a nail. Thus, the natural effect of specialization is a shift of assessment focus to those aspects of an individual that matter to that particular specialist.

A horrific example of the potential consequences from this syndrome comes from a recent child welfare tragedy in Illinois. Illinois DCFS has mandated treatment for children who are survivors of sexual abuse. This is generally a good thing in that it forces private providers to make sure they address these children's needs. However, in one case, each time the child was taken to her treatment, she would have a violent tantrum. Because she lived in a congregate care environment, the response was to send more staff to escort her to her appointments. One day when she tantrumed, the staff restrained her and in that process suffocated her. She died.

Originally, it was thought that the lesson of this tragedy was that we had to become more skilled at restraining children safely. However, this lesson misses the fundamental reason for the tragedy. Specifically, the young girl was being taken to a form of trauma treatment that focused on "making meaning." In this "best-practices" approach to trauma work, the survivor is encouraged to talk through the experience until they can make sense of what happened and move on. Unfortunately, this young lady had an IQ of around 50. Given her cognitive capacity, this girl would never be able to effectively "make meaning" of her traumatic experiences. All that was happening was that her "therapy" was essentially retraumatizing her each time she was forced to talk about the sexual abuse. She communicated in the manner that most developmentally challenged children communicate—through her behavior. With her tantrums, she was telling everyone that therapy was not working for her. Perhaps if people had "listened" to her behavior, rather than enforced the treatment mandate, a different outcome would have occurred.

The Happy Face Syndrome

The term mental health stems from an attempt to shift attention away from the problems associated with psychiatric and psychological problems and disorders. This change started as mental hygiene and was one of the first efforts in what has become known as the political correctness movement in language. The philosophical underpinnings of this approach are derived from the social constructionist perspective that claims no verifiable reality but only perceptions that are formed from social consensus. In other words, if we all can agree that some object is a table, then it is called a table. There is no separate "objective" reality. Thomas Kuhn's (1962) book, *The Structure of Scientific Revolution*, is perhaps the best read for individuals who are interested in learning more about this philosophy of science. Metaphorically, Kuhn argues that science is a ship on an ocean. The ship sails off in a particular direction with the captain and crew, believing progress is being made. Periodically, a set of crewmembers grows tired or frustrated with the pace or direction and seizes control, which is called a paradigm shift. The new captain and crew sail off in a different direction. The ultimate problem for the enterprise, however, is that there are no shores. Scientific progress is, therefore, a social construction—progress is in the eyes of the believers. Taking this model to its logical end, you don't really need to change anything other than how you talk about things. You may notice that this is the philosophy that also leads us to politically correct language.

Advocates of remaining perpetually positive, even in the face of difficult circumstances, found a home in the strengths-based treatment movement. In the extreme, oppositional behavior, and even interpersonal violence, becomes assertiveness or the ability and willingness to express feelings. The argument for a positive, strengths-based perspective is compelling. Certainly, it is not hard to understand that children and adolescents may be less than enthusiastic to come to meetings or sessions in which the focus remains on all the negative things in their lives. Certainly, some such approaches to psychotherapy could allow practitioners to pathologize nearly any and every behavior. On the other hand, it is naive to think that by simply relabeling problems as positive, we can effectively address all challenges.

We have completed several studies that have demonstrated the statistical independence between symptoms of psychiatric disorders and

strengths in predicting levels of functioning and high-risk behaviors
(Lyons et al., 2000; Oswald, Cohen, Best, Hensen, & Lyons, 2001).
In other words, the more depressed a child becomes, for example,
the lower *his or her* functioning tends to be and the more likely he or
she is to engage in high-risk behavior. Independent of the severity of
symptoms, if the child has strengths—for example, a musical talent or
a loving family—the higher *his or her* functioning remains and the less
likely he or she is to engage in high-risk behavior. This suggests that
both needs and strengths are important. The sole reliance on one or
the other limits one's possibilities for a successful intervention.

The Ostrich Syndrome

The Ostrich Syndrome is related to the Happy Face Syndrome, but
results from a different set of circumstances. Sometimes, service providers choose to intentionally not identify needs. There are two reasons for this deliberate failure to detect needs. First, if you don't see
the problem, then you don't have to do anything about it. Second, if
you fail to detect and document needs, sometimes you can sometimes
protect yourself from problems of accountability. Like the proverbial
ostrich, if you just stick your head in the sand, the problem will not
exist.

Perhaps the most common needs that fall into this category are
problems associated with substance use and abuse. In nearly every
state where I've worked, the level of detected substance use of youth
placed in residential treatment falls below 10 percent, which is comparable with, or in some cases lower than, the general population of
youth. Few people actually believe that these very high-need youth
have no more problems with substance use than the do the children
in the general population; however, you will seldom see any evidence
of substance-use problems in the treatment records, particularly once
the youth has been placed. To document continued problems would
admit that youth can obtain and use alcohol and drugs at the residential facility, which represents an accountability problem. Thus, despite
the actual presence of the need, the system continues to move forward
pretending that there is no problem.

In the long run, this reasoning falls quite short of the ideal of service
delivery. The mere presence of these unmet needs can interfere with
our ability to meet other needs. One example is that chronic mari-
juana or alcohol abuse can complicate the treatment of depression—
it is not possible to alleviate the depression until you get a handle on
the substance use. If anything has been learned about this form of

dual diagnosis, it is that sequential treatment (e.g., first psychiatric treatment, then substance abuse treatment) is not effective.

The Fuzzy Pathogen Syndrome

Although there are libraries full of theories of the causes of mental health problems, little is actually known about the precise nature of causality when it comes to the symptoms of mental illness and subsequent impairments in functioning. Examples of the range of hypothesized causes include parental behavior, intrapsychic conflicts, too many or too few neurotransmitters in the synapse, rewards and contingencies of reinforcement, poverty, and specific genes.

There are really no known pathogens in behavioral health. This creates a scenario in which literally thousands are possible. In psychiatry, research on theoretical psychopathology has often focused on treatment effects. If a treatment works, the effects of that treatment must somehow address the causes of the illness. In medicine, this logic is, at times, compelling. For example, it is clear that insulin saves the life of persons with type II diabetes. The fact that providing insulin to the body can essentially replace the functions of a nonworking pancreas is good evidence that diabetes is a disease caused by the lack of insulin production in the body.

However, other circumstances in medicine are more complicated, such as the example of antibiotics. Antibiotics clearly work against some infections, but would that mean that the antibiotic is replacing a function of the body, as in the case of insulin? Well, sort of, but not really. The antibiotic is actually killing specific bacteria that have taken up residence in the body. Of course, in this example, too, there is an understandable link between the chemical action of the treatment and the putative cause of the disease.

There are notable limits to this logic. Let's consider the case of insomnia. Imagine that you've had a very stressful day. Your boss is angry with your performance and is considering firing you. Your spouse is mad at you for other reasons. You cannot sleep as you lie in bed worrying about things. You can take a sleeping pill that will likely put you to sleep. Does that mean that your insomnia was caused by things related to the chemical action of the sleeping pill? Probably not. Does it mean that the sleeping pill might be blocking the symptoms of stress that are keeping you awake? More likely. What if you get up and read for an hour and then go back to bed. Was the reading addressing the root causes of the insomnia? What if you did one of the enumerable other strategies to help you sleep (e.g., eat something, make love, clean out a closet, or watch a boring television show). Are all of these things operating on the same causal pathway?

There is another way in which putative causes are identified in the field. Although generally not taken seriously among people who actually provide services, there are a number of theories of psychopathology that have arisen from laboratory research with college undergraduates. Learned helplessness and hopelessness depression are two examples of these types of theories. These college undergraduate laboratories are very specific environments that create findings that generally do not replicate to the outside world. Learned helplessness is a great example. Although this is a theory that does not replicate and has generally been given up on by theoretical psychopathology experts, it lives on in college undergraduate texts and popular culture.

I was recently at a meeting at a residential treatment center in Illinois. The staff told me an interesting story about their on-grounds school. In the previous year, they had significant problems with school attendance. Youth would often feign sickness to avoid school, or, if they did attend, they would exhibit many behavioral problems. Often they would be suspended or sent back to their cottages. The orientation and priority of the school at that time was that compliance was the primary goal. Getting the kids to behave was the key function of the teachers, the principal, and the school social worker. It was a near disaster. By applying pressure, the center was able to force the local school district to replace the principal, the school social worker, and a key teacher. With the new school staff, the objectives of the school changed from behavioral control to individualized efforts to make learning appealing. Not surprisingly, attendance has gone way up and behavior problems have gone way down. Program staff now often report not even having to remind and escort youth to school. This was a dramatic cultural shift with huge implications for the education of these youth. It also is a clear reminder that environments create disruptive behaviors and only environments can ameliorate these problems. Are we to assume that the original school's philosophy was the original cause of these children's problems? Of course not.

It is useful to review the three major classes of causes—predisposing, precipitating, and maintaining. Predisposing causes are underlying characteristics that make an individual vulnerable to the development of a specific type of psychopathology. Genetic and familial factors are generally considered to represent possible examples. Precipitating causes are the "straw that broke the camels back." Stressful life events are often seen as precipitating causes; these are causes that trigger the initial manifestations of symptoms. Maintaining causes are factors that perpetuate the continued manifestation of symptoms. Codependence and enabling are factors that have been identified as maintaining causes. Disability incentives (e.g., workman's compensation, sympathy, and welfare) also are sometimes proposed to maintain psychiatric symptomatology.

The Imagined Cure Syndrome

As discussed previously, one of the major models of mental illness is a disease. That means that mental health would be the absence of that disease. Therefore, the focus of mental health treatment is to cure the identified mental illness. Don't we all wish it were so simple? Of course, once something is actually identified as a disease, it loses its status as a mental illness. For example, the identification of syphilis as the underlying disease for general paresis "unmasked" what was thought to be a mental illness and reclassified it as a medical condition.

For most significant mental health challenges, it is likely that a full cure is a relatively rare outcome. It is rather more likely that children and families learn to live with their challenges more effectively and deal more effectively with problems as they arise to prevent delays in healthy development. Even depression, which in many ways fits a disease model, is likely a chronic disease. In these circumstances, lifestyle changes to support prophylactic treatment and ongoing support are important considerations.

The Endless Treatment Syndrome

There are a significant number of clinicians who provide mental health services who are unable to define when services would no longer be needed. For many of these clinicians, therapy is seen as a lifelong enterprise. Let's say a person goes to therapy because of some difficulties he or she is having in a relationship. Once that is resolved, a pattern of similar issues is identified in other relationships. If these issues are resolved, others will reveal themselves, because no one is ever without issues. In this way, the clinician becomes somewhat of a life coach.

Ken Howard, the renowned psychotherapy researcher, was a dear friend of mine. On more than one occasion during our conversations, he expressed the opinion that most therapists, after practicing a couple of decades, stopped providing treatment. Rather, these older therapists saw people that they had seen for a very long time. There was no longer a pretense of the "work" of psychotherapy between the psychotherapist and *his or her* patient; the therapist simply had become a part of these individuals' lives. Although Ken had attempted to retire from an active psychotherapy practice, he found he could not avoid continuing to see some of these individuals until they moved or died.

Although this syndrome is less problematic with children due to their age, it still influences how the system is understood. In the Therapist Illusion Syndrome, we discussed that service recipients appear to purchase sessions, whereas therapists view themselves as providing long-term treatment. The child- and family-level manifestation of this syndrome is that the process that therapists are trying to sell is essentially continuous and without end. In our planning work with New York State, we found that only 10 percent of children receiving outpatient services ended services with agreement between the family and therapist that the treatment was over, and about two-thirds dropped out. In other words, they stopped coming against the advice of the therapist. One could argue that they felt that they had completed therapy, but that the therapists did not agree. Given an expectation of endless treatment, most people will be noncompliant. Even among RTFs, we found that 27 percent of children were non-compliant with the end of treatment. In many of these cases, parents pulled their children out of the residential placement against the advice of the RTF treatment staff.

Summary and Next Steps

The tensions and syndromes outlined above are among the most significant barriers to achieving the vision of an accessible and effective service system that respects the basic tenets of the system-of-care approach. In chapter 3, a vision of how to manage the tensions is presented and a two-prong strategy of prevention and service system management is outlined. The first step is to make a decision regarding what location on the continuum between poles of each tension the service system should balance itself. Then, a prevention strategy based on community development and a treatment service system management strategy with a focus on clinical outcomes are presented. In chapter 4, the community development model is detailed in view of the goal of stopping preventable emotional and behavioral problems from becoming serious enough to warrant formal intervention. However, it is clear that despite even the most comprehensive and coordinated approaches to prevention, children will still develop serious emotional and behavioral disorders. Therefore, there is no doubt that specialty behavioral health care treatments will be needed. Chapter 5 presents an alternative way of thinking about how to manage these services through Total Clinical Outcomes Management (TCOM) strategies. How TCOM strategies can be used to reduce or eliminate the syndromes described above is presented. Chapter 6 discusses how the present system components can be incorporated into the TCOM approach. Finally, chapter 7 discusses strategies and mechanisms that support service system evolution.

CHAPTER 3

DEVELOPING THE VISION:
FINDING THE BALANCE

Before beginning to discuss the focus of this chapter, it is important to summarize the state of children's public mental health services in the United States. At present, there is a disjointed system for children that functions well in some places, but functions very poorly in others. It is, at times, heroic; at other times, it appears to be corrupt. The experiment of managed behavioral health care has been largely a failure, but the fee-for-service system was not really any better. Direct grants to providers do not appear to result in notable improvements. There are some innovative programs that appear to be responsive to local community needs, but these are few and far between. Thus, it may help to reconceptualize our approach to the public mental health system for children.

As described in chapter 2, one of the key considerations in effectively evolving the system of care is to make the business model fit the clinical model for the service system. As such, it is useful to review the recent history of financing mental health services. If we go back to the original thinking behind managed care, it went something like this: for decades, decisions about the nature, setting, and duration of treatment occurred in negotiations between the service recipient and the provider. A person would experience some type of problem and either seek out or be referred to a provider of behavioral health care. The person would tell that provider his or her problems, and then the provider would say what he or she thought was happen-

ing and how treatment should occur. Sometimes the provider would
bill the person directly; however, most times a third party paid for
most or all of the services—either an insurance company, Medicaid,
Medicare, or the state. Although there is still a substantial amount
of self-pay for behavioral health care services among wealthy service
recipients, for the most part, there is a separate negotiation about
payment for services between the provider and a third party. This is
almost completely true for people living near or below the poverty
line. Individuals with limited financial means cannot afford behavioral
health services and, therefore, are completely reliant on services or
programs to meet their needs that are paid for by insurance, the government, or charitable organizations.

Of course, the public mental health system is particularly complicated because, in addition to the standard insurance perspectives,
there are often additional interested parties including child welfare,
juvenile justice, and the schools. It is not uncommon for the following
scenario to unfold: a juvenile is arrested and appears before a judge.
A psychological assessment is presented that identifies that the youth
has a serious emotional or behavioral problem. The judge then orders
that youth into residential treatment. However, the parents do not
have the means to pay for it. Generally, the county of the youth's residence must cover the costs of this treatment.

Each of the child-serving partners has a different perspective
regarding the behavioral health treatment of children. Mental health
systems tend to focus on symptom management of the children and
adolescents, and, to a less extent, on the functioning of the family.
Child welfare systems tend to focus on finding a safe place for the
child to live; permanency is a driving force in these systems. Juvenile
justice systems tend to emphasize community safety. To them, keeping citizens safe from dangerous juveniles is a priority.

There are several problems inherent in a multipartner system.
First, unless the service recipient is *very* knowledgeable about their
rights and their choices and has the ability to assert him- or herself
in conversations with highly educated specialists, the negotiation
between the service provider and the recipient is quite imbalanced
in terms of available information and confidence about the accuracy
and interpretation of this information. In these circumstances, the
various system partners have enormous power in this discussion to
indicate that the required treatment is what the provider (or other
system partner) prefers rather than the optimal treatment for the
recipient.

Other problems besides information imbalance plague the public mental health system. It is usually the case that the party responsible for paying for a treatment is different than the party receiving the treatment. Generally, the state or an insurance company has the responsibility to pay for treatments. When this third-party payer has too much control over the decision-making process, other problems can develop. If the payer has a rather narrow focus on reducing expenditures or keeping expenditures consistent and predictable, then effective treatments can be curtailed in the name of cost containment. Privatized managed behavioral care has been a disaster in that the shareholders of the managed care firm benefit by not serving persons with behavioral health needs, but only by failing to serve. The less spent on services, the better the profitability of the enterprise. The perverse incentive of privatized managed care is that denial of services results in the best possible financial outcome for the managed care company.

In the early days of managed care, giving firms enormous profits was seen as morally acceptable because it was a firmly held belief in many health policy circles that behavioral health care was primarily a luxury and that the system was very top heavy with an overemphasis on intensive and expensive treatments such as psychiatric hospitalization or inpatient substance abuse treatment. There were several research findings that justified that belief. First, there was little data that showed a relationship between mental health need and service use (Lyons, Howard, O'Mahoney, & Lish, 1997). When Medicare attempted to create prospective payments to hospitals by diagnostic characteristics, diagnosis-related groups (DRGs) were developed. Psychiatric DRGs could not be implemented because diagnosis had no relationship to hospital length of stay. Medical/surgical DRGs successfully predicted hospital length of stay and expenditures for nonpsychiatric services. This lack of relationship was used as evidence that psychiatric services were not clinically rational. However, it is now known that this was a conceptual problem with the research. Psychiatric diagnoses are not the clinical factors that drive decision making in behavioral health (Lyons, Stutesman, et al., 1997). Second, economists noted that behavioral health services were quite elastic (Bechtel, Ofir, & Ventura, 1990; Lyons, Howard, et al., 1997). In other words, mental health utilization is strongly influenced by price (Taube, Kessler, & Burns, 1986). In most economic models, price elasticity is seen as indicative of a luxury, not a need. People will spend what they have to address a need. People will spend what they perceive they can afford in order to obtain a luxury. Finally, an enormous amount of stigma remains attached to behavioral health and behavioral health providers (U.S. Surgeon General, 1999). A significant proportion of the U.S. population still considers mental health treatment as unnecessary or ineffective. These three factors combined to allow policy makers to look the other way while shareholders of privately held managed care firms took millions of dollars directly out of the U.S. behavioral health care system.

In the children's system, the untoward effects of the multiparty market take on very complicated manifestations. Schools are mandated to pay for any treatment that is required for the child to learn. However, school systems do not want to pay for treatment unless parents are able to successfully document the relationship between the child's mental health and his or her school performance. Judges in juvenile court, furthermore, can order almost anything in terms of treatment or intervention for a child; however, the courts do not have to pay for anything. Child welfare systems often develop a parallel behavioral health care system for their children alone, or else try to shift costs to Medicaid or state mental health whenever possible through the use of hospitalization and residential treatment.

The problems of the current system evolve from the basic design of that system. In order to effectively and comprehensively address these issues, it is desirable to reconsider the fundamentals of the public mental health system for children. To develop this vision, we must first consider the role of mental health services. This role should be defined by our understanding of what mental health involves.

Understanding Mental Health

My metaphor for good mental health is the following. Life is a journey. In that journey of life, we all need to carry our own bags. However, we also need to recognize when they are just too heavy, there are too many, or we are just too tired to keep carrying them. At these times, we need help carrying our bags. However, once rested, we need to repack them—jettison things we no longer need, pack more efficiently, and learn to pace ourselves.

Some of us are better packers than others. Some people find it very easy to move beyond carrying all the things they collect during their life experiences, or are able to pack them efficiently so they don't weigh them down. Others seem unable to get rid of anything. They carry everything that's happened to them with a significant emotional weight. Of course, some people are given more to carry than others. In that way, life isn't fair at all.

Now, if we don't try to carry our own bags, over time, those who we ask to help us get tired of carrying both their bags and ours. We become a burden. Of course, we can hire somebody to help us carry our bags, but that's expensive and only a few of us can afford this for any length of time. If we don't have enough money, then we have to get a third party to pay for the help. There are people who will simply never be able to carry their own bags. As a society we pool our resources to make sure that these individuals get the long-term help that they need to assist them on their journey. Further, the fact that they need assistance does not mean that they should just sit in one place so that they minimize the burden on the rest of us. They should be able to keep moving forward to the destination of their choice, just like the rest of us.

Sometimes there are too many people trying to help carry the bags of someone in need, or there are disagreements over which bags need to be carried. This is particularly a problem with children. Parents have certain responsibilities to help their children in the early stages of their journey. Schools also have certain responsibilities. When children's needs go beyond these two sets of helpers, additional help can either facilitate the child's journey, or all the helpers can become frustrated as they get in each other's way. Some helpers may get so frustrated that they stop helping. Others are only willing to help if their specific conditions are met.

There are some implications of this model of mental health for the approach that is taken toward service delivery:

1. Everybody has problems. There will never be a time when anybody is problem free.

2. Addressing traumatic and emotional experiences so that they have less impact on our current and future life is a priority.

3. Learning to deal with the problems we have and the ones that will likely come up in the future is more important than understanding them. To the extent that understanding them helps us to deal with them, such exploration is fine. However, it is not an end in and of itself. Sometimes forgiveness may be more important than understanding.

4. We all need to move forward with our life goals and objectives. No one else can do that for us.

5. Distance traveled is only one way to evaluate a person's journey. Things that happen along the way are as important as the journey's length and destination.

To extrapolate this metaphor for mental health into the functioning of the mental health service system, it becomes necessary for the services to be geared toward fostering independence so that the benefits of the intervention last long after the treatment has stopped. Services should be practical and focused on skill development. Outcome expectations should be developmentally informed and consistent with individual interests and capacity. These implications are quite consistent with system-of-care philosophy, but begin to go beyond it.

Now that we've developed our definition of mental health, it is useful to return to the system-of-care model and understand how it requires evolution if we are to achieve our vision of establishing an accessible and effective public mental health system for children.

Guiding Principles: Expanding on Child and Adolescent Service System Program Principles and Philosophy

Child and Adolescent Service System Program (CAASP) principles have become the foundation for systems-of-care initiatives around the country and receive consensus support as the conceptual foundation for the children's public mental health system. You are unlikely to get much argument with the proposition that services for children and families should be designed with these principles in mind.

Although the CASSP values and principles represent an important area of consensus within the children's mental service system, these principles only represent the focus of service delivery and do not establish principles for the system of care from its multiple perspectives. In other words, what is missing from the existing system-of-care principles is a full embodiment of the notion that, as a system, it includes multiple, different partners. Each of these partners has a unique set of responsibilities to the system, and, therefore, enters the system with a unique perspective. In order to fully manage the entire system, it is necessary to establish an understanding of the core values and guiding principles of at least the following additional perspectives: state and county mental health agencies, children's mental health service providers, and families. These principles must incorporate the business aspects of service delivery. Using an approach consistent with the CASSP philosophy, it is possible to derive principles that incorporate other perspectives to guide the development of a children's public mental health system of care.

Chapter 1 presents the CASSP core values and guiding principles in Table 1.2. A review of these principles suggests that although they establish a foundation for a system-of-care approach, they do not go far enough in understanding the values associated with the various perspectives within the children's system. In sum, the CASSP guiding principles require the following of a system of care: a comprehensive and culturally competent array of services that are integrated, coordinated, and managed and are provided in an individualized way while still keeping the child in the least restrictive environment possible. Family members should be fully involved in all aspects of the system. The rights of children and families must be respected.

Although there is little argument about these principles, disagreements more likely arise from discussion of how to get to this idealized system. Of course, disagreements are a natural aspect of all systems. They arise from the fact that different partners within a service system have different perspectives. The honest pursuit of one's own perspective can fairly easily place one in conflict with another partner's perspectives. As discussed in chapter 2, tensions that result from honest disagreements on perspective cannot be eliminated; they can only be managed. Creative management of these tensions can, in fact, be the source of energy for innovation and evolution. We will return to this topic in chapter 7.

The first step in the creative management of tension in a system of care is to explicate the additional principles under which system partners operate. In the development of a working paper for a coalition of residential providers in New York State, I completed a series of focus groups with representatives from each of the primary perspectives operating within the children's public mental health system. The result of these focus groups led to the identification of additional guiding principles for a system of care that are applicable to any state or locale.

State Government Perspective

The key issue for understanding the perspective of state government is that it operates in an essentially political environment as the messenger/executor of the government as directed by the governor and legislature. The state government represents all of the residents of the state and is responsible for the just allocation of tax revenues across all of the competing options. The state's mental health authority primarily serves to implement the directives of the state government. To some degree, the state agency also represents citizens and residents with mental illness and their families within the state; however, this representation is by no means exclusive, because many other

Table 3.1
State Government Perspective Principles

1. The state is responsible for the well-being of all of its residents and must weigh all decisions within the broad context of the overall benefit to residents, citizens, and taxpayers.

2. The mental health authority represents the state to residents of the state, those with mental health challenges and their families, and providers who address these challenges. This authority must operate within the legal, regulatory, and policy directions established by the governor and the legislature.

3. The authority has limited resources and must allocate those resources based on need within a complex political environment.

advocacy organizations and individual citizens all communicate with the state government. Table 3.1 presents the principles of the state government perspective.

For the most part, the state mental health authority is responsible for funding and monitoring services and the service-delivery system. This places the state authority in an oversight role with the county-level processes. The one exception to this general rule is that some state authorities do provide direct services through the state-operated hospitals. The dual oversight and service provision role may complicate some aspects of the agencies' work. A state agency that has both oversight authority over community providers and operates a direct service program might find itself in a conflict-of-interest position on certain issues. It is difficult to maintain credibility as an oversight agency when such conflicts exist.

County Government Perspective

County government shares the three principles of state government in that the county represents the residents, citizens, and taxpayers of the county and must make decisions within that broad context. County officials are bound by the directives of county government and they must allocate limited resources within a political context. The major difference between county- and state-level government is that counties often do not have direct revenues and therefore rely on state revenues. However, counties often have direct payment responsibility for certain services, particularly residential treatment. For instance, if a juvenile court judge sentences a youth to a residential treatment center (RTC), the county has to find a way to pay for that placement.

There are other differences between state and county perspectives. County government involves fewer people, which allows for more personal relationships. Closer relationships offer both advantages and disadvantages to developing systems of care.

One of the complexities of making general statements about counties is that they can vary dramatically in terms of size and population. The size of counties limits options for system-of-care development. Some counties are so small that there is no economy of scale. I met the county mental health commissioner of a small rural county in eastern Oregon. He was also the only therapist in the county. Other counties are comparable with small states. Cook County, Illinois, serves a culturally diverse population of more than three million people. Geography, populations, and demographics influence what is possible and desirable.

In some states, counties are likely to have much greater control over decision making related to access to intensive community services. Counties are often the locus of level-of-care decision making. For example, in New York, counties operate Single Point of Accountability (SPOA) processes, which are team approaches to deciding whether children are placed in intensive community service programs or residential treatment. Many of these SPOAs utilize the Child and Adolescent Needs and Strengths (CANS) to guide this decision-making process. New Jersey's Partnership for Children has a similar process, with selection teams deciding on eligibility for the intensive community services brokered through county-based care management organizations (CMOs). The selection committees use a version of the CANS to support and model their decision-making process.

However, some counties also are direct service providers. When the county directly provides the intensive community services, this is a noteworthy deviation from models in which the county serves primarily a triage or level-of-care, decision-making/utilization management function. Just as with states, managing and providing services places the county in a potential conflict of interest. Such a conflict would only exist if noncounty agencies were providing or seeking to provide similar services in that county.

Table 3.2 contains the principles identified through discussions among representatives of county government. Review of these principles reveals how much more similar the county personnel perspective is to that of children and families in their community than is possible from the state perspective. In addition, concern

Table 3.2

County Government Perspective Principles

---

1. There are no exclusions from a system of care. All children and
   families should be eligible. Similarly, there are no extrusions from a
   system of care. You cannot terminate or discharge a child or family
   from a system of care.

2. Child-serving agencies must work in partnership at the local level,
   directed by the parents or substitute parents to address the needs of
   children. These partnerships take time to develop.

3. Service planning should be based on identified needs and strengths,
   not on what services are available.

4. A primary goal of a system of care should be to prevent placements.

---

about residential placements is a clear priority, both clinically and
economically.

Family Perspective

Families with children who have serious emotional and behavioral
problems face enormous challenges. The time involved in addressing the individual needs of the child is substantial. Often, schools
require a parent to come in each time a child acts out. Suspensions
and expulsions may require a parent to stay with the child when he
or she is not in school. Attendance for clinical services can result
in scheduling and travel complications. All of these factors make
keeping a high-need child at home difficult for the parent/caregiver.
As such, in addition to an individualized, coordinated array of services, families often require additional help in overcoming barriers
to access.

The U.S. Surgeon General (2001a) has identified stigma as one of
the most significant barriers to services. For parents with children
who have emotional and behavioral problems, this stigma can include
feelings of inadequacy and blame. As discussed in chapter 2, the
mental health field is not that far removed from blaming constructs
or the notion that parenting failures cause mental health problems in
children. Even the subtle communication of such thinking can be a
major barrier to service delivery with families. As seen in Table 3.3,
reactions to historical and recent feelings of disrespect come through
in the identified principles from the family perspective. The emphasis
of these principles is on supporting the role of parents in managing
decisions around services for their children.

Table 3.3

Family Perspective Principles

1. Parents should be recognized as the experts regarding their own children.

2. Services should be provided at the convenience of the family. Barriers to access should be identified and minimized.

3. Families should have choices in services and providers. Family decision makers should be given the information they need to make informed choices.

4. Services should be provided in a way that respects individual family members and does not blame families for the presence of mental health problems.

Provider Perspective

Providers are often confronted with dual priorities. On the one hand, service delivery is a business and, like any other business, must be profitable in order to survive and prosper. On the other hand, clinical decision making should be based on both the proper assessment of problems and knowledge of the most effective treatments. This decision making is thought to exist outside of any business considerations. As seen in Table 3.4, the provider perspective emphasizes that the child mental health service system should be guided by a set of principles that emphasize clinical judgment exercised within an environment that responds to family wishes and financial pressures, with an equitable distribution of risk.

Table 3.4

Provider Perspective Principles

1. The system of care should support the ability of providers to exercise their clinical judgment consistent with family wishes, and professional, ethical, and evidence-based standards.

2. It is desirable and often necessary to establish an expected flow of cases to allow for appropriate program planning and staffing. Other system partners should be aware of providers' needs in this respect.

3. Reimbursement for services, regardless of the specific funding mechanism, should be sufficient to support the recruitment and retention of high-quality staff.

4. Business models for specific programs should be designed to be consistent with the clinical objectives of those programs.

5. Competing demands from different system partners should be resolved between those partners, and providers should not be financially penalized for problems that result from these conflicts.

Now that principles have been drafted for each of the primary perspectives represented in the system of care, the next step toward the reconceptualization is to determine where to balance each tension on its continuum. Decisions on how to balance the tensions must be made while respecting the principles of each of the system partners.

Finding the Balance: Managing the Tensions

For each of the tensions identified in chapter 2, I propose a policy position on the continuum between the two opposing poles of the tension. Of course, solutions to these tensions do not exist, and no position in the continuum between poles can possibly be ideal from everyone's perspective. The goal is rather to find the fulcrum between the opposing perspectives that is acceptable to the broadest range of service system partners and, most importantly, that creates opportunities for accessible and effective services that maintain their focus on the well-being and healthy development of children and families.

System-Level Tensions

Cottage Industries versus Systems of Care

The advantage in this instance goes to the system of care. Integrated services require collaboration and coordination. Service integration is much easier to perform with a more defined management organization. However, it is not necessary to abandon small or solo providers. In fact, there can be some competitive market advantage to having multiple small providers. If multiple providers are available that provide the same service, then real choice is available to both families and payers.

The balance of the tension between cottage industries and systems of care should be at the level of service system financing. In an effective and efficient system of care, a fiscal agent would broker services and could decide to utilize these providers for services for specific children and families. This is a care management function. In this way, the system integration occurs at the child-family team service-planning level and is brokered seamlessly by a care manager who is knowledgeable of and has access to all the necessary services. An example of this model is New Jersey's Partnership for Children. In the Partnership, CMOs are funded in specific geographic locations—counties, for the most part, except in areas where a single county is too small for economy of scale. These CMOs receive funding from the state to do assessment and care management. The care management activities include brokering services for enrolled families. In this model, for example, respite providers can be solo providers who subcontract with the CMO.

The goal should be blended funding at the local level that supports a comprehensive approach to assessment and service management. The actual service-delivery system can remain complex and include both small and large providers. However, the organization that manages the financial resources must be an assertive purchaser of services. In other words, the purchaser must monitor the outcomes of services and insist on accessible and effective interventions.

Multiple Models

There is no easy resolution to the process, but over time, a resolution must be sought. It appears that several theoretical perspectives have something to offer, and coming up with an integration of these would be an important breakthrough for the field. In the meantime, an emphasis on the use of evidence-based practices may be the best solution (Hoagwood, Burns, Kiser, Ringeisen, & Schoenwald, 2001). Any theory that generates a treatment approach that can be demonstrated to work in both randomized clinical trials (i.e., efficacy) and in field applications (i.e., effectiveness) is acceptable. However, the focus is not on the theory, but on the results of the treatment. Theories would be epiphenomenal. The system would be agnostic as to theory and only embrace treatments and services for which evidence of benefit exists. Further, an additional principle is that families should be allowed to choose among treatment options for which evidence of effectiveness exists. This requires developing systems in which such choices actually exist.

This model is not dissimilar to how treatments in medicine work. Oftentimes, the actual mechanism of an effective treatment is not known when the treatment is first introduced. The theories of mechanism of therapeutic effectiveness are important to the science of medicine and, potentially, to the development of new treatments. However, this theoretical work is of little practical value to the day-to-day operations of the service-delivery system.

A corollary issue of the multiple model tension is that most professionals are trained in only one model. Given the divergence of models for which evidence of effectiveness exists, it is likely necessary to reconceptualize how training is accomplished. Training based on the theory of practice may need to be replaced, or at least augmented, by training based on the technical practice of evidence-based treatments.

Central versus Local Control

For most decisions, particularly those at an individual child and family level, local control is of greater value than is central control. Thus, most decision-making power should be left at the local level, where decision makers are most informed about local circumstances. However, central (state) authorities must have oversight responsibilities to help ensure that local authorities remain accountable to children and families. More specifics on how to address this tension are discussed later in the book under the concept of matrix accountability, but the basic idea has the following logic: it is desirable to allow child- and family-level decision making to occur at the local level. Central control over case management-level decision making is likely to be insensitive to local considerations including racial, ethnic, and cultural diversity. However, because local authorities are subject to the same corrupting influence as is any other authority, accountability is a critical balancing factor. In the matrix accountability model, the central authority's primary responsibility would be outcome monitoring and management at each local level. The central authority also would have the responsibility of identifying evidence-based practices and supporting their implementation. Local outcomes would be benchmarked with other local authorities across the state, allowing for the identification of local areas of excellence or need. Thus, the central role at the state and federal levels should be technical assistance and oversight.

An issue related to the central versus local control tension involves the provision of services by central authorities. In general, I believe that it is a bad idea to have funding authorities also provide services. As such, central authorities (i.e., states) should not be in the business of providing services directly, because it creates conflicts of interest and, as will be seen later, unnecessarily complicates matrix accountability. The most common manifestation of this problem involves state-operated psychiatric hospitals. Although both the number and size of these facilities have dwindled over the past several decades

(Nierman & Lyons, 2001), many states continue to operate psychiatric hospitals as the ultimate safety net. This creates a mission split in the state mental health agency, in which part of the mission of the bureaucracy is focused on funding and accountability, and another part of the mission is directed toward the service-delivery business. These two sides of the agency compete with each other for limited funds and other resources. Thus, the state hospital operations can work at cross-purposes with community-based initiatives in the same state agency.

Budget Silos versus Blended Funding

Figuring out how to blend funds for all children's services may be the mythological ideal toward which we should strive. As Daniel Burnham, the architect responsible for Chicago's beautiful lakefront parks said, "Make no small plans." However, although specific examples of notable success on this matter exist, broadly speaking, actually blending funding is probably as likely as finding Eldorado or the Fountain of Youth. As discussed in chapter 7, incremental approaches to the ideals represent a realistic and acceptable change strategy. In the absence of blending funds, it would be desirable to establish and maintain close collaboration and perhaps even some integration at the program level across partners in the system of care. For example, in several areas it has been possible to get all child-serving systems to use comparable assessment and outcome management tools, which helps to build a common language of assessment and service planning. Coordinating expenditures on overlapping programs can be nearly as effective as blended funding. In other words, programs that are jointly funded by multiple agencies or programs funded by one agency that are operated within the other agency's infrastructure would fit this model. However, it requires strong relationships among child-serving agencies.

As described previously, New Jersey's Partnership for Children offers an interesting compromise with regard to blended funding. In this initiative, funding is combined across the Department of Mental Health, Department of Youth and Family Services, and the juvenile justice system. This funding targets the highest-need children in designated geographic areas. The funding is used to create the CMO in these areas, and each partner can refer up to three youth each month into the CMO level of care. The CMOs offer intensive community services using a wraparound philosophy. Other programming is left intact within each of the three partner agencies, so that their independence of mission is maintained while collaboration in serving the highest-need children with multiagency involvement is enhanced.

I have witnessed states move between a single department that houses all child-serving agencies to separate departments for each partner and back again. In the past five years in Illinois, the Department of Mental Health became the Office of Mental Health in the Department of Human Services. This year it became the Division of Mental Health. In many states, there appears to be a natural cycle of forming and dismantling versions of a Department of Human Services. Whether child welfare, mental health, and juvenile justice are in the same or different departments does not really matter. It is far more important that programming at the community levels supports integration among these partners. A state can allow blending of funds at the community level and achieve the same purposes as having blending at the highest levels of the bureaucracy. In other words, funding from multiple sources flows to the county organization, which then blends it in child-family teams. In many ways, this type of approach is most likely politically much more palpable. Everyone maintains their turf at the state, but can share bragging rights about successful models of integration in the community.

School Districts and Service-Delivery Boundaries

Defining "local" in a consistent and meaningful way should be a critical goal of service system reform. The local definition should encompass publicly funded mental health services, child welfare, schools, and juvenile justice. Thus, each of these four primary child-serving systems should be organized in a consistent geographic fashion. This is an achievable goal, but would require considerable political courage. (Note: I honestly don't think that's an oxymoron.)

Any proposed solution to this complex tension is bound to sound glib. That being said, perhaps the simplest solution might be to form consortiums of school districts that share common boundaries with regard to the public mental health and juvenile justice system. These consortiums of schools would maintain the financial and geographic integrity of original school districts while easing the challenge for other child-serving partners to collaborate with the schools. In most states, child welfare services could be reorganized to fit these geographies, if they do not already. Juvenile justice organization is sometimes limited by where courts are located. However, an interim solution to common geography would be to organize representatives from each partner to represent shared geographies.

This proposed solution would be similar to the Local Area Network (LAN) model, which is used in Illinois. LANs are formed in geographic regions that contain catchment areas. The primary function of the LAN is to convene a meeting of all child service system partners in the area to talk about the coordination of their services. Unfortunately, the effectiveness of the LANs has been limited by the fact that they have little direct funding. System representatives attend the meeting out of a spirit of collaboration and a fear of being left out. To the degree that the LAN has some decision-making power (and some do), then the degree of participation is generally higher.

Insurance Model versus Biopsychosocial Model

To solve the tension between the insurance model and the biopsychosocial model, we need to broaden both the definitions of eligibility and the processes of assessment. The emphasis on psychiatric diagnoses that predominates the insurance model is insufficient to support either the biopsychosocial model or the person-in-environment model; however, the insurance model is not necessarily incompatible with these more complex views of human behavior, disorder, and disease. As discussed later in this book, assessment strategies that are comprehensive and include aspects of a person's life outside of specific symptoms and psychiatric disorders are required. It is possible to then match services and strategies to this broader assessment strategy and maintain the basic logic of the insurance model—services should be based on documented need, but the needs can transcend those of the individual child.

A second innovation would be to transfer the locus of insurance from the child per se to the family. In other words, the family, not the individuals within that family, would receive the insurance coverage. This change is particularly important for children served through the Medicaid extensions (parents are not included) and families with child welfare involvement. In this way, insurance could become consistent with a family focus, and some of the challenges that result from only having insurance for the child but not the parent could be addressed. This change in focus would encourage the development of family-based treatment approaches that would likely be more efficient than child-based programs. Often, the younger siblings of high-need children develop similar needs. By incorporating all family members into the initial treatment approach through integrated insurance coverage, these children would receive service prior to their emotional or behavioral functioning deteriorating to the point of individual eligibility.

The tension between the insurance model and the biopsychosocial model can become particularly complicated around issues of eligibility for nontreatment services. For example, stable housing is a foundation of intensive community treatment. You can identify, assess, and plan to serve a child and family, but then that family looses its housing. They might move to a different school district or catchment area and the service-planning process must be started anew. However, housing services do not fit a health insurance model. Thus, housing support is important, but is not likely to be covered by the same funds and mental health services, even under the broadest of blended funding models. In these cases, coordination of services with different funding streams and eligibility requirements is needed. Case management strategies should broadly encompass the full range of possible needs that can impact a family's health. It is reasonable to expect that the public mental health system adequately pay for these case management functions. It is also reasonable to expect the housing and vocational service systems to actively collaborate with the case manager and the programs to facilitate coordination and access.

Eligibility versus Prevention

Public health conceives of prevention strategies as either universal or targeted, and this distinction offers the road map for the management of the tension between eligibility and prevention. Universal approaches are population based and I discuss these within the context of community development. The service system must be eligibility based. There are two reasons for this. First, there is growing evidence that children without needs are not helped by mental health services and may, in fact, be harmed by such services (Lyons, 2003). Second, we live in an environment of limited resources. Often there are severe limitations on the availability of services and, in situations of limited resources, some rationing strategy is required. Rationing based on the level of need is by far the fairest way to manage limited resources.

I have come to believe that universal (prevention) and targeted (treatment) approaches are so different that they require different providers and agencies. We currently have a habit of funding service-delivery agencies to provide prevention services. We also have the same federal and state agencies responsible for both prevention and treatment of specific problems. Substance Abuse Mental Health Services Administration (SAMHSA) funds both treatment and prevention activities. The state agency that funds the public alcohol and drug abuse treatment system also funds prevention activities. I have come to believe that this may not be the optimal strategy. I realize that this is likely to be an unpopular opinion. However, if service agencies were actually successful at prevention, they would put themselves out of business. It has been my observation that service agencies tend to use prevention programs to improve their visibility and identify more cases, which is actually marketing and case finding. Neither of these services is bad—in fact, both can be useful; however, they are not prevention. As elaborated in chapter 4, it is my belief that the prevention of mental health problems requires community development initiatives that have little to do with mental health. Community development is an entirely different intervention and cannot be supported adequately by the public mental health service delivery system. Community development strategies must be developed independently.

An advantage of the community development strategy is that if one embraces the implications of it fully, then federal and state agencies that provide treatment services should get completely out of the prevention business and reallocate all money spent on prevention to the treatment system. That could lead to a notable increase in available funds to support treatment system improvement. Mental health advocates would then lobby for investments in the kinds of community development strategies that could support the prevention of emotional and behavioral problems among children. The net effect would be an increase in funding to the public mental health treatment system.

Program-Level Tensions

Business Model versus Clinical Model

With regard to the tension between the business model and the clinical model, I would place the emphasis on first establishing the clinical model of treatment. Once the treatment model is defined, then a business model can be developed and monitored to ensure that it supports the clinical model and does not result in untoward effects on service delivery that interfere with the clinical model's objectives. That is, the clinical model should drive the business model.

As an example, pretend that you want to manage length of stay with children's RTC services to ensure that children do not stay past an optimal episode of care. The admission and discharge of the child from the RTC are the most expensive parts of the stay. At admission, you want to ensure that a careful assessment is completed, that the child's adjustment to the RTC is carefully monitored, and the treatment plan is adjusted accordingly. Likewise, the period just before discharge is expensive because you want to ensure careful coordination with the subsequent placement and, if the child is returning home, that care is taken to ensure that the parents are informed about what was learned during the RTC episode of care. In this case, you could create a business model whereby the per diem for the first and last months of an episode of care are highest, with a declining per diem reimbursement from month two until the month of discharge. You could structure the slope of the per diem change to provide incentives for specific lengths of stay. These slopes could be adjusted based on the expected trajectory of recovery for a particular child (see chapter 5). Other examples of fitting the business model to the clinical model abound. For example, home visits are often reimbursed at a higher rate than are office visits. This strategy provides incentives for clinicians to reach out to children and families who have challenges attending office-based treatment.

One of the reasons that business models have been developed independently of clinical models is that, until recently, funding sources were agnostic as to the treatment approach used. With the increasing identification of evidence-based practices (EBPs), the actual clinical models that should be used are becoming clear (Burns & Hoagwood, 2002). Manualized EBPs actually allow for a thoughtful development of a business model that can support the effective treatment.

Accountability versus Quality Improvement

I would propose to balance the tension between accountability and quality improvement in favor of quality improvement. However, the solution can be accomplished in an accountability model if accountability requires attention to ongoing efforts at quality improvement. The National Committee for Quality Assurance uses this balanced approach. For accreditation, organizations have to demonstrate that problems were identified and that solutions were attempted and assessed. Thus, the accountability model holds agencies, programs, and providers to learning organization cultural standards. The expectation is that data are collected and utilized in the management of services. Documentation of both the data and the utilization of findings from the data are required.

One also can shift the balance toward accountability in circumstances in which the outcomes are auditable. One of the challenges of mental health services is that a large number of possible outcomes involve the assessment of internal subjective states (e.g., sadness, fears) experienced only by the affected individual. Clinical outcomes, therefore, can sometimes be inaccurate out of concerns about possible accountability. Clinicians also might feel that the incentives lead them to overrate needs at admission and underrate them at termination. Service recipients can worry that if they make too much progress, they might lose their benefits. If the outcome measures are auditable, these issues of misrepresenting clinical status for business or eligibility reasons can be identified and addressed. As is discussed in chapter 5, the Mental Health Services and Policy Program routinely uses audit methods to encourage accurate clinical status assessments in the projects that it manages. By increasing everyone's confidence in the accuracy of clinical assessments, audits support the use of outcomes for accountability.

Leadership Salaries versus Line-Staff Salaries

Leadership salaries are only a problem in comparison with the low wages of direct service staff. If we are to develop and maintain a high-quality public mental health system, it is necessary to pay direct service staff salaries that are sufficient to retain them in direct service roles. This requires higher salaries than those currently being paid. There are a variety of ways in which salaries can be increased; however, any solution likely requires some central authority intervention. Either state regulators will have to require providers to pay higher minimum salaries, or public mental health workers will have to organize and bargain collectively. However, employee unions can be a problem when they negotiate for less work rather than more pay or when they block progress as a threat to the status quo. It seems unlikely that agencies will start paying higher salaries to line staff until pressure is exerted through either regulation or job action. I do not see this problem helped by reducing the salaries of the chief executive officers of large child-serving agencies. That strategy would simply drive qualified leaders out of the profession.

Of course, the salaries of service-delivery staff are an important consideration within the design of the business model. With the increased implementation of evidence-based treatments, the credentials and training of the individuals who are qualified to provide the treatment can be built into the reimbursement model for that treatment.

Donors can help to address this issue. Most child-serving agencies use charitable donations as a significant portion of their operating budget. On several occasions, I have recommended to colleagues of mine who are running large agencies to use charitable donations to support the development of their human capital (i.e., staff development and retention). Uniformly, these leaders tell me that donors want to see the tangible effects of their contributions—buildings, libraries, computers, and so forth. I continue to believe, however, that donors can be educated about how child services require a significant investment in human capital.

Liability versus a Learning Culture Environment

Although we do live in a litigious society, the perceived risk of liability is far higher than the actual risk. In addition, there is little evidence that monitoring effectiveness and attempting to use data to improve services increases the risk of lawsuits. In fact, there is reason to believe that a strong learning culture environment might actually reduce an agency's liability risk and, even if sued, increase the likelihood of success in the court room (Senge, 1990). Thus, this tension may be more an issue of perception than actual risk. I have come to believe that some individuals use the liability risk as an excuse in a misguided attempt to avoid accountability. Confidentiality issues are sometimes raised in a similar way. Although confidentiality is important, there are many effective ways to maintain confidentiality while maintaining accountability and a learning culture environment (Senge, 1990). However, resistant partners and employees will raise issues of liability and confidentiality in an attempt to sabotage these efforts. Leadership must resolve to move forward on an initiative despite resistance in order to identify and clarify legitimate concerns, two strategies to address this tension.

Clinician versus Administrator Tension

There is a need to develop a profession of behavioral health administrators. Although some clinical training may be desirable so that these administrators are knowledgeable about the processes of treatment, such training is by no means sufficient to prepare individuals to be effective administrators and, in fact, it is possible that clinical training is somewhat of a disservice to the development of an administrator. Therefore, training programs for administrators is a needed area of development within the educational system.

These training components would have a variety of core competencies, including the following:

- Bookkeeping and budgeting
- Strategic planning
- Personnel recruitment and retention
- Financing
- Fund-raising and grant writing
- Management
- Organizational development

Child- and Family-Level Tensions

The Unequal Information Tension

In our current system, professional ethics is intended to prevent the information imbalance between providers and recipients from unduly influencing the provider's behavior. The appropriate resolution of this imbalance is clear in the children's mental health system. A trained and ethical professional is supposed to be fully trained in all possible treatment approaches, offer those approaches to recipients, and allow them to decide which treatment approach to select. Unfortunately, as discussed in chapter 2, clinicians generally are not trained in all approaches. Clinicians' choices and behavior are limited by the business models under which they work. Clinicians have personal preferences, styles, and beliefs that influence how they practice. Thus, they likely will continue to be able to provide only a subset of possible treatment options, limiting their motivation to fully inform recipients with regard to choices.

Regardless of the problem of providing real choice, and despite the good intentions of many ethical and even noble clinicians, there is simply no way that professional ethics alone can balance the negotiation between someone knowledgeable in a particular perspective and someone distressed and not trained in behavioral health. Thus, unless recipients are highly educated and very assertive, the imbalance of any treatment negotiation is inherent to the process. This imbalance leads to only one real choice for service recipients in many situations: they can refuse treatment—and that's generally what happens.

The imbalance of information also affects the other child-serving systems and their interactions with the family and the system. Judges are not experts in behavioral health care, but are expected to make decisions based on the best interest of the child and community. If an assessment states that a child needs a "structured and secure environment," the judge may feel duty bound to order a child to a residential treatment facility without exploring intensive community options.

Child welfare caseworkers often find themselves in situations in which parents and other family members are hesitant to be forthcoming about problems. In focus groups with parents of high-need children, I have repeatedly heard the complaint that if you are open with child welfare workers, they are much more likely to find incriminating evidence to support taking your children away from you. This fear creates relationships based on mistrust rather than trust. From the child welfare worker's perspective, if you do not know what is going on and you cannot trust the only available informants, then the reasonable decision for the child welfare worker may be to ere on the side of caution and pick the most restrictive environment in order to maintain the safety of the child. From the parents' perspective, if they tell the child welfare worker too much, their child may be taken away. Both concerns coincide to lead to a greater likelihood of removal of the child from the home.

Ideally, parents and families would have the same information as do the professional experts. The ideal solution to the unequal information tension is minimization of the imbalance. The solution to managing this tension includes several universal and targeted strategies. Improved education of all citizens, particularly parents and youth, with regard to mental health and its treatment is an important universal strategy. Decreasing stigma and increasing knowledge in the general population will have the positive effect of balancing the information disparity in favor of parents and youth.

However, even with a massive public education initiative, it will always be the case that as new knowledge and treatments are developed and new procedures are required to access these treatments, experts will maintain their information advantage. Therefore, strategies in which parents with recent personal experiences in the system support new parents offer a second method for shifting this balance. A number of these programs exist around the country. All the SAMHSA system of care sites have professional parents who facilitate entry of new families into the system. The New Jersey Partnership for Children has established family support organizations (FSOs) to correspond to the CMOs within specified geographies. The FSO parents work with incoming families to provide information and begin to balance the information disparity. In all of these applications, the parent professionals are paid. This type of program is unlikely to be successful if it is run entirely using volunteers.

Provider Convenience versus Recipient Convenience

The fulcrum for the tension between provider convenience and recipient convenience must lie midway between the conveniences of each of the main parties in the service system. In most cases, our current system favors the provider; thus, movement in the direction of greater recipient convenience is required. The rebalancing of this tension in favor of recipients means expanding hours for outpatient services and including weekend availability. Supporting transportation and child care for young children in the family who are not in treatment would facilitate improved convenience. For some families, home-based services represent greater convenience; however, for other families, home-based services are experienced as an intrusion. Increased sensitivity to these individual differences across families is required. In the end, all that is really required is that parents and youth be fully informed as to their choices and encouraged to assert their preferences.

Parents versus Professionals—Who Cares More?

Professionals must learn that regardless of the struggles a parent may be going through, in all likelihood, that parent will be far more likely to maintain a long-term relationship with a child than any paid caregiver. Most clinicians understand fully that no matter what feelings a therapist has for a child in their care, that therapist cannot replace the parent. In the vast majority of cases, a provider who comes to believe that they are somehow better for a child than that child's parent should be considered to be experiencing an ethical lapse.

Our culture sometimes gives an ambiguous message with regard to supporting and respecting parents' rights. For most treatment decisions, parental consent is required. However, in some situations, no parental consent is required. Take, for example, the case of abortion. Although the elimination of parental consent for this controversial procedure is intended to support pregnant teenagers who might be subject to abuse if their parents knew of their pregnancy, the vast majority of parents are unlikely to be abusive. They may be mad, ashamed, hurt, or any other of a variety of emotional reactions, but very few will harm their daughters. Policies founded on rare exceptions are generally poor policies. In those rare circumstances, judicial review procedures can be used. Thus, it is a questionable policy to undermine parents' roles in their daughter's life by sanctioning a message from the government that basically states that a teenage girl cannot trust her parents to not abuse her should she become pregnant. Regardless of one's position on abortion rights, it seems to me that parental rights might trump other rights, at least to an extent.

Federal regulations stipulate that children over the age of 12 cannot be compelled into substance abuse treatment—it must be voluntary. Although giving youth an opportunity to chose whether or not they want to receive treatment is a good concept, this regulation can provide some challenges to parents whose children have serious substance abuse problems and are in denial about the implications of those problems. Some greater level of parental control, or at least options to exert control at least until the child becomes sixteen, seem warranted.

Situations in which children are removed from their parent(s) because of allegations of abuse or neglect provide the greatest challenge to the tension between parents and professionals. There are clear cases in which some individuals who bear children are simply not fit to be parents. In these situations, the termination of parental rights is appropriate and necessary. The challenge is to identify these parents and distinguish them from parents who are undergoing significant problems that interfere with their current ability to parent, but will not prevent their eventual ability to resume parenting roles.

What Youth Want versus What Others Want for Them

Ultimately, in a free society, we are unable to compel adults to do something that they do not want to do or to not do something that we do not want them to do. We can only reward them for doing things we value and punish them for doing things that we, as a society, do not allow. The situation is somewhat different for children. Parents often compel children to do things that they do not want to do. That is a major aspect of good parenting. The problem lies with the transition from child to adult—adolescence.

Adolescence is a time of significant emotional turmoil, when young people are struggling to come out of the control of parents and into self-control. This transition is often a messy one. Adolescents seek more freedom than they can handle and place themselves in jeopardy of adverse events, or fail to seek any freedom at all and stunt their emotional growth.

These developmental considerations must inform solutions to this tension. Young children likely require only relatively minor input into decisions about mental health treatment. They are likely to be insufficiently knowledgeable about themselves and their well-being to make sound decisions. Therefore, adults, particularly parents, must make these decisions for them. However, as a child becomes a teenager, more autonomy of choice is important, and more respect for individual preferences of the youth must be accorded.

Child Focus versus Family Focus

Consistent with shifting the balance of tension toward parents, shifting the tension between a child focus and a family focus toward favoring families would be a good thing, with some caveats. For the most part, children are dramatically affected by the circumstances of the entire family. Having a separate adult mental health service system to address the needs of parents when it overlaps with the needs of their children creates problems.

The caveats to favoring families somewhat over individual children involve situations in which the best interests of a child are clearly compromised by other members of the family. These situations include problems with parental divorce when the two parents are unable to prioritize their child's interests above their marital difficulties. They also involve situations of abuse and neglect. In these circumstances, a child focus makes sense; however, these are less common than the range of circumstances in which a family focus is more sensible.

One implication of this shift means that providers also must be skilled in the treatment of adults and understanding adult development. It is insufficient to populate the child service system with providers that only understand children. Given the significant impact that adults have on children's lives, such specialization might be too narrow in some circumstances.

As with the earlier tension between children and parents, a second implication is that a funding mechanism should be designed that addresses the needs of all members of the family concurrently. Having disjointed child and adult service systems is problematic. Perhaps the distinction should be individual (for emancipated adults who seek treatment alone) and families (for everybody else). Thus, there would not be a public children's mental health system. There would be a public family mental health system.

Parent Responsibility versus Parent Blame

The solution to the tension between parent responsibility and parent blame may be more semantic than substantive. Parents are responsible for their children. Even parents with very challenging children maintain that responsibility unless they relinquish their parental rights. The problem is the language of blame that sometimes overlaps with the communication of responsibility. As mentioned in the definition of mental health, a focus on what can be done as opposed to the exact cause, helps to minimize the anxiety and anger that can result from this tension.

As a culture, we give a rather confusing message to parents and children with regard to parental responsibilities. In some states, laws are on the books to punish parents for the misbehavior of their children. In other states, parents without sufficient financial resources must give up guardianship status in order to get residential treatment services for their child.

The consumer movements motto of "no blame, no shame" is an important goal. Blame and shame create and maintain the stigma of mental health challenges. This stigma blocks children and families from getting services that can help.

Psychotherapy as a Product versus Psychotherapy as a Process

The packaging of psychotherapeutic services must be rethought. Presenting psychotherapy as a product to service recipients may be a very good model. The idea would be that a person comes to therapy for certain results. Monitoring the treatment to achieve that result is a reasonable strategy for determining the length of treatment. Presenting recipients with this way of thinking about treatment, along with the tools they need to monitor the desired effects (see chapter 5), is recommended.

My friend Ken Howard was fond of proposing that everyone should have an annual mental health checkup, much like a physical checkup. The idea would not be to initiate treatment, but rather to take stock on one's circumstances and issues and make plans for the next year. This is just one of a number of ways in which behavioral health services could be reconceptualized. Short-term treatments exist and are sometimes advertised, although not consistently. It is ironic that early research with health maintenance organizations demonstrated that individuals with a 20-session limit on outpatient psychotherapy actually attend more sessions than do people with unlimited-session benefits (Manning, Wells, & Benjamin, 1987). Rethinking the process from the consumer perspective could do the field a substantial amount of good. Our notion of an open-ended process just doesn't sell that well to the general public. Only a small proportion of those with real needs are willing to buy this product. We need to repackage outpatient treatment in a manner that better fits what the consumer wants, or do a better job of explaining exactly what we are selling.

A Modest Proposal—Identifying the Tools for Change

With apologies to Jonathon Swift, a set of comprehensive strategies to improve our system of care for children and families does exist. We have the tools. We have the technology. It is my own modest proposal that we need only to develop the vision to understand the full ramifications of the approach and the will to implement it. I believe that there are two components to this vision. The first has a prevention focus and, as suggested earlier, involves community development. There is a substantial body of research to suggest that community characteristics influence the well-being and development of community members. Therefore, creating mentally healthy communities would be the universal approach to addressing public mental health. Chapter 4 discusses a vision for community development, with an intention of preventing the development of some emotional and behavioral problems and creating natural supports for problems that inevitably do develop.

However, even with a very successful community-development strategy, there will always be a need for specialty mental health services. The key is to make those services as accessible and effective as possible. The primary strategy to accomplish this goal is a system that I call Total Clinical Outcomes Management (TCOM). OK, so another acronym isn't really what we need, but let's dissect the words in this one:

Total indicates that the use of outcomes is embedded in all activities at all levels, from the individual case with the child and families as full partners, to the program level, the agency level, the network level, and even the full system level. All partners in the system of care share the same language and same vision with regard to desired clinical outcomes.

Clinical indicates that the use of outcomes is focused on the healthy development, well-being, and functioning of the child and families. Consumer satisfaction is relevant to the degree that it is associated with clinical outcomes. System level, service use, or provider outcomes are of secondary or even tertiary importance.

Outcomes indicates that the focus is on those factors that are related to characteristics of the individual child or his or her family that are either indications for the use of a particular approach or are reflections of the proposed impact of that approach.

Management indicates that these outcomes are used in all aspects of operating the system of care, from individual case planning and monitoring, to supervision, program management, funding and system management.

The concept of TCOM is a comprehensive one in which the measurement and management of information regarding the characteristics of individual children and families is the single most important focus of managing treatment interventions at all levels of the system of care simultaneously. This strategy is discussed in much greater detail in chapter 5.

In summary, two rather distinct approaches may lead to solutions to many of the problems facing the public mental health system and those it is intended to serve. The first path involves the evolution of healthy communities. The goal of these communities is to prevent children and adolescents from ever having to enter the formal public mental health system. Chapter 4 describes some aspects of this approach. However, despite the best efforts of community development, it is most likely impossible to prevent the development of all emotional or behavioral disorders, and thus an accessible and effective specialty behavioral health system is critical. The key consideration is how to manage this system in a way that eliminates syndromes and yet also supports both accessibility and effectiveness. I propose that the key to achieve this vision is to shift the focus away from utilization of services and toward outcomes. Further, a total commitment to using outcome information to manage the system is necessary; that is, TCOM. The basic tenets of this approach are described in chapter 5.

CHAPTER 4

BUILDING HEALTHY COMMUNITIES

Although the concept of preventing mental health problems through community action is not new, we do not really know a great deal about how such prevention might work. Efforts to prevent mental illness have their modern roots in the Community Mental Health Act of 1963, which mandated each Community Mental Health Center to establish a prevention component. Most of these prevention activities centered on community education and what might be considered "pretreatment" interventions. Although there is a large body of research on these types of prevention, the findings are not particularly encouraging.

Part of the prevention problem comes from the broad definition of mental health problems. Included in this definition is everything from major mental illnesses such as schizophrenia and bipolar disorders to adjustment reactions that can occur after traumatic events. Therefore, when thinking about creating health communities, it is best to consider exactly what types of mental health problems can be prevented and what types of problems cannot.

I would argue that currently not enough is known about mental illness to prevent biologically based psychiatric disorders, often referred to as serious mental illness (SMI). SMI refers to disorders such as schizophrenia and major affective disorders (i.e., bipolar and unipolar). I would also include dementias and antisocial personality disorder (APD) in this categorization, although APD may be somewhat controversial with regard to its primary biological basis. The prevention of a biological disorder likely requires either a genetic or biologically based prevention strategy. In addition, there is good reason to believe that the effects of trauma can be reduced with rapid intervention, but this is more of a rapid-treatment deployment approach than a universal prevention activity (Hembree & Foa, 2003; Wolmer, Laor, & Yazgan, 2003). The focus of prevention activities that I consider in this chapter is therefore less about preventing major mental illness or the long-term impact of trauma and more about preventing emotional and behavioral problems associated with problems of living. The idea behind prevention is that if you can reduce problems of living or help people to better cope with problems, then you can prevent the behavioral health problems associated with life stress when the situations arise.

To date, most efforts at prevention have been either mass media or psychoeducational, or what I might call "pretreatment" prevention activities. Using the media to reach a large audience (e.g., the antidrug commercial, "This is your brain on drugs") is a common strategy to increase awareness, and it likely has an important role in addressing the problem of stigma of mental health problems. The other types of prevention activities generally seek smaller audiences and involve some strategy designed to convince people to change key behavior, which is why I refer to them as "pretreatment"; they seek to perform some type of transformation on individual members of the target audience. Although these types of prevention activities have inherent value in the system, it would seem that with a conceptualization of prevention that focuses on reducing factors that place individuals at risk for significant stress, the greatest impact would come from making life less stressful for people. This seems more the domain of community development than mental health services per se.

That is not to say that mental health professionals have no role in prevention; they simply do not occupy the focal role. Healthy communities must have the ability to respond rapidly to disasters and traumatic events that affect a large number of people. There is indeed substantial evidence to suggest that the rapid mobilization of trauma services has a very beneficial effect on reducing the long-term impact of the traumatic event (James, 1989; Weintraub, Pynoos, & Hall, 2001; Yehuda, 2002).

As mentioned previously, shifting our theory of prevention outside of the behavioral health profession has the potential benefit of bringing more resources to bear on the problem of children's mental health. An organized community development strategy that attends to preventing risk factors for emotional and behavioral reactions to stressful living would not need to be funded by the specialty mental health system. Separate and significant funding streams already exist to address community development.

Guiding Principles for Establishing Healthy Communities

As with the Child and Adolescent Service System Program (CASSP) principles created to guide the development of systems of care for children with serious emotional disorders and their families, if we are to shift the focus of prevention activities to community development, it is reasonable to propose guiding principles for establishing healthy communities. The following represents an initial offering of these principles.

Principle 1: Prevention Activities Must Have a Community Focus Rather than an Individual Focus

In order to develop healthy communities, approaches to health-promotion intervention must be community focused rather than individual focused. Public health strategies have been relatively successful in a number of areas, including smoking cessation, HIV transmission reduction, and cancer awareness. Expanding these efforts to include approaches relevant to emotional and behavioral health is a relatively new aspect of public health. New initiatives that attempt to reduce violence and bullying are being tried around the country. The ability to respond rapidly to traumatic events has been enhanced dramatically over the past decade. Treating school violence and teen suicides using this model appears to be effective (Weintraub et al., 2001).

As a warning, the public health efforts to reduce substance use through the Drug Abuse Resistance Education (DARE) initiative appear to be a failure (Burke, 2002). If anything, this approach may be associated with increased alcohol and drug experimentation. The evaluation of the DARE model shows that community-focused interventions are not necessarily bound to succeed just because they have a community focus. Figuring out what works for which target problem is an important priority for public health research (Sherman et al., 1998; Stovell, 1999).

There should be a national public health priority to identify community-focused strategies that reduce circumstances closely related to the development of emotional and behavioral health problems. Research identifying the characteristics of healthy communities and their institutions should be a funding priority.

Principle 2: All Children Are Included

"No inclusion, no exclusion" is an important principle in healthy communities. The idea behind this principle is that all children experience challenges and difficulties, and creating an environment that allows for these problems to be addressed with all children is an important aspect of creating healthy communities. Any child living in a community is a member of that community.

This principle has a number of important implications for understanding the interface of the community to the service system. First, eligibility for services, at least at the least-intensive level (e.g., counseling and psychotherapy), should not require a specific level of need. The most common eligibility criteria used is the presence of a *Diagnostic and Statistical Manual of Mental Disorders*, 4th edition (DSM-IV; American Psychiatric Association, 1994) psychiatric diagnosis. This requirement has at least two unintended consequences:

1. It forces all children who are seeking help to be labeled with a psychiatric disorder.
2. It forces all providers to claim the presence of a psychiatric disorder in order to obtain reimbursement for services.

The first unintended consequence is a problem of stigma. Needless to say, children likely do not understand that they are even given a diagnosis let alone what implications their diagnosis might have; however, becoming diagnosed with a psychiatric disorder is not a high priority among most teens (U.S. Surgeon General, 1999).

The second unintended consequence is a problem of honesty versus advocacy. This is a sensitive topic in the mental health service system. Understandably, providers do not like the implication that they may use inaccurate diagnoses in order to be paid for services. Thus, to minimize any direct accusations of impropriety, I like to personalize this issue when discussing it publicly. In some aspects of my clinical training, I was encouraged to pick the diagnosis that was least stigmatizing and most likely to result in reimbursement. I do not think I am alone in this experience. Although this strategy makes sense from an individual advocacy perspective—that is, you are able to provide services for the affected individual—the ramifications of this issue can be troubling. In my work around the country, I have observed the following phenomenon:

1. **Provider-specific diagnostic selectivity:** At one program, all children receive a diagnosis of adjustment disorder with problems of conduct; in another program, similar children receive a diagnosis of conduct disorder; in still another similar program, children generally receive a diagnosis of oppositional defiant disorder.

2. **A general discounting of the meaning of diagnosis:** At the system level, there are enormous datasets of Medicaid claims data that are sometimes used for policy research. Unfortunately, almost nobody actually believes that the diagnoses included in these datasets are reliable or valid. At the individual child and family level, the diagnoses are often seen as a formality and may not even be shared with the family.

3. **A disconnect between diagnosis and treatment planning:** With a diminished emphasis on diagnoses as meaningful information, they become less utilized in treatment planning. Often, treatment planning can occur without any formal DSM-IV diagnosis being rendered. Although assessment is critical, diagnosis specifically becomes less relevant. The general exception to this rule is when a psychiatrist is involved in medication management. Although sometimes the diagnosis is informed more by treatment response than by diagnostic interview, there is likely to be a direct relationship between diagnosis and treatment in these circumstances.

As the field moves toward implementing evidence-based practices, many of these effective treatments are targeted for specific disorders (Hoagwood, Burns, Kiser, Ringeisen, & Schoenwald, 2001). Although psychotropic medication management has shifted from a disorder basis to a target symptom basis, accurate assessment of these symptoms remains a key to effective treatment (Weisz & Jensen, 1999). One strategy to address this problem would be to remove the link between the presence of a diagnosis and reimbursement for the service provided. Thus, although comprehensive assessments should be required to ensure that the needs of children and families are met with effective, high-quality services, there should be no diagnostic eligibility requirements for outpatient services provided in the community. All children and families would be equally eligible for these services.

A possible strategy also would be to provide reimbursement based on an established link between the assessment and the intervention. The range of options for evidence-based treatments is not yet broad enough to permit this strategy, but there is every reason to believe that in a few years, it should be possible to have a clear map between assessed needs and recommended treatment approaches.

Principle 3: The Geography of the Child-Serving System Should Be Consistent across All Child-Serving Partners

To develop an effective organizational structure, it is a fundamental necessity to have all participants in any system of care share geographies. The primary problem in this area in the existing system is the lack of geographic compatibility between school districts and service system. As discussed in chapter 3, this is a major impediment to effective system management. It is critical that regular school programming and school-based interventions are coordinated regarding other approaches to address children's mental health needs.

All child-serving systems should share a common geography. The most rational approach would be to organize all services by county, because there is already governance organized at the county level. The next best approach would be to organize all services by school district. Although our local school-funding mechanisms are a factor in maintaining large disparities in public education across the United States, the school district model and its concomitant taxing authority remains popular in many parts of the country. Therefore, given the politics of school funding, this strategy might be the easiest strategy to implement. Single mental health agencies could be integrated with several school districts, but multiple agencies should not be integrated within a single district. Child welfare caseworkers and juvenile courts also should be organized in a consistent manner. The example of the Local Area Network organization described in chapter 3 represents one possible interim solution to this problem.

Principle 4: Parents Must Be Partners in Community-Development Strategies

As discussed in other sections of this book, parents have primary responsibility for the healthy development of their children. Further, parents generally know their children better than does anyone else, regardless of differences in training and expertise. Consistent with CASSP principles, parents should be represented in community-development strategies. This is a complicated issue, as anyone who has participated in a school referendum that intends to raise property taxes can attest.

Our representative government is founded on the principle of one person, one vote. Parents have one vote, although they represent additional citizens—their children. A family of four has two votes, but four citizens. At the same time, voters without kids often feel like community services that have a child focus do not provide anything positive for them. Child-focused developments may be less popular than are developments that benefit all adults. Thus, children are not fully represented in our democracy. For this reason, parents must organize to advocate for policies, programs, and services that are in the best interest of children and families. In representative democracies, particularly those with substantially less than 100% participation, advocacy is an important tool. As the Surgeon General's (1999) report notes, one of the most significant changes in the past several decades has been the rise of consumer and family movements. Although these movements have gained significant power nationally, in some locales, the power of consumer- and family-advocacy organizations is still limited. Not surprisingly, family advocacy is often least visible in those local areas with the greatest needs. It is incumbent on the national advocacy organizations to help identify and organize parents and other family members in these geographic areas to improve advocacy throughout the country. In the meantime, national and state consumer and family organizations should advocate for communities that cannot yet advocate for themselves.

Although I have often observed significant professional ambivalence about consumer and family involvement, I have also witnessed its power to transform meetings, agendas, and outcomes. Several years ago, I suggested consumer representation to the Executive Committee of our Department of Psychiatry—a suggestion that was strongly voted down because several other representatives said it was "just too difficult." Like any form of democracy, building consumer and family representation into the process is difficult and, at times, can be emotionally and practically messy. However, the benefit is worth the price of the struggle.

There is also a political reason why professionals should be eager to see the growing power of the consumer and family movement. Because professionals are paid for their work, they are in an essential conflict-of-interest position when it comes to advocacy. When professionals advocate for increased services for children and families, the same professionals can benefit financially. Because of this financial aspect, professional advocacy becomes no different than any other form of lobbying. Consumer and family advocacy, however, does not suffer from this form of diminished credibility. Therefore, family and consumer advocacy groups can have much more moral authority than can any professional advocacy group.

Principle 5: Any Parent Who Wants to Work Should Be Able to Work

A person's job is generally a significant aspect of his or her health and well-being. Substantial evidence has shown that working offers significant health and well-being benefits, above and beyond the financial benefits of a paycheck. A job can provide a person with a sense of him- or herself, and can provide opportunities for self-fulfillment and experiences of self-efficacy. Full employment—that is, everyone who wants or needs a job is able to have one—is an important social goal. The existing data on working mothers supports this principle. For example, Scarr, Phillips, & McCartney (1991) report little effect of maternal employment on child development and attachment, but did find that steadier employment and higher income streams can have positive effects on child development.

Some people will view this guiding principle as controversial in that there is a significant division in our society with regard to the role of mothers. Some feel that any policy that supports working mothers is an indirect tax on mothers who stay at home with their children (e.g., Family Research Council, www.frc.org). This concern is an important one, because mothers who are able to stay at home to raise their children should not be penalized for their decision to be stay-at-home parents. However, if we expect families to take care of themselves, it sometimes is necessary for mothers to work. Any other position is naive. If, as a society, we decide that we want at least one parent to stay home to raise children, then we would have to reinstate our previous welfare system that essentially paid mothers to parent. We already know that this approach failed and created enormous dependency and a nearly permanent underclass.

An irony of our political circumstances is that one end of the political spectrum (liberal) tends to prefer direct cash payments to support women parenting at home, whereas the other end (conservative) does not. However, some representatives of the conservative perspective view subsidized child care as a tax on stay-at-home moms. Conservatives must choose between the values of fiscal conservatives (personal empowerment through gainful employment) and social conservatives (traditional families with stay-at-home moms). Given the fact that so many families experience divorce during child rearing and that, in many of these circumstances, the only viable parent is a woman, it is not feasible to achieve both values. Sadly, undercutting subsidized child care as a threat to traditional family values is actually at odds with the goal of maintaining intact families. Empowering women to work and parent while supporting mothers who want only to parent seems like a feasible vision that might actually help to keep the families with working mothers together.

Principle 6: All Families Have the Right to Safe, Stable, and Affordable Housing

Stable housing is the foundation of community inclusion. Families living in poverty have a difficult time maintaining housing. Housing transitions cause all sorts of other transitions that can be quite unhealthy for children. For example, it is not uncommon for children to have to change schools because they have moved even relatively short distances across school boundaries. Unstable housing is a major source of complexity to community services. Homelessness is devastating for families. The National Center on Family Homelessness (1999) estimates that by age eight, one out of three homeless children has a diagnosable psychiatric disorder. Nearly two-thirds are witness to violence.

The greatest increase in homelessness over the past decade has come as an increase in the number of homeless families. It is currently estimated that about 40 percent of all homeless persons are families with children (National Center on Family Homelessness, 1999). The common pathway to homelessness for families is a problem with domestic violence, divorce, and/or job loss. Initially, unstable housing sometimes leads to "doubling up," a situation in which two families move in together in order to pool resources. Although these circumstances can provide single parents with some initial support, they often become quite stressful due to the complexity of living together as a family with another family.

The typical homeless family consists of a single mother with two or more children. More than half of these mothers have never been married; therefore, financial and other resources from fathers have often never been available to the family. Most mothers of homeless families have experienced at least one of the following historical risk factors: foster care, running away, physical or sexual abuse, or had a parent with an SMI in their own lives (Bassuk et al., 1997). Thus, we have the information necessary to know who is at risk for these problems. In addition, substance abuse or dependence is common among these women (Robertson, 1991). Studies suggest that at least half of all homeless mothers have significant mental health problems (Hoffman & Rosenheck, 2001).

The children in homeless families are particularly vulnerable (Burg, 1994; Graham-Berman, Coupet, Egler, Mattis, & Banyard, 1996). Most are not consistently in school. Special needs are common, and those with special needs generally do not get those needs met consistently. Older children—particularly boys over 12 years of age—are often prevented from staying with their families in shelters or other programs, and homelessness is quite often followed by separation of parents from their children (Cowal, Shinn, Weitzman, Stojanovic, & Labay, 2002). Shelters are the most common form of service for these families. Although most families report a generally positive experience in shelters, the allowable stays are usually insufficient to make it possible for families to obtain permanent housing. In addition, research suggests that communal living circumstances (as is found in shelters) can create communal mothering, in which there can be a gradual deterioration in the family over time (Hoffman & Rosenheck, 2001). When the family leaves the shelter, the parental role may be further diminished as a result of these experiences, making parenting, particularly of older children, even more difficult. In addition, shelters are breeding grounds for infectious diseases and often are situated in antiquated buildings with high lead content (Burg, 1994).

In sum, the children of homeless families are the most vulnerable population of children in our nation. The mothers of these children also have great need. Although housing instability may be unavoidable in a free, capitalist society, homelessness is preventable. Homelessness of families—generally, single-parent families with multiple children—is unconscionable.

Summary

Given the above set of principles, strategies are needed to help achieve the vision of how to create healthy communities. Although there are many possible pathways to this goal, I will focus on three that I believe are central: the creation of jobs in the communities with the greatest needs, the development of healthy schools, and the management of stable and affordable housing for families with significant challenges.

Creating Jobs in the Community

At least two things have to happen if we are to approach full employment opportunities for parents of children with serious emotional and behavioral challenges. First, jobs must be created that single mothers with high-need children can actually perform adequately. Second, sufficient, safe, and affordable day care options must be created to allow these mothers the freedom to work.

Although there is very little empirical research on this topic, anecdotal experiences and focus groups with parents of children with serious emotional and behavioral disorders identify several significant barriers to employment. The two primary barriers are the time away from home and the flexibility of the position. The essential challenge for parents is that parenting a high-need child requires time at fairly unpredictable moments. The school may call when the child acts up and require the parent to come and pick the child up; or the only available appointment time to see a counselor is during the workday. If a parent works a distance from home, the time of the commute is added to the workday, to make the time away from home prohibitive. It is even more difficult to be responsive to the emergent needs of the child (or school) if the travel time is long. Some employers are more flexible than are others. Parents with high-need children require some flexibility in scheduling their workday, so that they are available to their child and the child-serving system.

Given these two primary barriers, the apparent solution is for the parent to find a job in or near the neighborhood where they live that offers flexibility in terms of workday. Generally, small business enterprises in local neighborhoods fit these criteria. The neighborhoods with the highest rates of utilization of public mental health services are the same neighborhoods that have the highest rates of child welfare involvement, substance abuse, crime, and school dropout rates; and they are the areas that are least likely to have employment opportunities (Shen, 2001). This phenomenon has been called the jobs-housing imbalance (Cervero, 1989, 1996). This imbalance refers to the fact that, in general, poor people cannot afford to live in places near where jobs exist, and affordable housing is generally not found near places of employment (Gober, McHugh, & LeClerc, 1993). Transportation to and from work is a major barrier to sustained employment for parents, in that it involves additional time and expense. This barrier is even greater for parents who move to work from welfare (Sawicki & Moody, 2000).

Most job-training programs focus on preparing the trainee to work for someone else. However, if no jobs exist that are sufficiently convenient and support parenting, this strategy will have limited success. An alternative solution in terms of community development is small business incubation. Incubation efforts involve transforming individuals who want to develop their own businesses into successful entrepreneurs. In their book, *Incubating New Enterprises, A Guide to Successful Practice*, Lichtenstein and Lyons (1996) offer a technical guide to thinking about creating employment opportunities through entrepreneurship. Although business incubation does not directly address the employment needs of the parents of children with serious emotional challenges, it offers a strategy for creating more jobs in the areas most likely to have the greatest need. In addition, special incentives could be used to create job opportunities for parents with special needs.

The Enterpreneurial Development System

The Enterpreneurial Development System (EDS; Lichtenstein & Lyons, 2001) approach advocated by these authors has been utilized to stimulate the creation of new business in areas with large minority populations or few other resources. The EDS is a transformational approach that considers all aspects of the potential entrepreneur's life and business situation, to allow for a comprehensive approach to helping new businesses along a development path toward sustainable profitability.

Although it is beyond the scope of this book to address business development in depth, a brief review of the EDS model might clarify the challenges facing business development in financially struggling communities. Lichtenstein and Lyons (2001) begin by identifying the following four categories of required resources for business success:

> **The business concept:** This is the entrepreneur's idea or innovation for a product or service that meets some market need or takes advantage of an opportunity.
>
> **Physical resources:** These include such things as raw materials, office or production space, and equipment. These resources must be available and affordable.
>
> **Core competencies or skills:** All businesses need leadership or employees who are able to do the tasks necessary to effectively bring a product or service to market. These skills include management, operations, marketing and sales, financial, legal, and administrative, as well as higher-order skills such as creativity and problem-solving abilities.
>
> **Market(s):** This refers to the universe of customers for the product or service and how the business reaches them. It can include distribution and transportation issues.

Even a cursory review of the above concepts demonstrates why business incubation can be difficult in poor neighborhoods. Minority entrepreneurs can have a number of context-specific challenges in terms of access to resources and markets. Lichtenstein and Lyons (2001) identify nine categories of obstacles to accessing and utilizing the aforementioned resources:

1. **Resource availability:** Resources either do not exist or are of low quality.
2. **Resource visibility:** Resources that could be available are not identified.
3. **Resource affordability:** Resources are prohibitively expensive.
4. **Transaction barriers:** Nonfinancial barriers make it difficult to obtain or use resources. This can be a particularly important barrier for minority entrepreneurs (see, e.g., Durr, Lyons, & Lichtenstein, 2000).
5. **Self-awareness:** The entrepreneur does not know or understand his or her needs.
6. **Accountability:** The entrepreneur will not take responsibility for problem resolution.
7. **Emotional coping:** The entrepreneur cannot manage emotional responses to problems.
8. **Skill:** The entrepreneur lacks a key skill necessary for the business to succeed.
9. **Creativity:** The entrepreneur cannot innovate solutions to problems.

According to the EDS model, business incubation is a transformational process, not a transactional one. Traditionally, enterprise development work has been transactional. An entrepreneur needs capital—a venture capital supplies the necessary funding and is built into the ownership of the company. Transactional approaches generally assume too much (e.g., all that the entrepreneur needs is capital) and focus too little on the complex interaction between resources and barriers experienced by the entrepreneur.

Transformation is achieved by helping the entrepreneur to identify his or her business resource requirements and to identify and work through the obstacles to obtaining and utilizing the aforementioned resources. The final, and perhaps most important, step in the process is the identification and development of the individual entrepreneur's skills. By providing a template for new businesses to identify resources and obstacles and to assess and develop the entrepreneurial skills of the individual, EDS incubates small business enterprises. Metaphorically speaking, the concept is to not fall prey to the easy temptation of giving small business people a fish, but rather to engage in the more difficult task of teaching them to fish. EDS provides the infrastructure for the development of an entrepreneurial community that can directly address the jobs-housing imbalance.

A Case Example of EDS

Tom Lyons, Ph.D., the Fifth Third Bank Professor of Community Development at the University of Louisville, tells the following story about how successful business incubation can work in a poor community. This story is about a woman in Wisconsin who ran her own housecleaning business. She had a team of women who worked six days a week cleaning people's houses. She had plenty of customers to keep her crew busy, but she wasn't making a profit. She did her own self-diagnosis and decided she wasn't making a profit because she didn't yet have enough customers. In order to expand her customer base, she believed she needed to hire, train, and equip a second crew. However, this would require money (capital) that she did not have. She concluded that she needed a bank loan to start the second crew, which she would be able to pay off when the profits started rolling in.

She went to the banks in town and was unable to get a loan at any of them. In some cases, she couldn't afford the interest and collateral requirements. In other instances, the banks were not inclined to make the loan because she was a woman operating a "marginal" business (although they didn't say so in so many words). In the language of the diagnostic matrix, she required a physical resource—financial capital—and faced affordability obstacles and transaction barriers (female business owner, not a high-growth firm) to getting this resource.

The entrepreneur decided to try the local business incubation program, which had a revolving loan fund and a mission to assist low-income entrepreneurs. She explained her problem to the incubator manager and asked for a loan. He was not willing to accept her superficial diagnosis, however, and asked her if they could review her business's financial records. When they did, they found her real problem. When she had priced her services, she had covered her costs but had not built in a profit. Therefore, no matter how many crews she had, she would never make a profit. Instead of giving her a loan, which would have only been squandered, the incubator manager helped her to reprice her services and deal with the customer-relations fallout of having to raise her prices. She has had a viable business ever since.

The resource that this woman really required was a core competency for business—the knowledge to properly price one's goods or services. The obstacles she faced were a self-awareness obstacle—she didn't really know what she needed—and a capability obstacle—she already had the physical resources she needed, she just did not know how to use them well.

In an EDS, the entrepreneur's skills are assessed in the beginning, so that a mistake like this can be avoided. Assistance providers (like the incubator program in this case) have the opportunity to help an entrepreneur proactively, rather than having the person come to them after it's too late. The woman in our case example was fortunate. She might have obtained a bank loan when she really wasn't ready, defaulted on the loan, and lost her business and her life's savings. Now, she can actually hire another team when she's ready, and increase her profits.

Continued evolution of effective national, state, and local policy on business development in communities with the highest rates of poverty and emotional and behavioral problems should be a priority. Linkage of these businesses to larger regional economies is important for sustainability. A particular priority on developing culturally sensitive business development strategies is indicated. Minorities—particularly African Americans—face unique barriers to business development and entrepreneurship (Durr et al., 2000). These authors indicate that African Americans can experience barriers unique to their racial status, including a lack of access to capital, a lack of business or technical skills, difficulty in establishing markets, personal problems, an absence of role models, a reluctance to approach-established sources of assistance, isolation, and instability in workforce involvement based on the business cycle (i.e., last hired, first fired). Thus, the challenges of business incubation are usually most acute in the areas that are most likely to have preventive effects on children's emotional and behavioral problems.

Developing Child Care Capacity

One of the greatest barriers to work for mothers is the availability, accessibility, and affordability of day care for preschool children. Thus, solving the jobs-housing imbalance creates a greater demand for child care. Often, multiple arrangements must be made that involve relatives and paid caregivers (Folk & Yi, 1994). Finding suitable day care can be particularly challenging for mothers attempting to leave welfare in order to work, because these women often work at or near minimum wage. In the foster care system, subsidized kinship care and assigning guardianship to relatives appears to be a viable alternative to permanent placements in child welfare. A similar strategy might be feasible to address the day care needs of low-income women. In subsidized kinship care, the state pays relatives to take care of children who have been removed from the care of their parents. A kinship day care model could easily be developed in which relatives are subsidized for assisting in taking care of preschool children of working mothers. Even small subsidies would have the effect of incubating day care options in high-need neighborhoods. If the relatives enjoyed the experience and benefited economically from the subsidy, they might even expand their efforts to providing day care for nonrelatives.

Developing Healthy Schools

Children spend an enormous amount of time in school, from kindergarten (or even before kindergarten) until they complete their education. Next to home, schools are the most important environments to support the prevention of behavioral and emotional problems. In addition, schools are the most common referral sources to most specialty behavioral health services (Lyons & Shallcross, 2000). Therefore, any comprehensive community development strategy intended to prevent the development of behavioral and emotional problems among children must consider the school environment.

Over the past several decades, a variety of programs have been implemented to help develop school cultures to support healthy learning environments (Rones & Hoagwood, 2000). These initiatives have been funded by both the federal government and states, and share some common characteristics, including teacher and parent involvement and skills development. Examples include the following:

    Positive behavioral interventions and supports (PBIS)

    School-improvement planning

    Flexible service delivery

    "No Child Left Behind"

    "21st Century Schools"

    Standards-aligned classrooms

Special education (least restrictive environment) (disability legislation)

Student assistance programs

Comprehensive school reform models

Of these, PBIS is the most comprehensive approach that maintains a primary focus on the prevention and treatment of behavioral and emotional issues while respecting the school's core mission of education (Carr et al., 2002; Scott & Eber, 2003). PBIS is a research-based systems approach that is designed to enhance the capacity of schools to (1) effectively educate all students, including those with challenging social behaviors; and (2) adopt and sustain the use of effective instructional practices. As such, this program is an excellent model for how to foster school environments that promote good mental health.

As shown in Figure 4.1, schools can be organized into levels or tiers. These tiers can be based on the degree of academic and behavioral needs of the students in the school. The largest tier consists of students without significant academic or behavioral needs, which represents the largest proportion of the school—in most cases 80 to 90 percent. These children will have normal problems of adjustment to development, and they also can serve as the healthy milieu to help the

Figure 4.1
Designing Schoolwide Systems for Student Success

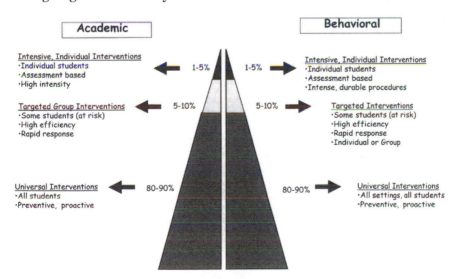

children with greater needs. This is the group of children for whom universal (schoolside interventions) would be intended.

Between 5 and 10 percent of children in schools can be expected to have some academic and behavioral needs. These are the children for whom targeted group interventions might be the most efficient and effective. These children would not be high risk enough to generate the iatrogenic group effects reported by Dishion, Bullock, and Granic (2002), but would still need some help in adjusting to problems that affect their lives at school.

The highest-need group comprises between 1 and 5 percent of the school. These are very high-need children who likely require intensive intervention both at school and outside of the school. School-based intervention is likely to be insufficient for these children and, therefore, these are the ones who are likely to enter the specialty behavioral health system of care.

In the PBIS model, the focus of the universal intervention is on the following key principles:

• The school as the unit of implementation
• Establishing a connection between social and academic achievement
• Building team-based leadership in the school
• Investing in capacity building
• Implementing and sustaining effective practices
• Making all decisions informed by data

This last bulleted item establishes that PBIS is in line with the Total Clinical Outcomes Management model elaborated in chapter 5. In order to pursue the objectives within each school, a PBIS implementation team is formed, which then develops the universal action plan. This plan is designed with the goal of reducing new cases of problem behavior and/or academic failure.

Among the elements of the schoolwide universal action plan are the following:

1. A common schoolwide approach to discipline that is proactive and positive.
2. A clear set of positive-stated behavioral expectations.
3. Clear definitions of behavioral expectations in both classroom and nonclassroom settings.
4. Procedures for teaching expected behavior to all students.

5. Design of a continuum of procedures for encouraging expected behavior.

6. Procedures for discouraging inappropriate behavior.

7. Procedures for ongoing monitoring and evaluation.

When I was first exposed to the PBIS model, I was struck by how similar this approach is to a good approach at parent training and family therapy. The key with parents is to get everyone on the same page in terms of what they expect of their kids and what they do if their kids do not do what they expect of them. This is really the same goal as PBIS, except that in school you've got the complexity of reaching a consensus in order to get a large group of teachers and other school personnel to all behave in the same way with regard to what they expect of their students and what they do when the students do not do what is expected of them. The following are examples of expected behaviors that have been developed in different schools:

Be respectful

Be responsible

Be there/be ready

Follow directions

Once these behavioral expectations are selected, they are carefully defined in the various school settings (e.g., classroom, hallway, cafeteria), and then curricula are developed to teach all students these behavioral expectations. Reinforcement strategies are identified that involve recognizing and rewarding students when they engage in expected behaviors. When a student is observed not engaging in the expected behavior, the continuum of consequences can go something like the following:

- Reteaching of expected behavior
- Follow-up with increased reinforcement
- Verbal reprimands
- Detentions
- Community service

The expectation is that these positive strategies will help to reduce problem behavior and prevent some students' behaviors from escalating to the point that they require special education assessments or referrals to treatment. However, PBIS recognizes that full prevention is not possible and thus tiers of intervention are established to allow for first a low-intensity group intervention and then a high-intensity individual intervention when problems are identified that cannot be resolved within the universal framework. The highest-intensity services follow a wraparound philosophy developed out of the system-of-care approach. Family involvement with the school in addressing identified problems is valued.

Although PBIS is just one strategy that can be used to support the development of a healthy school, the data on its effectiveness is quite positive and the experience with its implementation at various schools around the country has been equally promising. It incorporates many of the principles espoused in this book—child focused, evidence based, family friendly, assertively managed, and team directed. Regardless of the specific approach used, strategies that bring school personnel together to effectively address the emotional and behavioral needs of students in the service of their academic preparation is a critical goal toward building healthy communities for children and their families.

Creating Stable and Affordable Housing

A variety of programs have been developed over the past several decades that can serve as models for the solution to the problem of creating stable and affordable housing. In 1994, the Institute for Community Living, Inc., began operating the Emerson-Davis Family Development Center in a renovated college dormitory in Brooklyn. In 2000, this program won the prestigious Gold Achievement Award from the American Psychiatric Association (2000). The program enrolls single parents who are living in shelters or who have been recently hospitalized psychiatrically. All adult residents are homeless and have an SMI; about half are in recovery from substance-related disorders. This program reunites single parents with their children and allows them to live in the supported environment of the program. The program provides learning opportunities for both parents and children, focusing on activities of daily living and parenting skills. In addition, parents are expected to work, go to school, or enroll in a vocational training program. Once the family situation has been stabilized both economically and socially, permanent housing is sought in the community so that linkages to ongoing treatment can be maintained. The length of time a family lives in the center varies and is individualized to the family's specific circumstances. Stays have ranged from 2 days to 65 months.

The KidsStart program, created about 10 years ago by the National Center on Family Homelessness, now operates at 30 sites nationally. The program works directly with preschool children who are living in family shelters to identify and address developmental, health, and behavioral health needs. Included in this service is attention to trauma and its sequelae. The Substance Abuse Mental Health Services Administration has also funded a multisite demonstration project that involves a multifaceted intensive intervention with homeless mothers and their children. This project provides housing, support, treatment, and family preservation services.

The following factors are likely to be key design elements in any successful program that addresses family homelessness:

1. Temporary housing of an indeterminate length is provided.
2. All family members are allowed to live in this housing.
3. Special needs of each family member are identified and addressed.
4. The primary outcome goal is a transition to permanent housing that does not disrupt ongoing services to address special needs.

Of course, the fourth factor presumes that sufficient affordable housing exists in the neighborhood of the program, and that needed services and jobs are also available to persons living in that neighborhood.

Programs for families whose challenges lead them to seek shelter from homelessness are only part of the solution. With these families, the significant levels of need that either place the parents at risk for housing instability or result from the stresses of being homeless require specialty programs that link housing to services, including treatment services. However, creating a stock of affordable housing that is safe and stable for low-income and working-poor families is also a critical priority.

Additional Areas of Focus for Achieving and Maintaining Healthy Communities

The three priorities for community development discussed earlier—jobs, schools, and housing—by no means fully develop the principles and strategies necessary to achieve and maintain healthy communities that can prevent children from developing some types of emotional and behavioral problems. Other issues, although perhaps less compelling, require attention as well. The last section of this chapter addresses some of the additional issues.

Building Ties to the Religious Community

Major assets in many communities are located in the churches, temples, and synagogues of the community. Within a community's religious groups are people who can be sources of strength for others and resources to the community at large—and to children with special needs, in particular. The development of assets in religious groups and structures in communities to aid in achieving the vision of a healthy community is likely to succeed in identifying important community assets. The goal is to give the local religious communities the opportunity to fully participate in supporting prevention initiatives.

Currently, significant barriers exist between religious communities and mental health professionals. There are at least two reasons for this separation. First, mental health professionals are among the least religious of any vocational group. Therefore, opportunities for social contact in everyday living are often quite limited. Second, theories of the causes of behavior between religion and psychiatry and psychology can be dramatically different. In these circumstances, it can be difficult for representatives of either group to trust the judgment of the other.

Despite these differences, there is substantial evidence that has shown that for those individuals who are spiritual or practice religion, significant health and mental health benefits can be experienced through their faith and practice. In addition, religious groups often have a large number of caring people who can be enormously helpful as natural supports for children and families. Finding creative ways to work through the barriers that separate mental health from the religious communities may be a valuable community development strategy. If nothing else, work to reduce the stigma of mental illness might be addressed through forums sponsored by religious communities. This may be particularly useful in minority communities in which stigma is high (U.S. Surgeon General, 2001a), because in these communities, the religious organizations are often far more trusted members of the community than are the mental health service providers.

Building Leisure Options for Youth

A priority for community development must be the development of greater leisure options for children—particularly adolescents—so that options for fun and productive uses of free time are available. Poor communities, in particular, often lack resources to support and sustain recreational and other leisure activities. In our research on the Illinois

Mental Health-Juvenile Justice (MH-JJ) initiative, we found that having talents and recreational interests were strong resiliency factors for recovery from the symptoms of SMI and not being re-arrested for additional criminal or delinquent behavior (Lyons, Griffin, Jenuwine, Shasha, & Quintenz, 2003). Further, successfully linking these youth to community-based recreational services was associated with positive outcomes.

Intensive community treatment programs often have some flexible funding. Although further research is necessary to verify the relationship, there is every reason to believe that investing in the youth's participation in these activities appears to be worthwhile. Included in these activities would be athletic and artistic pursuits including lessons, interpersonal-focused activities (i.e., healthy versions of "hanging out"), hobbies (e.g., collecting or creating), and entertainment-focused activities (e.g., concerts and movies). Children and families with limited resources often do not have access to these essential activities; therefore, poor children often only have two options: hanging out with friends on the street or staying home.

Creating a Sense of Community

Having a community to be identified with is generally seen as an important goal for young people. Often they complain about aspects of their community, but they also can develop a sense of loyalty that makes the community "home," regardless of their specific housing situation. Therefore, consideration of strategies to increase children's and adolescents' sense of identifying with and belonging to a community should be undertaken. The goal of these strategies would be to allow youth to have a greater stake in their community's future.

Collaboration with Other Child-Serving Institutions

Although collaboration is a fundamental aspect of the system-of-care philosophy, it remains an illusive goal in many situations and actually, at least in many ways, more of an aspect of community development than of service planning and treatment. It is critical to support the development of collaborations with all other child-serving institutions in the community, so that coordinated efforts aimed at preventing emotional and behavioral problems when possible, and treating these problems effectively in all other situations, can be initiated.

The system-of-care philosophy often uses identified children and families to organize these collaborations. By meeting regularly with other system partners in child–family team meetings, collaborative relationships can be built over time, one family at a time. However, for purposes of discussion in this chapter, collaborations must eventually transcend individual children and families to encompass the full community institutions.

Several years ago, I had a meeting with New York City's commissioner of the Administration for Children's Services (ACS), the city's child welfare agency. After reviewing a study that we had completed on the prevalence of emotional and behavioral problems in the 33,000 wards of the city, I made the comment that about 75 percent of children had some behavioral health need and more than one-third had a serious emotional or behavior disorder. Therefore, the commissioner was not just running a child welfare agency; he also was running a specialty behavioral health care system. After we talked through the data, he told me that it was the most depressing meeting he had ever been in. Several months later, he quit ACS and became the Fire Commissioner. I tell that story with no disrespect for the commissioner; I admired him very much. The problems of child welfare are simply so daunting that even thinking about trying to integrate that enormous and complex system with the specialty behavioral health system for children can boggle the mind and lead even the most committed professionals to throw in the towel. However, incremental progress can be made with patience, perseverance, and a vision of the long-term goals.

Interface between the Community and the Specialty Behavioral Health Treatment System

An important aspect of a healthy community is the development of an interface between community institutions and the specialty behavioral health treatment system. This formal interface is necessary to improve the accessibility of the specialty system and build positive and lasting relationships between that system and the community it serves. An effective interface that supports the identification of problems and the effective referral and triage into the specialty system is important to the vision of an accessible system. There are four critical components to this interface:

- Mutual respect between the representatives of the community institution and those of the specialty behavioral health system.
- Awareness of the primary signs and symptoms of emotional and behavioral problems in children, so that referrals can be appropriately triggered.

- Clear, easy, timely, and efficient processes for taking an identified child and his or her family and linking them to appropriate services

- Feedback, so that the representative of the community institution knows what happens to the family after they have entered the specialty system.

Illinois has a statewide program that can serve as a model for the evolution of this type of interface with a community institution. The Illinois MH-JJ Initiative is a project in which a liaison from a community mental health agency develops a relationship with the area juvenile detention center. The liaison then helps the court and detention staff to identify youth who are currently experiencing either a depressive disorder or a psychotic disorder. The liaison involves parents of referred youth and then screens the youth. If one of these disorders is observed, then links are made to the community services to facilitate treatment for the youth's psychiatric disorder and other services to facilitate healthy development and reduce the risk of reoffending. Evaluation of this program supports its effectiveness at identifying appropriate youth, linking them to services in the community, helping to reduce their psychiatric symptoms, and substantially lowering their likelihood of being re-arrested (Lyons et al., 2003). In the process of achieving these objectives, the MH-JJ liaison establishes the four critical components outlined above. He or she builds relationships with court personnel and detention center staff, trains these staff to detect potential mental health problems, manages referrals to limit the efforts required of others, and reports back on the progress that youth make once they are in the program.

Similar models—all of which involve some sort of consultation and liaison relationship between a mental health specialist and a community institution—are possible for every institution. The responsibilities of the liaison are to build trust and reduce stigma, raise the visibility of mental health services, and ease the process of referrals into the system for children and families identified through each institution.

Summary

Community development involves a broad and complex set of strategies with three primary goals. The first is to develop healthy and productive citizens in the community. The second is to enhance the effectiveness of community institutions in addressing mild problems so that they do not require formal mental health intervention. When the first two goals are not achieved, the third goal is to rapidly and easily help children and families who are experiencing mental health challenges to link with specialty mental health services in their communities.

CHAPTER 5

THE MEASUREMENT AND MANAGEMENT OF OUTCOMES IN A TOTAL CLINICAL OUTCOMES MANAGEMENT APPROACH

Total Clinical Outcomes Management

The process of defining Total Clinical Outcomes Management (TCOM) began in chapter 3. TCOM can be thought of as a set of strategies that allow for the management of the service-delivery system across all levels, from the individual child and family to the program, the organization, the county, the state, and perhaps even the country. The essential idea is that all decisions at all levels of the system should be informed by knowledge of the needs and strengths of the child and family.

Is TCOM really new? In some ways, these strategies have been around for more than a decade. In other ways, these strategies have never been fully implemented. Over the past decade, there have been numerous calls for improving the use of outcomes in behavioral health care. In fact, the Community Mental Health Act of 1963 mandates evaluation of all programs funded by the federal government provided by community mental health centers (CMHCs). There have been specific calls for the use of outcomes in children's services (e.g., Steinwachs, Flynn, Norquist, & Skinner, 1996). In actuality, the collection of outcomes data is nothing new. However, although this mandate gave many evaluators a career start (including me), evaluation was never effectively embedded into the CMHC service-delivery system. There were a variety of reasons for this failure:

- **Technological limitations:** Computer technology was just being introduced in the 1960s and 1970s. Minicomputers were popular at CMHCs, but their data entry was difficult, data storage was limited, and processing time was significant. I worked at Ravenswood CMHC in Chicago in their evaluation unit in the mid-1970s. During that time, they had a state-of-the-art minicomputer. Its removable disk drive was the size of a wedding cake and could only hold about six months' worth of data. Annual reports were a nightmare. Paper and pencil approaches, although still robust, were hard to aggregate and analyze in a timely fashion.

- **Measurement constraints:** There were two common trends in the selection of measures at this time. The more common of these approaches was to identify measures used in research and insert them into clinical operations. As is discussed in depth below, this strategy does not work well. The second trend was an approach called Goal Attainment Scaling (GAS). The GAS strategy was novel in that it was designed to allow for the individualization of outcomes. The problem was that the GAS approach was so individualized, no two individuals could even be compared. Thus, beyond tracking the progress of one individual at a time, there was no ability to compare providers, programs, or systems. The primary problem, however, was that clinicians at this time did not see the relevance of outcomes measures to their work with individual cases. In the most frequently practiced approach to outcomes management, measures developed for research are selected and an effort is made to insert them into service-delivery operations. Outcomes measures have not been relevant to clinician's work, particularly with regard to work with individual children and families.

- **Resistance among providers:** When I first joined the faculty at Northwestern, Ken Howard was just implementing his ground-breaking work on psychotherapy outcomes. At that time, the outpatient therapists would complain that by asking outpatients about their therapy experiences, Ken's work was "diffusing the transference relationship." In other words, by allowing psychotherapy clients to communicate with someone else about their therapy, even indirectly, the relationship with the therapist would be damaged. It turned out that psychotherapy clients generally appreciated the opportunity to describe their experiences. Ironically, if it had any effect, asking about clinical status and satisfaction may have enhanced the therapeutic relationship (Howard, Moras, Brill, Martinovich, & Lutz, 1996).

- **Lack of understanding among administrators:** In part due to the Clinician as Administrator Syndrome, whereby the longest-standing clinical line staff become program and then agency administrators, there was little interest or expertise in evaluation among the administrations of CMHCs. The exception to this rule was when someone working as an evaluator moved into a higher administrative position at an agency. In these circumstances, evaluation was often treated with a different level of respect. In most situations, administrators are not knowledgeable about outcomes management technology and confuse it with research and evaluation activities.

- **Evaluation was an unfunded mandate:** Although the initial CMHC legislation called for evaluation, there was no mandate that it be timely or relevant. Thus, it was quite easy to meet the mandate and never do anything meaningful. Further, there was no specific funding for evaluation. Because evaluation in these settings was new, there were few expectations that it would be useful. At times it was useful, but there were no financial incentives for it to be relevant. The primary effect of the legislation was to create a caste of program evaluators.

- **The evaluator's dilemma:** There is an interesting conundrum for evaluators in the public sector. Funding for services was often achieved through the promise of results. For example, agencies would convince a funding source to pay for a new service on the promise that it would work. However, actually monitoring the new service to discover whether or not it really did work put the agency, and therefore the evaluator, in a bind. If the evaluation showed that the program was ineffective, then those parties who sold the program in the first place (usually the evaluator's boss) would look bad. If the evaluation showed that the program worked—well, we already knew it was effective; that's why it was funded. This is commonly called the evaluator's dilemma and, in certain situations, it is truly a Gordian knot that makes evaluation data either moot or dangerous.

For these reasons, and probably others that I've failed to identify, the evaluation efforts of the 1960s and 1970s were not integrated into clinical practice. Although the technology has improved substantially and there are areas in which outcomes are used in relative "real time," there are few places where a TCOM approach has been fully implemented. One of the closest approximations to TCOM would be the quality assurance component of Multisystemic Treatment (MST). To implement MST, an agency is required to participate in an intensive program that monitors outcomes and the fidelity of the implementation. Of course, this approach is only applicable within MST programs and thus does not support cross-program or system-level outcomes management.

Why Should We Believe that TCOM Could Work?

The potential power of TCOM can be found in several examples of service system reform undertaken within the past decade. The first effort of this type involved a community reinvestment strategy to improve services within the Illinois Department of Children and Family Services (DCFS; Lyons, Mintzer, Kisiel, & Shallcross, 1998). At the time of the reform, 55,000 children were state wards served under a total budget of $1.5 billion. About $450 million was invested in mental health services, and about 80 percent of these dollars were used to fund psychiatric hospitalization and long-term residential treatment. At the time, more than 6,000 wards were placed in residential treatment center (RTCs) costing $80,000 to $350,000 per year for each child. This overuse of RTCs created a two-tiered system in which a child either received too few services in the community, or the child functioned poorly enough to qualify for placement in an RTC.

DCFS wanted to implement a community-reinvestment strategy consisting of reducing RTC stays and investing the savings in intensive community services. Initially, they asked RTC providers to identify step-down candidates. However, instead of identifying the children most likely to succeed in foster care programs, RTC providers tended to identify children who were not responding to treatment in their facilities, a strategy that had tragic consequences. For instance, an RTC might say, "Don't take 'Mary,' she's doing well in our program and you would disrupt her treatment. Instead, take 'Johnny;' we aren't helping him, maybe you could." One step-down candidate was identified who was in a hospital level of care and aggressive with staff and peers, prone to running away, and on five different medications. He had grandparents who loved him, so they offered to try if no one else would. About six weeks after he was moved from this intensive treatment setting to a small town in Illinois, he killed both his grandparents.

This tragedy made it clear that residential treatment providers were unable to effectively do the work of identifying appropriate candidates to successfully move from RTC to a community placement. RTC had a conflict of interest in that they were being asked to make decisions in the best interests of the system that would have a potentially negative impact on their programs. What was needed was an objective strategy for defining which children should be placed in residential treatment; which should not; and, among those currently placed, which children should be stepped down to a less-intensive setting (e.g., a foster home). For this purpose, the Childhood Severity of Psychiatric Illness (CSPI) was created as a consensus approach to identifying children who were appropriate for residential treatment (Lyons, 1998).

The first step in the development of the CSPI was to hold multiple focus groups with child welfare caseworkers, community providers, residential providers, parents, youth, and advocates. The purpose of these focus groups was to identify factors that inform good decision making within the children's mental health service system. From these focus groups, a consensus measure was developed. Initially this measure had three primary dimensions—symptoms (informing the type of treatment approach), risk behaviors (informing intensity of services or settings), and community caregiver capacity (informing intensity of services or settings). A planning study was undertaken using this measurement model, and it was demonstrated that more than one-third of all children currently placed in RTC could return to the community (Lyons, Mintzer, Kisiel, & Shallcross, 1998). The CSPI was then implemented at placement review and step-down, and within 18 months of the initiation of the reform. Through the use of the CSPI, the census of RTC was reduced by nearly one-third, saving tens of millions of dollars for reinvestment in community services.

Six years later, the congregate-care population stands at about 2,200 children. Part of this overall reduction came from a reduction in the number of children who were wards of the state (down to about 33,000). However, a large part of the effect results from clearer definitions of which children should be placed in this form of treatment and assertive management of these placements by DCFS. This example clearly demonstrates how managed behavioral health care, and the financial perversions that come from it (e.g., the draining of resources from the public mental health service system into the pockets of company shareholders), is not necessary if a purchaser of services takes a more assertive role in system decision making. If the assertive purchasing is directed by the needs of the children rather than concerns about the costs of services, then state agencies can be very effective in managing their systems of care.

It is noteworthy that a reduction of about 2,000 children placed in congregate care over an 18-month period forced a number of providers out of business. Anyone who follows state politics knows this type of dramatic change is difficult because an agency might simply call their legislator and warn that the state is trying to close a big business in that legislator's district. Few agencies complained, and none effectively. In fact, a number of programs voluntarily went out of business. I believe the reform worked politically because it always stayed focused on doing the right thing for the children who were wards of the state. Early in the process, I attended a meeting of RTC chief executive officers. I made the comment that if the reform was successful, the RTCs should be prepared to have a population of children that was more acute than before. If you remove the low-need children from the mix, you only have high-need children left; therefore, the average acuity goes up. One chief executive officer said something to the effect of "John, you have to realize that we use the easy kids to subsidize care for the harder ones." As soon as this statement was out of his mouth, everyone in the room realized that this is an unethical practice. You cannot treat a child who does not need treatment only so you can afford to treat one that does. We all agreed that the better strategy was to make the reimbursement model work for serving higher-need children.

As a second example, for the past five years we have been managing a decision support project for the Illinois DCFS for all crisis service providers in the state (Leon, Uziel-Miller, Lyons, & Tracy, 1999; Leon, Lyons, & Uziel-Miller, 2000; Leon, Lyons, Uziel-Miller, Rawal, Tracy, & Williams, 2001). These 32 different agencies are responsible for crisis intervention and decisions regarding psychiatric hospitalization. We have developed a benchmarked decision model using five items from the CSPI (i.e., psychosis, depression/anxiety, attention deficit/impulsivity, danger to self, and danger to others) to predict psychiatric admissions. Initially, about 67 percent of admissions were reliably predicted. The two-thirds that could be predicted are not particularly interesting in that these are cases in which the crisis worker did what most other crisis workers would do with a child presenting similar clinical profiles. The interesting cases are the children who are either hospitalized without the level of clinical need that other children who are hospitalized present (i.e., low-risk admission) or the children who are deflected who have a level of clinical need more consistent with children who are hospitalized (i.e., high-risk deflection). Each program and crisis worker is given monthly feedback on cases that were either low-risk admissions or high-risk deflections. They were simply asked to explain what was different about this child's case that led them to choose a decision different from the prediction of what most crisis workers would do with a clinically comparable child. Over time, the consistency of decision making has improved, so that currently about 80 percent of hospital admission decisions are predicted

Figure 5.1
Percent of Hospital Admissions that Were Low Risk by Racial Group

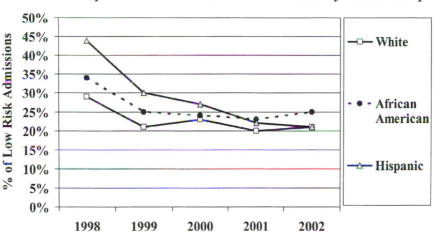

Source: Adapted from Rawal et al., 2003.

by the model. Interestingly, the major impact has been a reduction in the number of minority children who are admitted to the hospital, but are low risk. In other words, the process has reduced and nearly eliminated a racial disparity in hospital admissions (Rawal, Romansky, & Lyons, 2003).

Figure 5.1 presents the change over time in the number of low-risk admissions by racial grouping. Review of this figure reveals a clear racial disparity at the beginning of the outcomes management process. Without telling any crisis worker what to do on a given child's case, but by only asking them to explain why the decision was different from what other crisis workers would do, racial disparities were reduced and nearly eliminated over several years.

These are just two examples of the potential power of outcomes management approaches to facilitate program evolution. In the one example, money was saved and reinvested in intensive community services. In the second example, decision making was improved and racial disparities were reduced. Many other examples exist from both my experiences and the experiences of others. Information about the clinical status of children and families keeps the focus on the child and family and raises the level of the discussion in a powerful and important way. This is the strength of TCOM—it keeps the focus of the service system on the people everyone working in the system has agreed to serve.

The Need for a New Measurement Model

Despite expressed enthusiasm for outcomes measurement in most quarters of the children's mental health system (Steinwachs et al., 1996), success in implementing even simple outcomes measurement systems has been inconsistent at best. As mentioned at the beginning of this chapter, there are several reasons for the limited success to date of outcomes management. First, there is the hesitation to adequately fund the measurement and outcomes management process. This ambivalence may arise from a failure among program and system leadership to fully appreciate the potential value of data in program design, management, and improvement. In career selection, people who enjoy math and statistics often naturally evolve toward science, accounting, or even business. Mental health frequently attracts people whose interests lie in interpersonal pursuits. Given the clinician–administrator tension described in chapter 2, there may be an overselection of people who are somewhat uncomfortable with numbers and statistics found in the ranks of mental health administrators. However, there are likely other reasons for the absence of significant investment in outcomes management. In general, the public mental health system is woefully underfunded; therefore, anything that is seen as diverting from direct care can be a lower priority. The key to addressing the problem of insufficient investment in outcomes management infrastructure is to clearly establish the value of outcomes management strategies for the children's mental health service system.

A second problem has been that even when there are sufficient resources within a system, there have been difficulties fully implementing outcomes management strategies. Often, direct service staff do not see the relevance of outcomes measures for their work with individual children and families. This perceived irrelevance creates a circumstance in which the outcomes measurement process is seen as a paperwork add-on for an already busy staff. It is not seen as either helping them or the children and families they serve. Related to this problem is a general disdain for accountability. No one enjoys having someone "looking over their shoulder" at their work. Nor do clinicians like to be second-guessed about their decisions. When no mechanisms of accountability have ever been in place, clinical staff can be understandably resistant to participate in circumstances in which there is a potential that they might be made to look bad.

A third, but related, problem has been the complexity of selecting appropriate measures that can balance the need for comprehensiveness with the need for efficiency and brevity. The traditional approach has been to borrow measures developed within the research field and attempt to insert them into clinical operations. Although the standard outcomes for children's services can be quite simple (e.g., at home, in school, and out-of-trouble; Rosenblatt, 1993), the full range of outcomes applications requires more sophisticated measurement to support and model decision making with regard to services and levels of care as well as support quality assurance activities. Most measures developed for research do not accomplish the objectives of outcomes management.

Further complicating the selection of outcomes measures is that different perspectives (e.g., child and family, providers, administrators, evaluators) lead to different priorities for desired outcomes. Ideally, the selection of outcomes measures should be a group process with representatives of different perspectives. Among these perspectives, evaluators are likely to advocate for the selection of the most reliable and valid empirical measures from the existing research, administrators might emphasize the expense of any measure and its utility for quality improvement (QI) and accountability, service providers might stress meaningfulness and ease of use, and service recipients might advocate for measures with relevance and respect. Optimally, the selected outcomes measure should honor all of these perspectives.

Traditional Views of Outcomes Measurement

To better understand the challenge of developing outcomes measures for clinical applications, it is useful to understand the theories of measurement that underlie most of the currently available outcomes measures. The conceptualization and format of the measures and the formal definitions of reliability and validity are determined by the theoretical models that are used to develop measures. To date, there are two commonly espoused theories of measurement that guide the understanding of the psychometric properties of measures—classical test theory and item response theory.

Classical Test Theory and Outcomes Measurement

The essence of classical test theory is that the measure of any construct involves the use of a random sample of the population of all possible items that could be defined and identified to accurately measure the target construct. For example, if you were trying to measure depression, you would generate all possible questions relevant to the assessment of depression. Questions would cover all of the symptoms of depression such as sadness, irritability, psychomotor retardation or agitation, weight change, depersonalization, and so forth. You would then sample from this population of questions. The degree to which the universe of all possible items can be defined and adequately sampled to achieve a representative sample for this item population determines the quality of the measure. There are a number of statistical approaches that can be used to test these requirements, including item analysis and factor analysis.

Item analysis involves the study of the intercorrelations among sets of items—that is, the degree to which items in a set correlate with each other determines whether the items are actually measuring the same thing. For example, a correlation of 0.10 or less between two items suggests that they are measuring two different constructs and, therefore, are not members of the same population. Alternatively, a correlation of 0.90 or higher between two items suggests that they are measuring overlapping things and are therefore redundant. In other words, from a classical test theory perspective, one would argue that items with a high correlation are, from a statistical point of view, measuring exactly the same thing. A correlation of between 0.30 and 0.60 is desirable according to classical test theory (Nunnally, 1976). In other words, the items are measuring similar things, but are not too redundant.

Factor analysis can be used to identify the underlying structure of relationships among sampled items. The factor analytic approach, which is the statistical cornerstone of classical test theory, takes the correlation matrix and places some formal statistical rules on the size of correlations needed to support the claim that the items share a common construct or population. Scales developed through the use of factor analysis are often named based on the content of the items included. These scales, which are thought to measure individuals on unseen or latent continua, may or may not have any immediate meaning to service providers or recipients.

Reliability and validity considerations under classical test theory have been described in detail elsewhere (see, e.g., Anastasi, 1968; Nunnally, 1976). Although test–retest reliability and interrater reliability are important, classical test theory is most often used to evaluate measures of transient, subjective states that are neither observable nor stable. The only reliability option for an internal subjective state (i.e., only the person completing the measure knows how he or she feels) is internal consistency reliability. As such, internal consistency reliability has become a commonly used indicator of the reliability of this type of measure. Internal consistency reliability measures the degree to which items of a test correlate with each other. In this theory, the higher the correlation, the higher the reliability. As a rule, the more items there are on a test, the higher its internal consistency reliability will be. Thus, classical test theory, particularly when internal reliability is the only available measure of reliability, advocates the selection of tests with more items with overlapping content.

To encourage measures with many items, classical test theory also emphasizes measuring fewer constructs. A good measure, according to this theory, is not multifaceted. Rather, a good measure has a stable factor structure with a discrete, and probably low, number of factors. Each of those factors should have discrete validity with other measures of similar (or opposite) constructs (Anastasi, 1968).

Classical test theory generally views *face validity* as the least important of all forms of validity (Nunnally, 1976). That is, a potential test user should be able to read the items on the test and, "on the face" of it, the items should appear to be reasonable and relevant. The most important evidence of validity is captured within the broad area of information that is required to demonstrate *construct validity*. Thus, items do not necessarily have to appear consistent with what they are thought to measure as long as there is statistical evidence that these items are really measuring the construct in question. In fact, for some measures, items that might appear irrelevant can contribute to good measures. There are multiple examples of such items in classically constructed measures such as the Minnesota Multiphasic Personality Inventory (MMPI; Butcher, Dahlstrom, Graham, Tellegen, & Kaemmer, 1989) and the Substance Abuse Subtle Screening Inventory (Clement, 2002). The classic example comes from the original MMPI. One item that scores on the Paranoid Scale asks whether you ever cross the street to avoid running into someone you know. The average person says that they do; the person with paranoia says that they do not.

In sum, classical test theory implicitly defines longer measures of single (or few) dimensions as reliable and valid. Measures with too few items on each dimension or too many dimensions—particularly if they are not orthogonal (i.e., uncorrelated)—are more likely to be seen as flawed within this conceptual framework.

Item Response Theory in Outcomes Measurement

Item response theory approaches the measurement problem in a manner that is quite different from classical test theory (Drasgow &

Schmitt, 2002). Item response theory posits the existence of a latent
continuum, which is the measurable aspect of a particular construct.
The goal of measurement (at least in the outcomes field) is to reliably
and accurately locate a particular person on this unseen continuum
relative to all other possible individuals. A good measure from this
perspective is one that is sensitive in each and every relevant area of
this continuum. Therefore, the measure must have the ability to distinguish different people reliably, all along the continuum.

The statistical approach to item response theory can be quite varied
and complex, depending on the number of parameters used to define
the continuum. However, in all cases, the goal is to identify a set of
items that allows for the precise measurement of an individual on the
latent continuum or trait. The use of a single parameter model (e.g.,
item difficulty, which is used in Rasch scaling), is perhaps the most
common approach to measure development within this theoretical
approach, and can serve as a constructive example of the implications
of item response theory for test construction.

In Rasch models (e.g., Rost & Langeheine, 1997), the probability
of endorsing an item (if it is discrete) or the population probability
of ratings at each level (if it is continuous, such as a Likert scale) is
used to define where on the continuum the item is most useful to
distinguish respondents (i.e., the separation reliability). The relationship of the item's pattern of difficulty to the rest of the items defines
the degree to which the item lies along the latent continuum (i.e., the
fit statistic). A good test, from a Rasch perspective, has items that
separate individuals reliably, cover the range of the continuum, and
lie along that continuum. Thus, Rasch modeling and other statistical
approaches consider measures with more items on a single dimension to be more reliable and valid. However, Rasch model statistics
support finding the fewest number of items that accurately reflect a
single continuum. Thus, efficiency of measurement is respected in this
theoretical approach.

Item response theory approaches validity from a perspective similar
to classical test theory. Statistical relationships between and among
items trump other methods for evaluating measures within both
theories. It is possible that prediction (or statistical criterion) validity
is more highly valued in item response theory as compared with classical test theory; however, construct validity is again the single most
important validity criterion. Face validity in item response theory is
nearly irrelevant.

A Different Conceptual Model for Measurement

Despite the fact that more than 1,000 outcomes measures have already been identified and used in at least one published outcomes study (Ogles, Lambert, & Masters, 1996), it may be fruitful to consider still more alternatives, because most of these past measures were developed from one of the two models discussed above. Although the theoretical assumptions and statistical approaches of item response theory are dramatically different from those of classical test theory, from a pragmatic perspective, both theories implicitly value measures that have a larger number of items and measure a single dimension. This emphasis on longer, one-dimensional measures is a significant problem for outcomes measurement in mental health services, which aims to measure multiple dimensions in a brief time period.

The majority of services are thought to have important effects on more than a single dimension. For example, crisis intervention may reduce suicide risk, reduce the likelihood of violence, improve self-care, mobilize resources, and stabilize symptoms. Outpatient therapy is seen as having a potential impact on symptoms, subjective well being, and functioning. Thus, regardless of the specific intervention, comprehensive outcomes measurement requires a multidimensional approach to accurately capture the complexity of the impact of services (Lambert et al., 2000).

Second, there is little time available to implement the measurement process. In practice, neither clinicians nor service recipients are inclined to spend a great deal of time completing measures. Long and potentially redundant measures, which are valued by existing theories of measurement, are too time consuming. Many potential respondents, therefore, simply do not complete the measures. The value of an outcomes management initiative is directly proportional to the percentage of recipients that contribute complete data.

Third, the absence of obvious relevance to treatment planning can be problematic for the use of a measure. If a clinician does not see the relevance of a measure for his or her work, it becomes more of a burden. Service recipients likely have the same perspective. The absence of face validity also has potential legal ramifications. A prospective employee recently sued a company and its evaluator, citing—among other complaints—that items from a test did not appear to be relevant to the job.

Fourth, measures developed for research purposes tend to base their psychometric properties on uses within the research context, which is quite different from the service-delivery environment. We recently completed an evaluation of a pet therapy intervention in which girls in a residential treatment program for substance abuse learned to train volunteer dogs. The program organizers felt that the primary benefit of the intervention was to help boost the girls' self-esteem through mastery of the dog and the dog's unconditional love. Given this hypothesis, we borrowed Rosenberg's (1965) measure, which is the most commonly used self-esteem measure in research. By measuring self-esteem at program initiation and termination, we immediately observed dramatically falling self-esteem. Even with the first eight cases, the drop was statistically significant. The explanation of this phenomenon, of course, was not that the pet therapy was devastating these girls' self-concepts. It turns out that we were not actually measuring how these adolescent girls viewed themselves (their self-esteem); rather, we were measuring their public presentation of self-esteem—that is, what the girls chose to tell us about their view of themselves. The girls started out with substantial bravado, presenting themselves as nearly perfect in their own eyes. Following the intervention, they presented themselves in a far more balanced manner. Thus, it inaccurately appeared that program participation was associated with worsening self-esteem. In general, the research context in which many outcomes measures are developed does not consider the communication context in which the measures are used in practice.

Traditional theories that have guided measurement development emphasize the reliability and validity of measures. To accomplish a new set of goals, it is necessary to broaden the scope of our models of measurement to include guidelines for measures that relate to their utility in clinical operations. Measures intended for the evaluation of treatment outcomes should be easy to use and brief. Their output should be clear; unambiguous; relevant; easy to translate into treatment recommendations; and accessible to providers, consumers, and policy makers. These goals require a different model of measurement. Neither classical test theory nor item response theory fully informs the development of good measures for these applications.

Clinimetrics

In response to many of the problems with psychometric approaches identified above, measurement developers in medicine have utilized a theoretical approach referred to as clinimetrics. The stated goal of clinimetrics is to convert "intangible clinical phenomenon into formal specified measurement" (Feinstein, 1999, p. 125). Virginia Apgar is generally credited with developing the first measure from this per-spective (Apgar, 1966). Clinimetric tools are now quite common in medicine (e.g., Bloem, Beckley, van Hilten, & Roos, 1998; Gates, 2000; Hoff, van Hilten, & Roos, 1999, Stone et al., 2001).

Feinstein (1999) has enumerated six core principles to clinimetrics in comparison with psychometrics.

1. Selection of items is based on clinical rather than statistical criteria.
2. No weighting factors are needed; scoring is simple and readily interpretable.
3. Variables are selected to be heterogeneous rather than homogeneous.
4. The measure must be easy for clinicians to use.
5. Face validity is required.
6. Subjective states are not measured because they are severely limited in terms of source of observation.

Despite its utility and promise, clinimetrics in its current applications has some notable limitations (Marx, Bombardier, Hogg-Johnson, & Wright, 2000; Zyzanski & Perloff, 1999). Most clinimetric scales consist of a single item. When multidimensional phenomena are described, often a single item fails to communicate that complexity. For example, a Childhood Global Assessment Scale (CGAS) (Shaften et al., 1983), which ranges from 0 to 100 does not provide much information that is useful to the clinician beyond a rough sense of how the child is doing. In these situations, the single-item rating can become unreliable. In addition, single items are often somewhat gross and not particularly sensitive to change. This can limit their utility for measuring treatment effects. For these reasons, Zyzanski and Perloff (1999) and others have called for an integration of clinimetric and psychometric approaches to measurement.

A Communication Model for Measurement

Measures used within service delivery operations must be able to easily and accurately communicate relevant results. Feedback about performance is central to QI and outcomes management (Clark, Schyve, Lepoff, & Ruess, 1994; Koike, Unutzer, & Wells, 2002; Krulish, 2002; Schiff & Goldfield, 1994). This feedback requires the integration of measurement into the information feedback loop (Lichtman & Appleman, 1995). Thus, it can be argued that communication is a primary goal of measurement in clinical settings (Howard, Morass, Brill, Martinovich, & Lutz, 1996; Lueger et al., 2001). The communication occurs between recipients and providers about perceptions of clients' needs; between providers, program administrators, and evaluators about clinical status; between providers and payers about medical necessity for and benefits from services; and among providers and other partners about the goals and outcomes of an integrated children's system of care.

Communication theory is a broad and diverse field that informs improvements in outcomes management strategies. Although it is not possible to present a comprehensive review of the communication theory literature, there are three areas within communication theory that have particularly influenced the development of my approach to measurement development.

The first construct is the theory of communicative action. Simply stated, communicative action is a consensus-based approach that relies on mutual definitions of how to reach a goal (Habermas & Seidman, 1989). Kihlstroem and Israel (2002) found that group leadership actions based on communicative action theory lead to greater openness to diversity and individual experiences. Friedland (2001) posited that communication forms the primary ecology of postindustrial communities; this logic is relevant for the children's system of care. According to this theory, the foundation for a system of care would be effective action-oriented communication based on consensus among the partners in that system.

Second, White (2001) highlights communication as the basis for innovation in science. Within this context, the dissemination of evidence-based practices (EBPs) into the field requires consensus across the field that new practices are better than current practices. This kind of consensus cannot be reached by the publication of randomized clinical trials alone, but by ongoing interaction among service delivery, evaluation, and research (Drake, 2002).

Finally, Harris's work (2002) in organizational communication has laid out the importance of communication within business environments. He conceptualizes communication as a nonlinear process that plays a central role in effective leadership, organizational development, and establishing an organization's culture. Communication is especially important within the children's mental health service system. Given the organizational complexity of most children's systems of care, the system is in need of communication tools to serve these functions.

Application of the communication model within the children's services system will require the establishment of a common ground—
and a common language—among mental health, child welfare,
juvenile justice, and the school systems. With these goals in mind, I
have worked to develop a communication model of measurement. The
model builds on some of the tenets of psychometric theory (high face
and content validity, high interrater reliability, and high concurrent
and predictive validity) and the six principles of clinimetrics, adding
three additional requirements:

- All partners in the service-delivery system of care should participate in the development and uses of the measure.
- The goal of item selection is to include single items that represent
  each of the key constructs, identified by consensus, that inform good
  decision making and service planning in the service-delivery opera-
  tion.
- The levels of each item should be directly translatable into action
  steps for treatment planning.

In summary, a good communication measure should be clear, con-
cise, relevant, and comprehensive without being redundant. It should
use common, understandable language and be easy to use. Most
importantly, a measure should be useful for the three primary purposes for which one requires these tools in clinical practice: decision
support, QI, and outcomes monitoring.

Decision-support strategies help to ensure that clinically appropriate
decisions are made consistently at key points in the service-delivery
process. QI activities ensure that potentially effective interventions are
provided when indicated, and that needs are assessed accurately and
in a timely fashion. Outcomes monitoring efforts inform clinicians,
administrators, and evaluators about the impact of an intervention
or program. The measurement approach should allow for all three of
these tasks to be accomplished for every case, program, and system.

In terms of traditional psychometric properties, a good communication tool would have the following characteristics:

High face and content validity: It should be clear to all users what
the tool is attempting to assess and that the tool should assess all
things relevant to the clinical situation. Scoring should be easy and
should not require much interpretation.

High inter-rater reliability: All users must be consistent in the
application of the tool. Reliability across raters is important; internal consistency reliability is less valued.

High concurrent and predictive validity: The measure should be related to other measures attempting to assess the same constructs, and it should be related to good decision making and service planning. Further, it should accurately model clinical decision making. The measure should have a clear linkage to real decisions, both conceptually and statistically.

In addition to these three traditional psychometric qualities to which a communication-based measure should conform, the measure should also meet the following conditions:

Immediate meaning: If a measure requires complex scoring formulas in order to know what it means, its interpretability is severely restricted. A good communication measure should require minimal scoring in order to interpret its findings—at least on a basic level.

Relevance to the individual child/family: If a measure has limited relationship to individual case decision making, it is often seen as a nuisance addendum to the service-delivery process. A good communication measure should be directly related to the treatment/ intervention planning process.

For the past decade, I have been working to develop outcomes management tools using a communication model that blends the strengths of psychometric and clinimetric strategies to measurement development. Perhaps the most widely used tool of this type is the Child and Adolescent Needs and Strengths (CANS). Versions of the CANS have been used to develop assessment tools to guide service delivery for children with mental health needs, children with developmental disabilities, children involved in the child welfare system, and youth with juvenile justice involvement. In addition, a specific version for children three years old and younger has been developed. Development of the CANS is grounded, in part, in our prior work modeling decision making for hospital and residential services for children and adolescents.

CANS: Development, Function, and Structure

The CANS evolved from my work with the CSPI. The CSPI was developed to assess those dimensions crucial to good clinical decision making for intensive and expensive mental health service interventions. We have demonstrated the utility of the CSPI in reforming decision making for residential treatment (Lyons et al., 1998) and for QI in crisis assessment services (Leon et al., 1999; Lyons, Kisiel, Dulcan, Chesler, & Cohen, 1997). The strength of the measure has been that it is face valid and easy to use, but it also provides comprehensive information regarding the clinical status of the child or youth that can be translated into policy and/or treatment recommendations.

Item Selection and Structure

The CANS builds on the conceptual approach of the CSPI, but expands the assessment to include a broader conceptualization of needs and an assessment of strengths (Lyons, Uziel-Miller, Reyes, & Sokol, 2000). The CANS was developed using focus groups with a variety of participants including families, representatives of the provider community, case managers, and staff. The item selection process is congruent with the approaches used in clinimetrics. However, beyond including a clinical perspective, the goal of this measurement design process is to ensure participation of representatives of all partners to begin building a common assessment language.

The CANS consists of dimensions relating to both clinical needs and strengths. Anchors that are standard across these dimensions are used to rate the level of need or strength. The manual for the mental health version of the CANS can be found in the Appendix. The anchors themselves are worded in terms of the level of intervention needed, which enables the CANS to produce information that is instantly relevant for service planning. A unique aspect of the CANS is its item structure. Each item has four levels of rating and although these levels have anchored definitions, each is written to have comparable implications for action. For the needs, these action levels are as follows:

0   No evidence: No need for action.

1   Watchful waiting, prevention: Efforts are needed to monitor this need or engage in activities to ensure that it does not become worse.

2   Action: The need is interfering in a notable way with the child's or family's life and something should be done.

3   Immediate or intensive action: This is a priority for intervention. The need is dangerous or disabling.

Ratings of "2" or "3" define a need that should be addressed with any service, treatment, or action plan. Therefore, the connection between the assessment and service planning is clear-cut.

For strengths, the action levels are as follows:

0   A strength that can serve as the centerpiece of a strength-based plan.

1   A strength that exists and can be used in strength-based planning, but not as a focus.

2   A strength has been identified, but must be built.

3   No strength has been identified.

For strengths, all four levels have action implications. Ratings of "0" or "1" imply the use of the strength in strength-based planning, whereas ratings of "2" or "3" imply the need for strength identification and building efforts. When a particular child's situation does not quite fit the anchored definitions in the CANS manual, assessors are encouraged to use the action-level definitions to guide their ratings.

In terms of psychometric properties, we have found that research and practice with the CANS provides strong evidence of both reliability and validity. Following training, interrater reliability with case vignettes averages about 0.75. Interrater reliability with case records averages around 0.83. Interrater reliability with live cases exceeds 0.90. In addition, the CANS has demonstrated reliability at the item level (Anderson, Lyons, Giles, Price, & Estle, 2002). Audit reliability of the use of the CANS in practice has been above 0.80 in several statewide applications (Anderson et al., 2002; Lyons et al., 2003).

The CANS demonstrates concurrent validity with the Child and Adolescent Functional Assessment Scale (CAFAS; Dilley, 2003), the mostly widely used outcomes measure in the children's mental health system (Hodges & Wotring, 2000). It also is sensitive to change over at least three-month periods across a range of service (Lyons et al., 2003). Therefore, the CANS is a tool that supports the tenets of TCOM. It is useful at the individual child and family level and can be applied to decision support, QI, and outcomes monitoring processes.

Methods of TCOM

Use of Assessment Data for Eligibility

Because different services are intended for children and families with different needs, it is crucial for the measurement process to support eligibility standards. Eligibility criteria is a complex issue in our current service-delivery culture. As stated earlier, I do not believe in criteria for entry-level, office-based services. However, because there is a growing body of evidence to suggest that children who are not appropriate for a hospital and residential treatment service not only do not benefit from that service but may, in fact, be harmed by receiving the service, criteria are critical for more intensive services. An example of this type of service overuse would be initiating a substance-use treatment program with a youth who has no substance-use difficulties. There would be no benefit and a possibility exists that, through exposure to others who have substance-use problems, the youth might begin to affiliate with a substance-using peer group.

The complexities of this issue are several. First, as discussed elsewhere in the book, the mental health field has a long history of using clinical status information for advocacy rather than for accurate communication. Thus, once eligibility criteria are published, there can be a rather notable drift of assessments toward those criteria. This drift might be defensible from the perspective of an individual child and family—they are being provided with services that they might otherwise not receive; however, this is devastating to the system of care in that it creates significant distrust among system partners regarding the accuracy and meaningfulness of clinical status assessments. I recommend a combination of an open-team process to assessment to undercut this type of "gaming" in combination with the use of measurement audit techniques (Lyons, Rawal, Yeh, Leon, & Tracy, 2002). Teams are less likely to drift toward eligibility criteria than are individuals. The self-corrective nature of teams is particularly strong when the team process is open and representation on the team is diverse. Knowing that assessments can and will be audited creates an environment in which fraud with regard to clinical assessment can be treated with the same rigor as fraud with regard to finances. If we want to make the system about the children and families and not about the money, significant cultural shifts are necessary.

The second problem with eligibility criteria is that, ideally, eligibility criteria should be informed by evidence of the effectiveness of the service for which the eligibility criteria are designed. In other words, eligibility should identify those children and families most likely to benefit from the treatment or service. Particularly at this stage of service system development, integrating the relationship between eligibility and outcomes into eligibility criteria can be a bit of a chicken and egg dilemma. Until we have completed the analysis of the characteristics of children and families relevant to the effectiveness of the intervention, it is difficult to fully develop appropriate eligibility criteria that include both "rule ins" (i.e., characteristics that predict success of the intervention) and "rule outs" (i.e., characteristics that predict failure of the intervention). As an interim step, it is usually necessary to use either clinical logic or best practices guesswork about what the precise eligibility should be. In these circumstances, broader criteria make sense because they can provide a range of clinical profiles that can be evaluated for effectiveness of the intervention.

Use of Assessment Data in Service Planning

A key principle of TCOM is that the tools that are used for outcomes assessment should be fully imbedded in the service-planning process. Completing the assessment tools should inform and support this process. By making the measurement process an essential component of service planning, you directly address a primary resistance by staff to outcomes measurement—it now becomes fundamental to how they work with individual children and families, and is no longer simply a paperwork add-on that is detached from the service-delivery process.

Of course, the challenge here is that the selected outcomes tools must have direct relevance to the service-planning process. This is one of the primary motivations behind the communications-based method of measurement development. Because levels of the assessment tool directly and immediately translate into levels of action, it is simple to integrate assessments into the service-planning process.

Use of Assessment/Outcomes Data in Child–Family Teams

As discussed in chapter 2, one of the complexities of blending wraparound philosophy into the insurance model approach to funding public mental health services is figuring out the role of family members in making service-planning decisions. If you do not get the active participation of parents in the planning process, the success of any service plan will be severely limited. For this reason, wraparound trainers push the concept of allowing the family to decide what it is that they need.

Here is where confusion sometimes arises. Some wraparound advocates do not discriminate between what the family wants and what the family needs. Although a popular notion among family members, giving families anything and everything they might want is not likely to be a successful strategy in a resource-limited service system. Giving people whatever they want is not responsible when you have limited resources and other people who also have needs. Thus, rather than setting up families to believe that they should receive whatever services they want, it makes more sense to conceptualize the child–

family team as a negotiation between the family and the service system with regard to what is the best strategy for addressing the child's and family's needs. The key to success here is to ensure that parents are well informed and able to function as advocates for their children and families within this potentially complex negotiation. In this way, outcomes tools can facilitate this process. In many locales, for example, the CANS has been used within the framework of child–family teams to inform the negotiation about service plans. The family works with an advocate prior to the meeting to identify their child's needs and strengths and each parent's needs and strengths. This assessment is taken to the team to inform the discussion about strategies. In this way, the negotiation is informed by the family's view of their needs. The discussion then revolves around what strategies and services are available to address these needs and what strengths can be marshaled to support the healthy development of the child.

Using Outcomes in Supervision

One of the characteristics of the children's public mental health system is that, for most programs or service types, the staff who spend the most time with the children are the least trained, least experienced, and lowest paid of all staff. Unless there is a fundamental shift in how services are financed and organized, we can anticipate this characteristic of the current system to continue into the foreseeable future. At the same time, there are some advantages to this model of human capital. Younger, less-experienced staff are often highly motivated and enthusiastic. They see their work as important and pursue it with energy. On the other hand, this model has two primary shortcomings.

First, at the time of initial hire, it is not possible to know whether these new staff will have the skills, personality, and integrity to be successful. My very first clinical job was as a mental health technician at a private psychiatric hospital for children and adolescents. I was a 21-year-old, first-year graduate student with no clinical training. I showed up at the personnel office of the hospital, filled out an application, was interviewed by the head of personnel, and hired the next day. On the very first evening at this job, I was running a group therapy session. In retrospect, there is absolutely no way that I was qualified for this responsibility, save for the fact that I was willing. I don't think the personnel department of this hospital really had any ability to judge my potential. There was no training except for a presentation on hospital rules and regulations. Sadly, given the wages

and job circumstances of direct service staff in the public mental
health system, I do not think my experience is at all novel. I like to
think that the hospital made a good choice with my hire, but I know
they were not always so lucky. When a work colleague was arrested
for selling drugs to an undercover agent pretending to work for
the hospital, he was fired. One of the first things he did as a former
employee was to start calling former clients (teenage girls) and meeting with them socially.

Second, even when ideal candidates for positions are recruited and
hired, the new staff have little idea about how to actually do the work
of helping children and adolescents to achieve greater mental health
and higher functioning. Inexperienced staff need significant help to
achieve competence, and even more to achieve excellence.

Given these challenges of the employment model, supervision is a
critical function within the system. Use of a TCOM strategy within
the framework of supervision is a potentially powerful aid to address
the primary deficits of our employment strategies.

The first way in which TCOM supports good supervision is
through training in the completion and use of assessment tools. A
good assessment tool should (a) remind staff what they need to know
about a child and family in order to do their jobs, and (b) structure
the information in an efficient manner to support communication
with others about these characteristics. Training new staff to use an
outcomes management tool reliably reinforces job training. While
doing a training in New Jersey, a director of a county care management organization came up to me and told me that when one of his
new staff was grousing about having to come to a training for one
of the assessment tools, she asked him, "What is this anyway?" He
responded, "This is your job description. If you don't know these facts
about a child and family, you simply won't be able to do your job."
Great answer. This statement is a clear reflection of the principles and
philosophy of TCOM.

Anecdotally, we have trained new staff in the reliable use of the
CANS. In most locales, there is a requirement that you must achieve
reliability of above 0.70. If you are not reliable immediately after
training, you continue to try. In several places, however, this requirement has not been enforced. In one situation in particular, several
years of experience suggested that the staff hired to provide case
management in an intensive community program who did not learn
how to complete the CANS reliably at hiring did not make it past the
90-day probationary period. Again, this experience is consistent with

the notion that the assessment/measurement strategy reflects an important aspect of the work.

The second way in which supervision should utilize outcomes is through the use of the assessments in ongoing supervision and in the trajectory of recovery. Assessments also can be used to monitor the service/treatment planning of staff. Change over time can be used to monitor both the success of any interventions and the need to consider alternative strategies when insufficient success is observed.

In TCOM, it is essential that supervision incorporates the outcomes assessment and monitoring as a central component of the supervision process. Supervisors should routinely get reports on assessments and outcomes status of recipients served by all supervisees. Supervisees should get comparable information so that they are prepared to utilize the information in their supervision experiences. Training supervisors on how to use outcomes in supervision is often an overlooked need.

Use of the CANS or another outcomes management tool in supervision can take at least two different forms. First, supervisees can bring assessment data and outcomes monitoring data to the supervisor to use in presenting the needs, strengths, or status of a particular case. Inclusion of standard assessments creates a uniform way to present children and families in supervision and speeds up that process for both the supervisor and the supervisee. Second, outcomes reports can be sent directly to the supervisor regarding the performance of the supervisee. This information can allow supervisors to benchmark an individual staff's performance relative to other staff that he or she supervises, all other staff, or both.

The latter approach's application in supervision only works if the individual supervisee has individual responsibilities with regard to a case that makes him or her responsible for the outcomes of that child and family. Thus, reports regarding outpatient counselors, therapists, or case managers would work fine. Reports for individual staff when team approaches to intervention are used make little sense. In these situations, feedback to all involved staff is more sensible. Thus, outcomes for a specific group home are best shared with all the staff of the group home rather than with any individual, with the possible exception of the director of that home.

Use of outcomes management in supervision is actually mutually reinforcing. As discussed above, it can be an important way to keep the focus of supervision on the child's and family's needs and strengths. In addition, the attention to the outcomes provided by the supervisor highlights the importance of these data and reinforces the need to ensure the timely and accurate completion of assessment and status tools. Enhancing the perceived value of assessments is a critical aspect of the successful use of outcomes data at all levels. Elsewhere in this book, the importance of making outcomes data meaningful at all levels—particularly including the individual child and family—is emphasized. Use of these data in supervision while informing and enhancing the supervision process also helps to ensure the ongoing use of child- and family-level data.

Use of Outcomes to Manage Programs

Program management can be enhanced through the use of clinical outcomes in a number of ways. Depending on the design of the program, individual staff outcomes can be monitored. For instance, the outcomes of staff therapists should be monitored in comparison with each other and benchmarks, when available. In a program that uses a team approach, aggregate outcomes across children and families can be used to monitor successes. In addition, cases can be identified with poor outcomes and analyzed in team supervision meetings.

The primary strategy for program managers is the support of QI efforts. QI should be an integral part of program management. Unfortunately, many programs see QI as something that has to be done for purposes of accreditation, rather than as a management tool. In these circumstances, QI projects are generally delegated to persons with little political influence in the program or agency. These attitudes can easily result in QI projects that have no impact.

In TCOM, QI is a fundamental tool of program management. The program head and agency leaders have clear authority over QI activities, the findings of all QI projects receive full hearing throughout the program and agency, and action plans in response to those findings are initiated.

The CANS is designed to support QI activities. One common strategy that we have used on a number of projects is to utilize the initial CANS assessment to monitor the fidelity of the treatment-planning process. Because ratings of "2" and "3" on the needs items of the CANS are consistent with action, the presence of these ratings should be followed by inclusion of strategies in the treatment plan to address these identified, "actionable" needs. Mary Beth Rautkis, Ph.D., at Pressley Ridge Schools, developed a treatment fidelity model to correspond to the CANS. Table 5.1 provides an example page from the rating system used in this fidelity model. In applications in a number of settings,

Table 5.1
An Example Page from the CANS Treatment Fidelity Index (TFI)

Circle the letter in each column that provides the best explanation. Do this for every CANS item identified as a "2" or a "3"

Key: "M" (Mostly) OR "P" (Partially) OR "R" (Rarely)

CANS Rating	Dimension: Mental Health	A — Client/Family needs were a focus of tx plans?	B — Recommended services & community supports were a focus of tx plans?	C — Client/Family needs were discussed in progress notes?	D — Recommended services & community supports were discussed in progress notes?	E — Services & supports provided helped promote positive progress in dimension?	TFI Rating
	Psychosis	M P R	M P R	M P R	M P R	M P R	1 3 5
	Attention Deficit / Impulse	M P R	M P R	M P R	M P R	M P R	1 3 5
	Depression/Anxiety	M P R	M P R	M P R	M P R	M P R	1 3 5
	Oppositional Behavior	M P R	M P R	M P R	M P R	M P R	1 3 5
	Antisocial Behavior	M P R	M P R	M P R	M P R	M P R	1 3 5
	Substance Abuse	M P R	M P R	M P R	M P R	M P R	1 3 5
	Adjustment to Trauma	M P R	M P R	M P R	M P R	M P R	1 3 5
	Attachment	M P R	M P R	M P R	M P R	M P R	1 3 5
	Situational Consistency	M P R	M P R	M P R	M P R	M P R	1 3 5
	Temporal Consistency	M P R	M P R	M P R	M P R	M P R	1 3 5

Notes: TFI rating

1- A rating of "1" is given for dimensions with two or more "mostly" answers, of which two must be from columns A and B. No "rarely" answers.

3- A rating of "3" is given for dimensions with four or more "partially" answers, of which two must be from columns A and B.

5- A rating of "5" is given for dimensions with four or more "rarely" answers.

Source: Adapted from the Child and Adolescent Needs and Strengths Treatment Fidelity Index (Rautkis & Sliefert, 2002).

this approach has provided useful information to support program enhancements. For example, using this strategy, we found that identified but unmet transportation needs were associated with re-arrest in our Mental Health Juvenile Justice (MH-JJ) initiative (Lyons et al., 2003). This discovery led to a shift in supporting transportation with flex dollars. In a different program, we found that although the case managers were identifying strengths, they were not incorporating them into the service plan. This discovery led to a series of in-service workshops on strength-based planning.

Use of Outcomes to Manage Systems

When clinical outcomes are applied to the management of entire systems, the combination is the most powerful use of TCOM. It is through these techniques that significant system evolution can occur. However, the magnitude and complexity of the data and required analyses easily can become overwhelming. The principles of system management include the following:

1. The outcomes management strategy must be meaningful to the individual provider. An approach that does not make sense at the individual child/family level will never be fully implemented.

2. System leadership must endorse and value the outcomes management strategy. A project without system leadership support, or only support from evaluation leadership, will flounder.

3. Data must be generated in a timely and interpretable manner to inform policy and system management. Although garbage in means garbage out, it is also true that over time, garbage out generates garbage in.

We are in the process of developing a TCOM system for residential treatment services in Illinois for children who are state wards. The process is instructive. The initiative was born out of a set of collaborative meetings that resulted from residential providers working more closely with Illinois DCFS in response to the changes that came from the residential reform in the mid-1990s. An outcomes committee arose from these meetings, and a set of provider representatives and DCFS staff together designed an outcomes monitoring system. DCFS then contracted with Northwestern to set up this system and manage it. The first step was to design a data acquisition and management system. Given the fact that there are 63 different residential providers who have at least one state ward in residence, we decided that a Web-based data entry solution was optimal. Northwestern contracted with a Web design firm. (Note: Do not cut corners and try to attempt this type of development on the cheap. Go with established professionals—it is more cost effective in the long run.) The firm, American Eagle, generated the first version of this system in January 2002. One of the primary goals of the system is to develop trajectories of recovery. In earlier work with the Oregon system, we had developed trajectories that were used to identify one site that was experiencing negative outcomes (i.e., on average, children were actually getting worse) and these trajectories were used to support and evaluate fixing that problem (Lyons et al., 2000). In Illinois, the goal is to develop the trajectories for provider profiling to study program outcomes, but also to allow for monitoring progress on individual cases relative to expected rates of improvement.

Figures 5.2 through 5.4 provide examples of these trajectories using the Child Functional Assessment Rating Scale (CFARS). As can be seen in Figure 5.2, the overall trajectory is flat. On average, across the system, children are not getting better, nor are they getting worse. However, when you study these trajectories by discharge disposition, as seen in Figure 5.3, you can see clearly that the children who go to lower levels of care (e.g., foster care) get much better whereas the children who go to high levels of care (e.g., Department

Figure 5.2
Child Functional Assessment Rating Scale (CFARS) Trajectories by Age

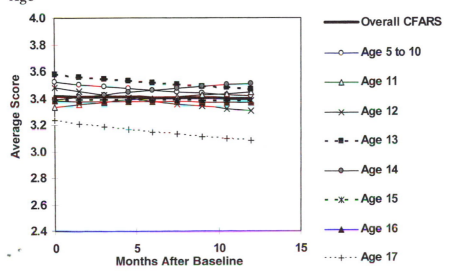

Figure 5.3
Child Functional Assessment Rating Scale (CFARS) Trajectories by Discharge Status

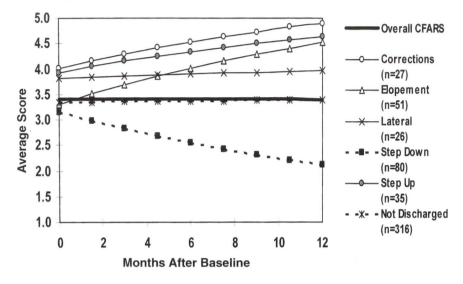

Figure 5.4
Child Functional Assessment Rating Scale (CFARS) Trajectories by Cluster Membership

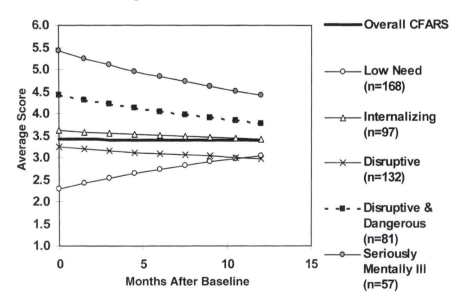

of Corrections) get much worse. Children who experience lateral moves have flat trajectories, indicating that their moves are not related to their change in clinical status. These findings should not be surprising, but they are certainly reassuring. In early analyses, you want to be able to document obvious findings to build confidence in the validity of the data.

Viewing trajectories by clinical characteristics of the child presents a still different picture (Figure 5.4). Cluster analysis with this population reveals the presence of five stable clusters: children with serious mental illness (SMI), those with disruptive behavior, children with disruptive and dangerous behavior, trauma survivors, and children who generally have low levels on all 16 items of the CFARS (i.e., low need).

Review of Figure 5.3 demonstrates that each of these clusters has very different expected trajectories of recovery. The children with SMI and the ones who are both disruptive and dangerous appear to experience the greatest improvements, but also start out with the highest needs. Low-need children actually get more symptomatic over time. It is noteworthy, however, that the initial assessment in this project is completed at the end of the first 30 days of placement. Therefore, it is possible that among the low-need children are those who experience a dramatic "honeymoon" period in new placements before their behavior problems become manifest.

The next step for this work is to begin to look at these trajectories by cluster for individual programs. Preliminary analyses suggest that low-need children who are placed in programs that are successful at treating children with SMI or disruptive and dangerous behaviors fair far worse than do low-need children who are placed in settings that have a greater proportion of low-need and traumatized, or disruptive-only children. If this finding holds up with the increasing dataset, it will have far-ranging implications for how children are placed into different programs. We also are finding relationships between admission characteristics and runaways. Because running away is the second most common discharge disposition next to step-down, it would be useful to providers to know which children are at greatest risk. We are developing a statistical model (using logistic regression) that will assign a probability of running away indicator based on initial assessment characteristics. The principle is to make sure that the system is as useful to the clinicians at each site as possible.

We recently added a component to the Web site that allows for the reporting of unusual incidents at each site. This feature expands the outcomes monitoring potential of the system by allowing us to monitor sentinel event outcomes. As can be seen by these examples, the process of developing, implementing, and utilizing this system is incremental and can be experienced as slower than some would like it to be. There is consistent pressure to have usable findings quickly. The danger is that these findings may not replicate with a full dataset. Balancing the need for information in a complex political environment with the need for accuracy is an important tension that must be managed carefully.

Developing and Implementing Decision Support Algorithms

Decision support is one of the three primary applications in outcomes management. Decision support refers to utilizing standardized assessment information to provide some guidance in making optimal decisions at key decision points in the service-delivery process. These decisions mostly involve issues of service planning—specifically, eligibility for particular programs or the intensity of services or settings.

Decision support involves the application of some form of a decision algorithm. A decision algorithm is a logical set of criteria that describe the clinical characteristics of children and families that would be best served by the available decision options relevant to the algorithm. Tables 5.2 through 5.4 provide examples of three different algorithms. The first algorithm (Table 5.2) is used by the Alaska Youth Initiative to guide decision making with regard to intensity of services. The second algorithm (Table 5.3) is used by the City of Philadelphia's Department of Human Services (DHS) to support decisions about eligibility for treatment foster care placements. The third algorithm (Table 5.4) is a draft under development by the Philadelphia DHS to support program placement within the juvenile justice system.

Over the past decade, we have collaborated on the development and implementation of decision support algorithms in a variety of settings. In most cases, we have utilized a seven-step process to ensure that the algorithms (1) capture the best practices in decision making, (2) remain generally consistent with the existing system functioning so as to not be overly disruptive, and (3) result in an improvement in the quality of the decision making within the system of care. The following steps describe an ideal process for developing decision support algorithms.

Step 1. Establish the clinical decision inputs

Step 2. Develop measurement strategy for inputs

Table 5.2
Decision Support Criteria Using the CANS for Determining the Three Levels of Care within the Alaska Youth Initiative (AYI)

AYI LOC Determination   Youth AYI Number_____   Date Completed _____

Criterion 1.	**OR**	A "3" on one **Problem Presentation** (not including Situation or Temporal Consistency) A "2" or greater at least two **Problems.**	☐ Meets
Criterion 2.	**OR**	A **Temporal Consistency** of "1" or greater A score of "2"or greater on **Cycling of Severity**.	☐ Meets
Criterion 3.	**OR**	A "3" on at least one **Risk Behavior** A "2" or greater on at least two **Risk Behaviors.**	☐ Meets
Criterion 4.	**OR**	A "3" on one **Caregiver Capacity** A "2" or greater on at least two **Caregiver Capacities.**	☐ Meets
Criterion 5.		A "2" on at least one **Risk Behavior**	☐ Meets
Criterion 6.	**OR**	A "2" or greater on **Monitoring** A "2" or greater on **Treatment**.	☐ Meets
Criterion 7.	**AND**	A "2" or greater on **Monitoring** A "2" or greater on **Treatment**.	☐ Meets
Criterion 8.		A "2" or greater on **Monitoring**	☐ Meets

AYI Level of Care:

Level III:	Meets criteria 1, 2, 3, 4 **AND** criterion 6.	☐ Meets
Level II:	Meets both criteria 1 **AND** 5 **OR** meets criterion 7.	☐ Meets
Level I:	Meets criterion 1 **AND** either criterion 5 or criterion 8.	☐ Meets
All other youth:	Not eligible for AYI.	☐ Does not meet

If a youth is admitted to AYI prior to completion of a CANS and does not meet criteria for CANS level I, II or III, the youth's plan must be developed for a "short-stay": brief services to stabilize the youth with discharge from AYI within 6 months.

For current AYI clients, clinical improvements should result in a decrease in the level of care over time. Ongoing case planning should reflect this process and result in an appropriate, timely discharge from AYI before the youth moves below a CANS level I. Movement below a CANS level I and loss of AYI eligibiity should not drive a crisis discharge.

AYI IDT Signatures:

Date of CANS:

Date next CANS:

Source: Adapted from the Alaska Youth Initiative (AYI).

Step 3. Complete a planning study assessing decision inputs

Step 4. Share results of planning study with key partners

Step 5. Establish initial algorithm

    a. Test impact of current system

    b. Assess relationship to outcomes

Step 6. Implement algorithm and monitor impact

Step 7. Adjust algorithm based on system experiences

1. Establish the clinical decision inputs. The first step in developing an algorithm is to determine what it is that you need to know to make an informed decision. To achieve this understanding, you first need to establish your decision options. It is one thing to develop an algorithm for psychiatric hospital admission versus deflection, and quite another to make an algorithm that covers a wider range of options such as (a) residential treatment, (b) intensive community, (c) intensive outpatient, (d) outpatient, and (e) no treatment.

Once the decision options have been established, it is necessary to identify the key information that is needed to make an informed decision about one of these options. There are at least three methods to accomplish this task: focus groups with partners and experts, review of the existing clinical and scientific literature, and/or case review using qualitative methods.

2. Develop measurement strategy for inputs. Once a choice has been made about what information is necessary to inform good decision making, it is necessary to devise a measurement strategy that allows for the reliable and consistent collection of the required information. This step is where he CANS method can be used. We have a large item bank from the various versions of the CANS and can either select items from this bank to cover all information inputs, or design new items to reflect additional information that must be obtained. Once a measure has been developed, it should be tested for reliability and feasibility within the context of the decision-making process.

3. Complete a planning study assessing decision inputs. This step may not be a technical requirement to establish an effective decision support algorithm, but it is likely a politically critical step because the full implementation of any decision support guidelines requires that the system partners "buy into it." A false step in implementing unworkable criteria without testing can stop a process cold. Therefore, in this step, you take the assessment strategy identified in the previous step and apply it to a sample of real cases. This is done

Table 5.3
Philadelphia Department of Human Services Treatment Foster Care (TFC) Eligibility Criteria

Criterion	Area	Rating	CANS ITEM
1 – Diagnosis	Presence of two ore more Symptom Areas Associated with a Serious Emotional/ Behavioral Disorder	"2" or "3"	17. Psychosis 18. Attention Deficit/Impulse Control 19. Depression/Anxiety 20. Anger Control 21. Oppositional Behavior 22. Antisocial Behavior 23. Adjustment to Trauma 24. Attachment 33. Severity of Substance Abuse
2 – Functioning	Notable Impairment in Functioning in at least one area	"3"	1. Motor 2. Sensory 3. Intellectual 4. Communication 5. Developmental 6. Self-care/Daily Living Skills 7. Physical/Medical
3 – School	Notable Impairment in School Functioning	"3"	9. School Achievement 10. School Behavior 11. School Attendance
4 – Risk A	Notable Risk Behaviors in at least one these areas	"2" or "3"	29. Danger to Self 30. Fire Setting 31. Runaway 38. Seriousness of Criminal Behavior 41. Sexually Abusive Behavior
5 Risk B	Notable Risk Behaviors in at least one of these areas	"3"	30. Social Behavior 40. Violence

IN ORDER FOR A CHILD/YOUTH TO BE DEEMED ELIGIBLE FOR TFC, S/HE MUST SCORE THE FOLLOWING:

Child/Youth must have at least TWO "2" or "3" for Criterion 1 – Diagnosis AND

> **a "2" or "3" for Criterion 2 – Functioning OR**
> **a "3" for Criterion 3 – School OR**
> **a "2" or "3" for Criterion 4 – Risk A OR a "3" for Criterion 5—Risk B**

Source: Adapted from the Philadelphia Department of Human Services version of the Child and Adolescent Needs and Strengths program for children involved with child welfare (CANS-CW) through the Best Practices Institute.

Table 5.4
Initial Draft of Philadelphia Department of Human Services Juvenile Justice Level of Care Criteria

Level I.　　　**Workforce Development**

    A. Not a "3" on both Seriousness and History of Criminal/Delinquent Behavior
    B. Psychosis is rated as a "0"
    C. None of the following Mental Health Needs rated as a "3"
        Attention Deficit/Impulse
        Depression/Anxiety
        Oppositional
        Antisocial
        Adjustment to Trauma
        Severity of Substance Abuse
    D. None of the following Mental Health Needs rated as a "2".
        Antisocial
    E. Not more than one of the following Mental Health Needs rated as a "2"
        Attention Deficit/Impulse
        Depression/Anxiety
        Oppositional
        Adjustment to Trauma
        Severity of Substance Abuse
    F. None of the following Risk Behaviors rated as a "2" or "3"
        Suicide
        Danger to Others
        Sexually Aggressive Behavior
        Social Behavior
    G. A School Attendance rating of "2" or "3"

ELIGIBILITY:　　　Referral to Work Force Development if youth meets criteria A through F. If child is referred from Truancy Court, criteria G also should be met.

        Priority Population: Youth with a "2" or "3" on either Talents/Interests or Vocational Strengths

Level II.　　　**Delinquency Prevention**

    A. Seriousness of Crime/Delinquent Behavior a "2" or less
    B. School Attendance, Achievement, or Behavior rated a "2" or "3"
    C. Psychosis is rated as a "0"
    D. None of the following Mental Health Needs rated as a "3"
        Attention Deficit/Impulse
        Depression/Anxiety
        Oppositional
        Antisocial
        Adjustment to Trauma
        Severity of Substance Abuse
    E. None of the following Risk Behaviors rated as a "3"
        Community Safety
        Suicide Risk
        Danger to Others
        Sexual Aggression

ELIGIBILITY:　　　Meets all three criteria A through D.

(continued)

Table 5.4
Initial Draft of Philadelphia Department of Human Services Juvenile Justice Level of Care Criteria (continued)

Level III.   **Extended Day Treatment**

    A. Seriousness and History of Criminal/Delinquent Behavior are not both rated "3" unless Community Safety is rated a "0"

    B. School Achievement, Behavior or Attendance rated as a "2" or "3"

    C. Psychosis is rated as a "0" or "1"

    D. None of the following Mental Health Needs rated as a "3"
        Attention Deficit/Impulse
        Depression/Anxiety
        Oppositional
        Antisocial

    E. Neither of the following Risk Behaviors rated as "3"
        Suicide
        Danger to Others

    F. One of the following Caregiver Capacity rated as a "3" or two or more rated as a "2"
        Physical/Behavioral
        Supervision
        Involvement
        Knowledge

ELIGIBILITY: Meets criteria A and B and at least one but no more than two of criteria C through F.

Level IV.   **Placement**

    A. Both Seriousness and History of Criminal/Delinquent Behavior rated "3"

    B. Community Safety rated a "1", "2" or "3"

    C. One of the following Mental Health Needs rated as a "3" or two or more rated as a "2"
        Psychosis
        Attention Deficit/Impulse
        Depression/Anxiety
        Oppositional
        Antisocial
        Adjustment to Trauma
        Severity of Substance Abuse

    D. One of the following Risk Behaviors rated as a "3" or two or more rated as a "2"
        Suicide
        Danger to Others
        Elopement
        Sexually Aggressive Behavior
        Seriousness of Crime

    E. One of the following Caregiver Capacity rated as a "3" or two or more rated as a "2"
        Physical/Behavioral
        Supervision
        Involvement
        Knowledge

ELIGIBILITY: Placement should be considered if youth meets criteria A and B
Treatment-based placement should be considered if youth meets criteria C, D, and E.

Source: Adapted from the Philadelphia Department of Human Services version of the Child and Adolescent Needs and Strengths for youth with juvenile justice involvement (CANS-JJ) through the Best Practices Institute.

in order to allow you to develop the initial decision model (i.e., algorithm) and test it. Depending on what you observe, you can fine-tune the decision model if it appears to overidentify (i.e., too many children eligible) or underidentify (i.e., too few children are eligible) cases. In general, if you are creating a two-level decision (e.g., yes/no, in/out, eligible/not eligible, hospitalize/deflect), you need at least 100 cases in order to have confidence in your model, and roughly a similar number of cases in each category. In most of our planning studies, we use 300 to 500 cases. One of the goals of this step is to see the degree to which your evolving decision algorithm is consistent with current decision practices. Implementing decision support criteria can be difficult, both practically and politically. If the new model suggests dramatic changes in which children are eligible or appropriate for particular services or programs, greater resistance from the system will be experienced.

Ideally, the planning study should be accomplished in the identical environment in which you wish to implement the decision algorithm. However, in instances in which you do not yet have a flow of cases or the flow is too slow, other strategies can be used. We routinely use retrospective review strategies to provide an initial test of algorithms using the CANS. Retrospective study with the planned tool is possible because the CANS assessment was designed to be used either retrospectively or prospectively with comparable reliability and validity. If records are flawed or limited, however, retrospective studies sometimes underestimate the actual levels of need identified prospectively.

4. Share results of the planning study with key partners. A key proposition for successful implementation of TCOM generally, and decision support algorithms specifically, is that the process is open and collaborative. There should be no secrets among system partners participating in these endeavors, and the focus should be on communicating needs and designing a system that is responsive to children and families. Trust is the foundation of successful communication and good communication helps to build trust. Building trust through effective communication is one of the reasons communication-based measures are more effective for TCOM applications. They support a critical component of the process: easy communication across system partners. In this step, it is important to allow key partners to have some say in the design of the initial algorithm.

5. Establish initial algorithm. Using either data from the planning study or a second data-collection process, an initial algorithm should be tested prior to implementation. This test should have two parts.

First, it should determine the extent to which the decision model will change referral and eligibility patterns in the current system. For example, in our planning study of residential treatment in Illinois, we found that approximately 33 percent of placed youth would be below the initial criteria and would not be eligible for this placement once the algorithm was applied. A one-third reduction is a fairly dramatic impact. In a planning study for treatment foster care, we found that 20 percent were below criteria. This finding, of course, is a less-dramatic effect. An ideal algorithm would have enough impact to justify its implementation, but not too much for it to create chaos in the system. An impact in the range of 15 to 40 percent is probably reasonable. Smaller than 15 percent change is hard to justify, whereas more than 50 percent of cases being reclassified would be disruptive.

The second effect to look for is a relationship between decision criteria and outcomes. Ideally, a good decision support algorithm should identify those children who are most likely to benefit from a particular program or intervention. Children deemed not eligible should not benefit. Otherwise, you would be creating a decision model in which children who could benefit from an intervention were being denied that intervention. That situation is counter to the TCOM philosophy.

6. Implement algorithm and monitor impact. The implementation of any algorithm can be complicated. Decisions must be made regarding who assesses the decision input characteristics, how and to whom this information is communicated, who applies the decision algorithm, and what processes are in place when system partners wish to appeal the decision supported by the model. In general, the decision support procedures should be designed to be the least disruptive to the system and provide those with responsibility the authority to exercise that responsibility.

Often third parties are best situated to apply the measurement of the decision inputs and the algorithm. In Philadelphia, the DHS implemented an independent CANS unit to assess children who were potentially eligible for treatment foster care and applied the eligibility criteria. In New York State, the processes know as Single Points of Accountability generally apply the CANS and determine level of care. In Alaska, providers completed the CANS, but the Alaskan Youth Initiative applied the decision algorithm. A number of models are possible, depending on the resources and structure of the existing system.

7. Adjust algorithm based on system experiences. The concept of TCOM is to use clinical assessments to manage the service system. Thus, the TCOM process is intended to enhance accountability of the system to the service recipients. However, consistent with the logic of matrix accountability, the TCOM measures and process must be allowed to evolve based on experiences with an evolving service system. No decision support algorithm should be seen as written in stone. It is always a work in progress, with feedback from the system informing the evolution of the criteria.

Developing and Implementing Outcomes Monitoring

Although somewhat overlapping with decision support, the steps involved in implementing an outcomes monitoring process are sufficiently distinct to require a separate description. Approaches to outcomes monitoring include at least three distinct strategies. Static estimation is the simplest form of outcomes monitoring. This strategy involves a one-time assessment of the impact of services on recipients. The standard approach for outcomes monitoring is consumer satisfaction. Change analysis—often called effectiveness analysis—involves the study of the impact of services or programs over time. Building trajectories of recovery is the most sophisticated approach to outcomes monitoring and involves the development of growth curves that represent observed and expected rates of improvement associated with service receipt.

In our book, *The Measurement and Management of Clinical Outcomes in Mental Health* (Lyons, Howard, O'Mahoney, & Lish, 1997), we outlined the stages of implementing an outcomes management project.

> Step 1: Determine organizational needs and capacity: what the organization needs, what can be managed, and what resources can be brought to bear on the project.
>
> Step 2: Determine what will be measured: when, how, and by whom.
>
> Step 3: Work the organization: get everybody on board who needs to be on board.
>
> Step 4: Pretest the instruments and procedures.
>
> Step 5: Train and initiate: get everybody reading from the same page.
>
> Step 6: Maintain and manage: keep data collection going, monitor reliability, and provide feedback to participants.
>
> Step 7: Analyze and provide feedback: understand the data and develop recommendations.
>
> Step 8: Re-engineer: use the findings to improve services and the outcomes management process.

1. Determine organizational needs and capacity. In this step, the goal is to use the vision and mission of the organization or system to determine the initial priorities and long-term goals for outcomes measurement and management. Organizations and systems vary in terms of their priorities and preparation for measuring outcomes. As discussed in chapter 7, I am a strong believer in planned incrementalism as a change process. As such, it behooves any organization or system to be sensitive to its current status as it rolls out any new processes and procedures. That being said, any organization or system that embraces a TCOM approach must take this implementation seriously and, while accepting a slow start, must maintain its long-term vision of full implementation.

There have been numerous attempts to develop and implement a standard approach to outcomes measurement. Although such approaches are desirable from a variety of perspectives—particularly in terms of evaluating systems and comparing programs and services—a single approach to measurement is undesirable from other perspectives. Perhaps an example will be instructive. The goals of psychiatric hospitalization are generally crisis stabilization and resource mobilization. As hospital stays have become shorter, the role of treatment in the hospital has changed to become focused mostly on adjusting medications regimens. It is unlikely that a psychiatric hospital stay will have much impact on the child's role functioning, so why should the hospital be accountable for the child's school functioning? On the other hand, the goals of an intensive community intervention are far different and likely include improved functioning as an outcomes priority. Measuring irrelevant outcomes is a waste of time and resources. For this reason, a single outcomes measurement strategy is unlikely to succeed.

2. Determine what will be measured. The three principles of selecting what to measure for outcomes first require the definition of the goals and objectives of the intervention to be monitored. You should measure those characteristics that either define positive and negative outcomes (e.g., symptom relief) or identify individuals who may be more or less likely to benefit from the intervention (e.g., coexisting substance-use disorders). There is no reason to measure things that are not relevant to those goals. The second principle is to ensure that the major audiences of the outcomes monitoring are defined and their interests are represented in terms of outcomes measurement. This is the first step in which key partner "buy in" can be established (key partners include parents and youth representatives). The third principle is that any decision with regard to what to measure also must be guided by what is feasible and practical.

3. Work the organization. Although critical, this step is often unappreciated. In order to achieve any implementation, it is necessary to get good participation (i.e., buy in) within the organization or system. There are a variety of factors related to this process. First, leadership is critical—leaders at all levels must embrace the goals of the implementation. However, it is also important to create opportunities for all participants to voice their opinions and concerns as well as opportunities to identify barriers to implementation. This process requires understanding how employees can support and sabotage the implementation process.

Rosen and Weil (1996) identified three types of employees when it comes to any technology innovation—Eager Adopters, Hesitant Prove-Its, and Resistors. The Eager Adopters are those staff who are always first to get involved in anything new. They are excited to be on the front line of change, and become frustrated when things do not change rapidly enough to suit their preferences. These are the staff who provide the enthusiasm and energy for any innovation. Part of effectively working the organization is knowing whom among the staff you can count on in this capacity. Engaging these people early in the process is desirable. Unfortunately, Rosen and Weil estimate that only about 10 percent of the workforce can be classified as Eager Adopters.

The majority of staff can be classified as Hesitant Prove-Its. These employees are willing to change, but only if it is clear that it is really going to happen and that the change is going to be of some benefit to them or their job. If you can demonstrate the utility of the TCOM approach, these people will be right on board with you. However, if you do not do your homework and it appears that the outcomes measurement or management is misguided in significant ways, these are the employees who will effectively end the implementation. Listen carefully to the feedback of these individuals during the pilot testing of measures and procedures. Rosen and Weil (1996) estimate that approximately 50 to 60 percent of the workforce can be classified in this group.

The remaining 10 to 15 percent of employees can be classified as Resistors. These are the individuals who will fight any change—often through sabotage and passive resistance if not through direct refusal. In my experience, these are the individuals through which only job action gets them on board. Full participation in the outcomes approach must be explicitly written into their contracts or job descriptions. Failure to participate must be taken seriously by organization or system leadership, and sanctions must be applied if the Resistors fail to respond to other pressures. Sometimes it can be useful to include a Resistor in the planning process, particularly if that person has considerable formal or informal power in an organization or system. However, it is critical to ensure that if this representation is sought, the individual is not allowed to derail the planning process.

In working the organization, you should take the opportunity to include representatives of the families that receive services in the process. If the organization does not already have formal representatives, it is an opportunity to formalize a relationship with a specific parent or parent organization.

4. Pretest the instruments and procedures. It is always best to pilot test any measures and procedures. This strategy is useful to identify early on any problems that may arise. By presenting the initial implementation as a pretest of the approach, it provides another opportunity for feedback from participants. To the extent possible, any pilot test should be as close to the full implementation as possible. In fact, you can refer to the initial month of a full implementation as the pilot month, and build in formal feedback opportunities. If you can adjust the approach "on the fly," then you may simply continue the implementation after this pilot period. To the extent that steps 2 and 3 were completed successfully, then this step should not result in major negative feedback.

5. Train and initiate. As mentioned above, steps 4 and 5 may be integrated into a single step. However, there are circumstances—particularly involving large system implementations in which the pretesting involves only a subset of the entire system—in which step 4 is used to sort out any potential problems before widespread implementation. In these situations, step 5 is clearly separate from 4.

Training on all tools to acceptable reliability is critical. We routinely require certification of all individuals who complete rating scales. A reliability criteria of at least 0.70 or above using training vignettes is our standard approach. In addition, we use booster trainings, periodic retest vignettes, and measurement audits to ensure sustained reliability of the tools.

For self-report measures, reliability issues are much more complicated. It is not possible to have a training program on the reliability of self-report measurements. Therefore, the following issues are critical:

1. All measures should be easy to read and understand. They should be respectful to the individual completing the form.

2. Cultural issues that might affect how different people respond to a measure should be investigated.

3. All procedures should be carefully explained to the individual completing the form. The reasons for requesting the information should be carefully explained. Opportunities for asking questions should be provided.

4. Results of measures should be shared. This is true for all measures, but is particularly important for self-report measures. If people take the time to complete a measure, they should receive specific feedback on what their responses mean.

6. Maintain and manage. The maintenance and management of an ongoing outcomes management process requires several things. Most important is the presence of an individual or individuals who are seen as champions of the process. Fred Newman refers to these individuals as the "persnickety." Someone must be paying close attention to the process and intervening when problems arise or when participation is not full. That someone must have sufficient power in the organization or system to get and maintain the attention of all participants.

In addition to the presence of champions, other factors are central to the ongoing success of a TCOM approach. Use is the most important factor. Full use, as described earlier in this chapter, is optimal. At the very least, people who put information into the system should be able to receive relevant and timely information back out. They may opt not to utilize the information, at least initially; however, it is essential that everyone participating has access to at least some feedback about the functioning and findings of the process. Ultimately, re-engineering (i.e., instituting policy or procedural changes based on findings) will get everyone's attention (see below), and often dramatically increases people's motivation to fully participate in the system.

7. Analyze and provide feedback. The analysis of outcomes data can be simple or complex. Simple analyses can involve graphs of pre- and postscores and counts of sentinel events. However, there are a number of complex statistical approaches that prove to be quite useful for outcomes management.

Logistic regression and discriminant function analysis can be valuable tools for decision support applications. In these approaches, clinical decision inputs are used as independent variables (i.e., predictors) and actual decisions (e.g., hospitalize/deflect, place in RCT/community) are the dependent variables. Statistical models can be created and then used to predict new decisions.

Hierarchical linear models, sometimes called growth curves, offer enormous potential for analyzing change in clinical status over time. These approaches are robust to missing data but require at least two time points for each case included in the analysis. With these models, trajectories of recovery can be calculated for groups or individuals. As demonstrated earlier in this chapter, these trajectories can be quite descriptive of change over time for different programs. Individual children can be compared with expected trajectories to monitor progress or the lack thereof.

Although sophisticated statistical approaches can be valuable tools in the TCOM process, it is important not to become so enamored with statistical approaches that you forget that the primary purpose is communication. Thus, consideration of the audience and its capacity to understand different types of analyses should influence decisions regarding choice of statistical analysis. It is often useful to initially design the feedback products (i.e., reports) and then determine the analytic strategies that best serve these products.

8. Re-engineer. Re-engineering based on the findings of an ongoing TCOM project can be a relatively complex task; however, it is the essential task of all QI activities. Therefore, much can be learned from the substantial literature on total quality management, continual QI, and other specific strategies for improving the quality and effectiveness of services. However, there remains a notable difference. In TCOM, the emphasis is on clinical outcomes of the service recipient rather than the process of care indicators (e.g., time between initial call and first appointment), ensuring that the focus of any change process remains on the shared vision: that is, improving the lives of the children and families we serve. From the TCOM perspective, a potential problem with a focus on "quality" is that it can shift the focus to the services rather than the people served. In most versions of QI, effectiveness is only one aspect of the larger construct of quality. In TCOM, everything is about improving effectiveness. For example, in TCOM, improving the credentials of program staff is only relevant if it improves the outcomes of the program. You wouldn't pursue this change unless you had evidence that staff credentials were somehow limiting the program's effectiveness (e.g., staff with higher credentials have better outcomes than do staff with lower credentials). In many versions of QI, improving staff credentials can be seen as a quality initiative in its own right.

Figure 5.5
Integrating Total Clinical Outcomes Management into Program Planning

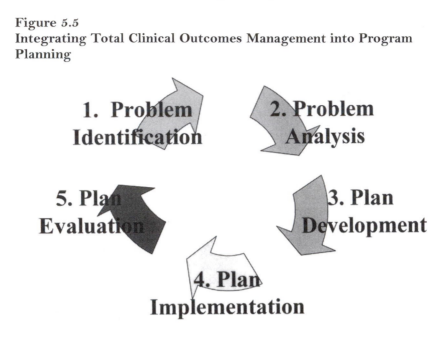

Figure 5.5 presents a modification of the Shewart cycle (Agency for Healthcare & Policy Research, 1993), which is a standard vision of QI. This figure identifies the five steps of re-engineering in TCOM. The first step is problem identification—what outcomes problem has been identified. The second step is an analysis of this outcomes problem in an effort to identify the potential causes. The third step involves the development of a plan to address the most likely identified cause(s). In the fourth step, the plan is implemented, and in the fifth step, the plan is evaluated. If the plan is successful, the cycle stops; if not, the process returns to step 1.

Addressing Syndromes through TCOM Strategies

One of the advantages of a full integration of clinical outcomes into program, organization, and system management is that it creates some options for addressing the syndromes described in chapter 2. Although these approaches likely cannot resolve tensions, syndromes are a different matter. The following is a discussion of some strategies to consider when encountering the untoward effects of the various syndromes.

Addressing System-Level Syndromes

The Political Dog Walk Syndrome

There are both positive and punitive approaches for dealing with the Political Dog Walk Syndrome. Politicians need to spread their influence around, but you can help them look good doing so if opportunities are presented that identify particularly skilled providers. On the positive side, if the politician is seen as rewarding outstanding performance, that is a win–win situation. Therefore, provider profiling and performance management strategies that allow for rewards or incentives (or even awards) can be ways of addressing the political needs and creating some motivation on the part of underachieving programs and agencies to improve.

On the punitive side, nobody wants to back a loser. Evidence of poor performance can be used to shift the political balance in some situations. No politician wants to be in the newspapers supporting a low-quality program or agency. In these circumstances, the use of broader communication strategies—including the mass media— might be considered.

The Field of Dreams Syndrome

Earlier in this chapter, we described strategies that address the Field of Dreams Syndrome with the example of how the Illinois DCFS evolved its residential treatment system. Managing the system based on the needs and strengths of children and families reduced the influence of existing service components to resist system change. Decision support strategies kept the focus on the children, and clinical outcomes data raised the level of the argument and reduced the power of underperforming system elements.

The Can't Fix Anything Unless You Fix Everything Syndrome

The Can't Fix Anything Unless You Fix Everything Syndrome is a tough one to address with only TCOM strategies. What is really required in this instance is the ability to communicate a vision of the long-term system changes and maintain the focus on the interim steps necessary to achieve this vision. However, clear and convincing data that demonstrate either the need for a change or the opportunities that could arise from a change can help to counter the arguments of naysayers. Strong leadership is the key ingredient here.

The What's Mine Is Mine and What's Yours...Well, That's Negotiable Syndrome

As with the previous syndrome, there are significant limits to how much TCOM approaches can help with the What's Mine Is Mine Syndrome. Collaboration has been described as an unusual act among nonconsenting adults; therefore, this syndrome may be, in large part, a function of being human. However, data can support collaboration in a number of ways. In New Jersey's Partnership for Children, all members of the system of care use the same assessment strategies. These common assessment strategies create a common language that all partners use to describe the needs and strengths of children and families. It is possible to blend services without blending funding, but it takes good communication and trust.

The Imperialism Syndrome

The key to managing the Imperialism Syndrome is the matrix accountability approach discussed later in chapter 7. Only by ensuring that all partners in the system are accountable to all other partners is it possible to reduce or even eliminate this problem. Generally, people are only imperial when they can get away with it. If it costs them in terms of impact, power, or respect, then they usually keep their urges to lord over others in check.

Program-Level Syndromes

The Colonel Sanders Syndrome

The Colonel Sander's Syndrome is managed through the effective use of decision support approaches matched with knowledge of what interventions are most effective for which types of children and families. There is a growing body of knowledge in this regard. In some cases, all that is missing is the willingness to exert the implications of that knowledge. If you want chicken, it's great to go see the Colonel. If you want something else, there are other choices. Ensuring that consumers have knowledge about these choices is the central aspect of limiting the potential untoward effects of this syndrome.

The Therapist Illusion Syndrome

The Therapist Illusion Syndrome is relatively easy to address. All it takes is consistent feedback to therapists with regard to the progress and outcomes of their cases. When information is aggregated back to therapists based on children and families rather than on the time the therapist spends providing services, there is no ability to maintain this illusion.

The Rose Reversal Syndrome

The Rose Reversal Syndrome is best dealt with through the use of fidelity assessments. Fidelity assessments should be a standard component of quality assurance/improvement activities (e.g., Nordness & Epstein, 2003). Assessing the fidelity of an intervention involves monitoring whether or not the program/provider is doing what is consistent with the program/intervention design. Any best practice, EBP, or contracted service can have a fidelity model developed for it. Anyone advancing a new intervention strategy should have an assessment of fidelity to the strategy available before replication and widespread implementation is permitted.

The Public Funding as an Entitlement Syndrome

The effective end of the Public Funding as an Entitlement Syndrome requires a cultural shift in our public mental health system. Accountability must be embraced by all partners in the system, and organizations or individuals who cannot accept accountability should not be included in the system. The goals of a service system should be about developing the shared vision that we can best help children and families in need by working together to ensure that the system remains focused on their well-being. Any successes experienced by partners in the system should be directly tied to their effectiveness of meeting this vision.

Child- and Family-Level Syndromes

The Expert Syndrome

The Expert Syndrome is addressed in several ways. First, developing knowledge within the general population—and service recipients, in particular—is an important strategy for reducing the information imbalance between experts and parents. Second, helping professionals to understand their roles in working with families so that they can communicate a greater level of respect is also important. Third, including parents—and possibly youth, depending on their age—in all aspects of their service planning provides an educational format for addressing this syndrome. Over time, they become increasingly knowledgeable about identifying their own needs and strengths, as well as service and treatment options.

The Hammer–Nail Syndrome

The Hammer–Nail Syndrome is best addressed by expanding the toolbox available to providers. The strategy that is most likely to be successful in this regard is to imbed training in multiple EBPs into all training programs. Comprehensive approaches to training on EBPs will help professionals to understand that they have different treatment options, with which they are experienced and comfortable, to address different situations.

The Happy Face Syndrome

I have found that the implementation of the CANS reduces the Happy Face Syndrome. With its simultaneous emphasis on needs and strengths and its implicit permission to allow for the presence of needs without implying any causality (and, therefore, blame), the tendency for people to place a "rose-colored glasses" frame on difficult circumstances is reduced. It is perfectly fine to have needs—everyone does. It is also likely that they have strengths. Needs and strengths are not opposite ends of the same continuum. For instance, it is not a strength to not be suicidal, but if someone is suicidal, the people around them should know about it and try to prevent a death outcome. There are differences between needs and strengths; both are important and they can coexist together.

The Ostrich Syndrome

The Ostrich Syndrome is directly addressed by accountability in the reliability of assessments. Audit methods can be used to identify those individuals who tend to underidentify needs. Retraining or other education-based sanctions can be used to encourage individuals to more accurately identify existing needs. However, having comprehensive service systems in which needed services are actually available and accessible would also go far to eliminate this syndrome.

The Fuzzy Pathogen Syndrome

One of the advantages of a TCOM approach is that it can be done in an entirely atheoretical fashion. You do not need to understand cause-and-effect relationships among needs, services, and outcomes in order to utilize this information to support service system evolution. Currently, we simply do not know enough about humans and their mental health to agree on one theoretical model. Getting bogged down in the debate is of little value to children with mental health challenges today.

The Imagined Cure Syndrome

The Imagined Cure Syndrome is addressed through an understanding of expected outcomes. We can readily demonstrate that addressing most children's emotional and behavioral problems is an ongoing process and that the elimination of all problems is unlikely and probably a naive goal.

The Endless Treatment Syndrome

The Endless Treatment Syndrome is related to the previous syndrome, in that it is necessary to develop a better understanding of how much treatment is enough. Traditionally, this has been an issue debated by professionals, but decided by service recipients. The vast majority of recipients decide for themselves that they have had enough and just stop participating in treatment. Professionals might benefit from spending more time listening to what consumers want, rather than trying to fit a treatment to a particular disease or disorder model.

Summary

This chapter is intended to serve as a primer for the TCOM approach. The rationale of TCOM is that only by placing the management emphasis of the case, the program, and the system on the health and well-being of children and families will it be possible to achieve an accessible and effective public mental health system consistent with the vision of the system-of-care philosophy. The selection of measurement tools is important, because they need to inform service planning and monitoring for individual children and families while providing reliable and valid data for decision support, QI, and outcomes monitoring activities in aggregates. The implementation process can be slow and is often difficult. The key ingredient for success is the commitment of leadership to the potential value of the approach. Maintaining focus on the long-term vision and goals during challenging times separates the successful efforts from the unsuccessful ones. Implementation of TCOM can help to eliminate the syndromes that have interfered with the ability to achieve the system-of-care vision.

CHAPTER 6

THE ROLE OF EXISTING PROGRAMS AND SERVICES IN AN EVOLVING SYSTEM

In building a comprehensive system of care for children and their families, much work has already been accomplished. Therefore, we are somewhere in the middle of progress toward a comprehensive and effective system of care for children. Consistent with McKnight and Kretzmann's (1993) notion of asset-based community development, there are considerable assets in the existing public mental health system that can serve as the foundation for the continued evolution of an accessible, efficient, and effective system of care for those youth who require comprehensive services.

There are also important political considerations at work. Many of the key partners in the system of care work within one of the existing structures. Therefore, most have considerable stake in the continued existence of these programs and structures. Once a bureaucracy is formed, it is exceptionally difficult to dismantle it. Just as we cannot be successful in developing a healthier family if we do not respect the needs and wishes of all family members, we cannot be successful in developing a more effective system if we do not respect the needs and wishes of the existing partners. Evolution is a more reasonable goal than revolution.

The purpose of this chapter is to begin the process of reconceptualizing some of these existing assets into their possible roles within a system of care. Then, within the framework of these evolving roles, we can begin to establish a conceptual approach to Total Clinical

Outcomes Management (TCOM) that would be applicable within each of these program environments.

Psychiatric Hospitals

As discussed in chapter 1, psychiatric hospitals are the historical foundation of the public mental health system. Until the 1960s, the only options for persons with mental illness who were poor were institutional care or no care at all. No system of publicly funded mental health services existed in their communities. The origins of public mental health for children are based in the psychiatric hospital. Although the treatment mission has shifted, psychiatric hospitals remain the safety net for protecting children and the community.

Originally, the idea of the psychiatric hospital was consistent with the notion of asylum and even today, the need for asylum is sometimes used as a justification for the hospitalization of children. The basic concept of asylum is a safe haven. When applied to mental health, the idea is that when stressful environments create mental health problems, removal of the person (in our case, the child) from the stressful environment can give him or her time to heal, gain perspective, and recover from the harmful effects of environmental stress. The problem with this notion is that there is very little evidence that the concept of asylum as an approach to treatment is helpful to people who must continue to live in stressful environments. Perhaps the most extreme example of the problem comes from what we have learned about stress reactions in combat. The farther you remove a stressed soldier from combat, the more permanent the psychiatric disability tends to become. Thus, you keep soldiers with "shell shock" close to the front line and return them to their posts as quickly as possible to minimize the "institutionalization" of any stress-related psychiatric symptoms that have developed. This policy was initiated during World War II and is still in effect today (e.g., Grossman, 2001; Sokol, 1989).

We have repeatedly demonstrated that decision making regarding children's hospitalizations is far more complex than is that for adults (Leon, Uziel-Miller, Lyons, & Tracy, 1999; Lyons, Kisiel, Dulcan, Cohen, & Chesler, 1997;). The primary issue is that the assessment of a child's risk of harm to self or others must be accomplished within the context of the parents' or caregivers' capacity to address the child's needs. A suicidal girl with parents who are knowledgeable about her feelings and issues, involved in her treatment, and able to provide an appropriate level of supervision could avoid hospitalization. The same girl with parents who were uninvolved or not under-standing her issues (e.g., "Go ahead and try to kill yourself. You're not that strong.") or who are unable to provide sufficient supervision would require hospitalization to ensure her safety. In this way, the use of the psychiatric hospital for a child is also based on the needs of his or her parents or caregivers. However, hospitals are designed to treat individuals while they are in the hospital. They are not designed to intervene in family systems. After all, it would be ridiculous to propose to "hospitalize" the whole family. However, family systems theorists would argue that by hospitalizing one child in a family, you are reinforcing or enabling the notion of an "identified patient" and making it more difficult for a family with problems to undergo sys-temic change. In fact, as silly as it sounds today, entire families were actually hospitalized in an experimental program in the 1960s at the Philadelphia Child Guidance Center (Salvadore Minuchin's program, which created systemic family therapy). Not surprisingly, this pro-gram lasted only a little over a year and closed due to the expense of the intervention and the difficulty in finding suitable, "hospitalizable" families.

Let me give you an example to help make this point. I was present-ing data in New York City on the use of psychiatric hospitalization. Our data suggested that only about 30 percent of children who were hospitalized in New York City would meet standard "medical neces-sity" criteria (i.e., danger to self or others or so symptomatic as to be dangerous). At one presentation, a psychiatrist said to me that I simply didn't understand the complexity of the issues involved. She complained about short hospital stays and said that she recently had a case in which it was not until the patient's sixth hospitalization that they could keep him long enough to remove him from all his medicine. During that hospital admission, they discovered that the reason he was engaged in sexually provocative behavior was that his mother was letting him watch an adult channel at home just to keep him occupied. The psychiatrist passionately felt that this case was strong evidence for long-term hospitalizations; that is, she believed that they could have gotten to the bottom of this patient's problem with the first hospitalization, even if it had to be extended for months. My argument was that it might have been possible to discover this particular problem (i.e., watching adult movie channels, becoming sexually aroused, and acting out on that arousal) even earlier, by actu-ally providing services in the home rather than by observing the child in the hospital.

Regardless of the conceptual and practical problems posed by psychiatric hospital stays for children, there are two potent advantages to this service setting:

1. Hospitals are safe. The 24-hour nursing services and security make it possible to work with a child or adolescent who is dangerous to him- or herself or others, either directly through suicidal gestures or violence or indirectly through the impact of severe symptoms of psychiatric disorders.

2. Hospitals generally possess the most sophisticated diagnostic potential, both in terms of machines and humans. From laboratories that rapidly and accurately assess biochemistry to magnetic resonance and positron emission tomography technology that provides interactive windows into the central nervous system, hospitals have the most sophisticated diagnostic machinery. They also tend to be staffed with the best clinicians, particularly in terms of diagnostics and assessment. In addition, hospitals are often able to pay higher salaries than are community-based providers, thereby attracting and retaining more highly trained clinical staff.

For these reasons, psychiatric hospitals must remain a key component of the system of care. Unfortunately, due to the early politics of the system-of-care movement, a "them versus us" attitude of community services versus hospital and residential services has developed in many areas. Because of this problem, combined with the tensions that arise between the medical and social models of behavioral health problems, hospitals are often not welcomed into system-of-care planning meetings, child–family team meetings, or other collaborations in the system of care. This is an unfortunate problem that can be easily addressed.

Decision Support Criteria for Psychiatric Hospitalization

Based on our experiences with the Childhood Severity of Psychiatric Illness and Child and Adolescent Needs and Strengths (CANS) tools, we have found that the following decision model supports appropriate use of psychiatric hospitalization:

Criteria 1:   A rating of "3" on at least one of the following dimensions:

A.   Psychosis

B.   Suicide risk

C.   Danger to others

Criteria 2:   A rating of "2" on any of the items in criteria 1 in combination with a rating of "2" or "3" on any of the following caregiver capacity characteristics:

A.   Supervision

B.   Involvement

C.   Knowledge

Although other algorithms may be used in specific local circumstances, these criteria identify the children who are most likely to benefit from acute hospital admission either through stabilization or the prevention of violence.

The key outcomes considerations for psychiatric hospitalizations should include risk reduction, acute symptom relief, resources mobilization, and linkage to community-based services. This last outcome is critical. We have observed in several states that the psychiatric hospital often serves as the portal to placements in out-of-community settings, particularly residential treatment. Maintaining the link between the community hospital and the community it serves is critical to the integration of hospitals into the system of care. An outcomes focus on this linkage should be a priority.

Home-Based Crisis Services

Both clinical and financial considerations have increased interest in alternatives to hospitalization. Clinically, it is desirable to prevent hospital admissions when possible, because hospital stays can be disruptive to school functioning and may be experienced as stigmatizing by the child and family. Financially, the widespread use of institutional placements—including psychiatric hospitalization—has resulted in a disproportionate share of the funding for children's services being spent on a small proportion of youth (Burns, 1991; Sondheimer, Schoenwald, & Rowland, 1994). One study reported 7 percent of high-end service users consuming nearly 45 percent of system resources (Lambert, Brannan, Breda, Heflinger, & Bickman, 1998). Elsewhere, we have reported that psychiatric hospitalizations are a common pathway into institutional placement (Lyons, Rawal, Yeh, Leon, & Tracy, 2002). Deflecting hospitalizations when clinically appropriate may allow for an investment in mental health services that covers a larger number of youth.

The goal of in-home crisis services is to provide families with resources to maintain their child at home and to more effectively cope with the persistence of many of their problems (Mosier et al., 2001). Preliminary work demonstrated success with providing community-based services to youth at risk for hospitalization. In one sample, after 8 weeks of home-based treatment, 90 percent of youth showed at least reliable and significant clinical improvement (Mosier et al., 2001). Children in the program reported symptom levels similar to those of children in outpatient treatment, indicating that less-intensive and costly treatment options could then be used (Mosier et al., 2001). In another sample, psychiatric hospitalization decreased by 23 percent with the use of intensive in-home services (Blumberg, 2002).

In the initial implementation of a mobile response service in the New Jersey Partnership for Children, we found that mobile, in-home services can prevent hospital admissions for all but the most acutely symptomatic and high-risk children (i.e., children with severe symptoms of psychosis and violence). Thus, depressed and suicidal children who are living in stable home environments may not require hospitalization. Impulsive children who can get linked to psychiatric treatment quickly and who can be provided with a safe environment also can be treated at home. The capacity of the family to manage the child's behavior—particularly risky behaviors—is the key to developing effective decision support strategies for these services.

In New York State, a six-week, home-based crisis intervention (HBCI) program has been established. We found that this program served children who were comparable with those who were admitted to community psychiatric inpatient units. No child died and only 8 percent of all HBCI cases ended up hospitalized, suggesting that this program was a good alternative to hospital admission.

Residential Treatment

Placement of a youth in a residential treatment center to address his or her emotional or behavioral needs has become increasingly controversial over the past decade (Bates, English, & Kouidou-Giles, 1997; Frensch & Cameron, 2002). More than any other program type, the implicit treatment philosophy of residential treatment can be in direct conflict with the principles of an evolving system of care (Burns & Friedman, 1990). Residential treatment has the highest per episode costs of any current component of the extant children's service system (LeCroy & Ashford, 1992). With per diem costs between $100 and $600 and lengths of stay ranging from months to years, these costs can be quite high. According to the 1999 Surgeon General's report on mental health (U.S. Surgeon General, 1999), residential treatment accounts for 25 percent of all spending on mental health services, despite the fact that it is only used by 8 percent of treated children.

Institutionalizing a relatively small number of children at considerable expense conflicts with the goals of managed care initiatives (i.e., devoting more money to less expensive services that serve more people). Institutionalization also conflicts with the widely accepted view, and a guiding Child and Adolescent Service System Program principle, that children should be treated in the "least restrictive environment" (Frensch & Cameron, 2002; Hussey & Guo, 2002; Rosenblatt, 1993). However, some children require placement outside of the home because their caregiver cannot cope with their illness or because their home environment is unsafe (Barker, 1998; Lyman & Campbell, 1996). Additionally, there is some evidence that many of the children who enter residential treatment have been unsuccessful in community-based services (Frensch & Cameron, 2002). In this environment, it has become increasingly important to understand the effectiveness of residential treatment interventions.

The basic concept of residential treatment is that a youth's well-being and development is best served by removing him or her from his or her home environment (or perhaps a homelike environment, as in foster care) to treat symptoms, risk behaviors, or functioning problems. This concept is not unlike the asylum movement in adult psychiatric services. Although asylum still has its advocates among children mental health specialists (e.g., Abramovitz & Bloom, 2003), it is generally a discredited concept. There is evidence that some symptom relief and risk behavior reduction does occur during residential treatment, but there is little evidence that gains made in institutional care translate into functional improvements upon return to the community (Lyons, et al., 1998).

Decision Support for Residential Treatment

In most conceptualizations of level of care by restrictiveness, only the hospital is more restrictive than is residential treatment. As such, these placements should be reserved for high-need children with no other alternative placements. In a variety of settings, we have utilized the following basic CANS decision support model for placement in residential treatment.

> Criterion 1: A "3" on at least one problem or multiple problems with a rating of "2." Problems include psychosis, attention deficit/

impulse, depression/anxiety, oppositional behavior, antisocial behavior, adjustment to trauma, and substance use.

Criterion 2: A "3" on one risk behavior or multiple risk behaviors with ratings of "2." Risk behaviors include danger to self, danger to others, running away, sexually abusive behavior, crime/delinquency, and social behavior (excluding social behavior is an option on this criterion).

Criterion 3: A "3" on one caregiver needs and strengths or multiple caregiver items with ratings of a "2." Caregiver needs and strengths include physical/behavioral, supervision, involvement, knowledge, organization, resources, residential stability, and safety.

To be considered for placement in residential treatment, a child would need to meet all three criteria, and intensive community treatment options must either have been attempted or be unavailable for the child.

In terms of outcomes consideration, a focus on the symptoms and behaviors that led to the placement would be the appropriate focus for monitoring change over time. Previously, I mentioned the project modeling trajectories in Oregon. Using the Childhood Acuity of Psychiatric Illness (Lyons, 1998), we originally identified reliable worsening at one particular program site. This led to an intervention at that site. Follow-up provider profiling demonstrated that although trajectories of recovery remained different for the existing programs, no program had children who on average became more symptomatic over time. Figure 6.1 presents the most recent trajectories by site.

In this same analysis, we found that children in state custody had flatter trajectories than did those who were still in the custody of their parents. Further analysis of this finding, along with conversations with program personnel, suggest that children who are still in their parents' custody often have great hope of getting out of residential treatment faster, and therefore work harder to control behaviors. Children who are in state custody often feel like they have no control over what happens to them.

Medication Management Services

In no other area of behavioral health have the treatment breakthroughs been more breathtaking than in the psychopharmacology field over the past 30 years. For children, medications with proven efficacy exist for attention deficit/hyperactivity, depression, and various forms of psychosis (U.S. Surgeon General, 2001b). The use of mood stabilizers to treat symptoms of bipolar disorder is promising, and the

Figure 6.1

Outcomes Trajectories for Residential Treatment Centers Using the Childhood Acuity of Psychiatric Illness (CAPI)

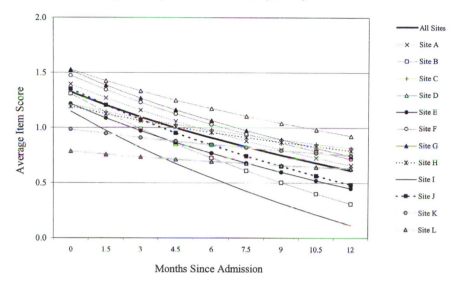

evidence with adults suggests that these will be effective treatments with adolescents as well.

In a review of the public mental health system in New York State, we found evidence that stimulant and antidepressant use was consistent with clinical indications and, if anything, underutilized given the level of observed needs among children served (Lyons, MacIntyre, Lee, Carpinella, Zuber, & Fazio, 2004). However, the use of antipsychotic medications—especially atypical antipsychotic medications such as risperidone—appear to be overutilized, particularly in congregate-care settings such as residential treatment and psychiatric hospitals (Rawal, Lyons, MacIntyre, & Hunter, 2004).

Clearly, psychotropic medications are a critical part of the system of care for children. Much like the psychiatric hospital, however, there has been a limited emphasis on the importance of these treatments— and the service-delivery systems necessary to support them—in the system-of-care literature. In my observations, I have noted three major barriers to the effective integration of medication management into the children's system of care:

- There is a dire shortage of board-certified child psychiatrists.
- There is an absence of accountability of psychiatry to other partners in the system of care.

- Current drug regulations allow for widespread use of medications
  in the absence of evidence-based indications for children and adolescents.

The initial focus of a TCOM approach likely would be on matching
the indications to the selected drugs. Decision support approaches
that build in empirical evidence for matching drugs to clinical indications should inform the analyses of these data. In terms of anticipated
outcomes, symptom relief and side effects would likely be the primary outcomes to monitor over time. Treatment fidelity in this area
would involve monitoring (1) whether prescribed doses are within the
appropriate therapeutic range, and (2) whether children are taking
their medications as prescribed.

It may be that until the shortage of board-certified child psychiatrists can be addressed, a rational plan for using pediatricians within
the children's public mental health system should be considered.
Pediatricians generally have a good deal of experience with the use
of stimulants to treat the symptoms of attention deficit disorder and
hyperactivity (Zito et al., 2000, 2003). Therefore, a model of utilizing
pediatricians for stimulant treatment and child psychiatrists for antidepressant, antipsychotic, and mood-stabilizing treatment might take
some of the pressure off of child psychiatry.

Outpatient Psychotherapy Services

Whenever a child experiences problems, the standard approach
is to refer them to counseling or outpatient psychotherapeutic
services. Although there is little doubt that this intervention can
be beneficial for some children, there is suspicion that counseling
and/or psychotherapy services are generally not particularly helpful for children (Andrade, Lambert, & Bickman, 2000). To evolve
outpatient psychotherapy services, I would make three recommendations.

First, I have already advocated that outpatient treatment providers should be allowed to serve anyone who comes seeking services.
This policy might increase the number of children and families
seeking services, but probably not by an overwhelming amount, at
least initially. Parents bring their children to treatment because of
experienced problems; therefore, finding a reasonable diagnosis can
be fairly easy. The point of removing the diagnostic eligibility is not
so much to improve access as it is to eliminate the need for therapists
to find some diagnosis in order to be paid. It is possible that access

could improve over time as a secondary effect of reduced stigma; however, whether such a relationship exists is not known.

Second, if the outpatient services have open access, then these services would serve important assessment and triage roles in the system of care. Thus, outpatient clinicians should be trained and skilled in assessment techniques (e.g., using the CANS) that guide level-of-care decision making in the system. In fact, the system's assessment capacity would be located in these settings. Locating system triage in the community would be superior to the current standard in which psychiatric hospitals often serve as the entry and assessment portal into residential treatment and other intensive services.

Third, it is critical that clinicians who are working in outpatient programs receive training in evidence-based practices and that clinics develop triage decision support mechanisms to ensure that children presenting for services are optimally matched to the type of treatment or treatments that would best serve them. Such a training agenda requires ongoing mechanisms for training both in educational settings and in practice settings. In addition, some mechanism for deciding what defines an evidence-based practice is necessary. I would recommend that a federal agency be identified or created that could establish a process much like the Food and Drug Administration uses for new drug treatments. If this is not feasible, then a nonguild organization such as the National Association of State Mental Health Program Directors could make recommendations. The conflict of interest limitation inherent to guild organizations (i.e., American Psychiatric Association, American Psychological Association, National Association of Social Work) is that they will be under enormous pressure to make recommendations that favor their own profession. Finally, individual states could create committees with broad representation that would review evidence and make recommendations.

Achieving these recommendations would require improving the speed of access into outpatient services. This might require expansion or it might require more intensive management of clinician schedules for when currently served cases stop coming for services, because no-show appointments result in significant inefficiencies. However, unless monitored closely, clinicians sometimes appreciate the free time associated with no-show appointments. Policies that limit the number of no-shows before ending the case could open more clinics' slots. These policies would have to be assertively managed by supervisors. Service recipients would have to be notified in advance of the policy and reminded regularly.

The most important TCOM aspect of outpatient services would likely be the application of fidelity models to ensure that evidence-based practices are being appropriately implemented in the field. If limited resources are available for TCOM, fidelity reviews may be more important than outcomes monitoring activities, although both would be beneficial to managing and improving the system.

Day Treatment

Programs included under the rubric "day treatment" are perhaps the most variable type of program model in the current system. Programming for day treatment ranges from educationally based curriculum for children who have difficulties in regular classroom environments to psychiatrically based programs that primarily focus on treatment and have a secondary emphasis on education. Thus, programs can vary widely with regard to their general emphasis on education versus treatment.

There is no substantial literature on the outcomes associated with day treatment. Although some literature does exist, due to the variation in program design, it is somewhat difficult to draw broad conclusions about this program type. Given this general absence of empirical data on effectiveness, it is reasonable to discuss the clinical logic of the program models described within this category.

Children generally are referred into day treatment through the school system. More than other components of the mental health service system, this program is intimately tied to the school system. This linkage with schools includes funding for the educational components of the programming. Day treatment programs that function as alternative schools are actually components of the special education system. They should contain specialized educational programming and low teacher-to-student ratios to make it possible to educate children who have behavioral and emotional problems that interfere with educational achievement. The primary objectives of these programs should be educational attainment. There is substantial evidence that children with serious emotional or behavioral problems become derailed in the school system. If day treatment can help these children to get back on a normal educational developmental track, the program would be a major success. A focus on education means that treatment must take a back seat. Thus, treatment in this program model occurs only in support of the educational mandate. Intervention in the school environment to support teaching would be indicated. Treatment of problems such as depression or anxiety that do not generally result in school misbehavior should be undertaken if the symptoms interfere with school performance. Identifying and addressing learning problems and developing teaching approaches that address individual learning styles would be a priority in these programs.

At the other extreme, day treatment programs that focus on treatment likely have a much different role in the system of care. As such, the length of stay for children in these programs should be short. Otherwise, considerable educational delays could result from removing children from a primary educational environment for a long period of time.

In two unpublished studies of brief interventions with children with serious emotional and behavioral problems, we studied the outcomes of a short-term psychiatric day treatment program and a 90-day crisis intervention/stabilization program. Children were divided into two groups—those who primarily showed internalizing problems of depression and anxiety and those who primarily showed externalizing problems of impulse control, oppositional behavior, and antisocial behavior. Figure 6.2 presents the outcomes for these program types

Figure 6.2
Comparison of Internalizing and Externalizing Children from Admission to Discharge in a Partial Hospital Program and a Home-Based Crisis Intervention Program. PH-Admit, Partial Hospital Program, Admittance; PH-Disc, Partial Hospital Program, Discharge; HBCi-Admit, Home-Based Crisis Intervention Program, Admittance; HBCi-Disc, Home-Based Crisis Intervention Program, Discharge

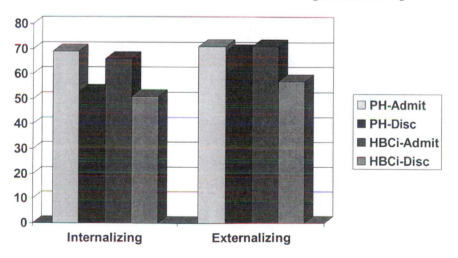

for each group of children. Review of these data reveals that children
with internalizing problems benefited from either program model.
Short-term day treatment or HBCI both were associated with reduced
symptoms. However, only the HBCI program was associated with
improvement among the children with disruptive behavior problems
(i.e., externalizing). Children with these difficulties did not improve
within the day treatment program. Interestingly, the average length
of stay for these children was more than triple (102 days) that of the
depressed or anxious children in day treatment (29 days).

The interpretation of these findings is consistent with what is
known about depression and anxiety versus disruptive behavior.
Depression and anxiety are called "internalizing" disorders because
they are very internally focused. Children with depression and anxiety carry these emotions with them wherever they go. It may be that
in these cases, it simply doesn't matter *where* you treat these children.
The comparable outcomes between day treatment and HBCI are consistent with this hypothesis.

Disruptive behaviors, particularly oppositional behavior, are
thought to be far more a function of the child's environment than of
an internal mental process. Thus, it is reasonable to suppose that the
environment in which the child lives to some degree contributes, or
at least maintains, the disruptive behavior. Therefore, it is possible
that in these cases, *where* treatment is provided is critical. Removing a
child from his or her environment and providing treatment outside of
that environment (e.g., in a day treatment program) is not as effective
for these children as is providing treatment in the home (or school
or community) environment that is actually supporting or triggering
the disruptive behavior. Again, the dramatically different outcomes for
HBCI versus day treatment for children with disruptive (i.e., externalizing) behavior problems are consistent with this hypothesis.

We can conclude the following about day treatment:

1. Long-term placement in an educationally focused day treatment
   program may be a valuable aspect of the array of educational
   options in a special education system. The criteria for acceptance
   into these programs should be a clear link between the behavioral
   health needs of the child and school achievement or behavior. The
   duration of treatment should be consistent with the academic cal-
   endar, to reduce educational discontinuity. If a child with disruptive
   behavior problems that are also prominent in the home is placed in
   a day treatment program, a component of the programming should
   include home-based intervention. Only "treating" the child in the

school when problems also exist in other settings would be less than optimally effective.

2. The logic in support of short-term day treatment programs is questionable. These programs make little or no sense for children with disruptive behavior problems. These program models appear to work for children with problems of depression and/or anxiety, but then so do a number of other treatment approaches. Perhaps the only suitable indication for these types of programs is the seriously depressed or anxious child who requires a full-day program to maintain safety or facilitate recovery from their disability. Children with disabling depression or anxiety do not represent a large segment of the children's system of care population. As such, creation or maintenance of these types of programs should not be a priority.

Day treatment should be a special education service that makes the education of the child its primary goal. Treatment and behavioral management strategies are used to prevent the child's emotional or behavioral problems from interfering with their educational attainment. Therefore, the primary outcomes for day treatment are assessments of academic achievement. Helping children return to working at grade level in their schoolwork would be the expected outcome. Symptom improvement or the reduction of behavioral problems would be a secondary outcome. Return to a mainstream classroom would be a primary dispositional outcome goal.

Intensive Community Services

The greatest investments in the expansion of children's services have been in the area of intensive community services. Although the types of services provided under this general rubric are varied and the models used to provide these types of services have still greater variation, there is communality across all such service programs. I use the term "intensive community services" to describe programs with the following characteristics:

1. **The program has a home and/or community-based component:** Not all services provided are office based. Staff routinely visit the homes of participating families or go to schools and other community locations.

2. **More than one unit of service is provided each week:** Multiple services or multiple units of single services are provided each week. The treatment approach is multimodal.

3. **The selection of services is intended to be flexible and individualized:** Different children and families receive different con-

stellations of the available service array. Although this intention to
individualize is not always met, the program design builds in flexibility and individualization of the service plan. There is an explicit
effort to avoid the Colonel Sanders Syndrome.

4. **Program eligibility explicitly directs serving children who
   would otherwise be served in hospitals or residential treatment
   programs:** These programs are generally expensive compared with
   other ambulatory treatment and inexpensive compared with long-
   term hospitalization or residential treatment. The cost of the program is justified by reducing or preventing expenditures on even
   more expensive service approaches.

5. **The array of services provided in these programs do not fit into
   traditional health services:** Financing models based on the health
   insurance model are problematic. Medicaid waivers are generally
   necessary for Medicaid to be a part of the funding stream for these
   programs.

Often these programs include efforts to pull together multiple
child-serving agencies into the funding and/or management of the
service. Sometimes funding for these programs will be blended from
child welfare, mental health, and juvenile justice sources. Occasionally,
school districts will participate as well. Even more rarely, agencies
that fund services for children with developmental disabilities will
participate. It is not uncommon for intensive community services to
not only be innovative in terms of program design, but also in terms
of organization and financing. This inventiveness complicates the
interpretation of evaluation data. Many things are going on simultaneously in the types of systems changes usually associated with these
types of services.

Substance Abuse Mental Health Services Administration (SAMHSA)
has funded a significant number of demonstration sites around
the country to stimulate the development of these services. These
SAMHSA site projects have only a five-year funding and, although
many of the originally funded sites have not proved to be sustainable
after federal funding runs out, other sites have successfully gained
traction and continue to provide services after the five-year start-up
funding.

Within the general definition of intensive community services, there
are a number of "name brand" treatment approaches. Perhaps the best
known of these is Multisystemic Treatment (MST; Henggeler et al.,
1997). As mentioned in chapter 1, MST is clearly an evidence-based
practice for delinquent youth; however, it is also a product. As such,

you cannot provide MST unless you have paid for the rights to it. To purchase the rights to provide MST generally requires hiring the company that provides the quality-assurance technology, to ensure that the treatment model is appropriately implemented. I once asked Scott Henggeler about this business strategy. His explanation was that because it was clear from the existing science that MST could be effective with a population of youth often thought of as "untreatable" (e.g., those with conduct disorder), it was his responsibility to ensure that any one claiming to provide this treatment was actually engaged in MST and not just calling what they do by that name. Thus, providing oversight and quality assurance was a means of maintaining the fidelity of the treatment approach.

There is a lot to be said for this argument. As discussed in chapter 2 (the Rose Reversal Syndrome), it is not uncommon for people to continue doing what they've always done, and just call it whatever is seen as the best practice of the moment. I have talked to several residential treatment center directors who claim that they provide "wraparound services" in their facilities. Review of the principles of wraparound in chapter 1 should make it clear that doing so would be impossible. In many ways, the MST model—with its strong quality assurance component—is one of the better examples of what might be considered something close to a full implementation of the TCOM approach. In general, the outcomes goals for intensive community treatment should be broad and include symptom relief, risk reduction, functional improvement, and improvement in family functioning and caregiver capacity. Returning the child to a pathway of healthy development would be the overarching outcome objective.

Mentoring

A key component of intensive community services, mentoring services have grown dramatically in popularity over the past several decades. It was difficult to decide whether to place mentoring in this chapter or in chapter 4, because it could easily be considered a form of community development. However, because individuals are now paid to mentor or at least to run mentoring programs staffed with volunteers, this service has become a component of the existing system of care. Mentoring programs certainly do not have the financial and political clout of hospitals, residential treatment programs, or even outpatient clinics; however, they hold a potentially important place in a system of care that attempts to keep high-need children at home, in school, and out of trouble (Rosenblatt, 1993).

There are a variety of mentoring models worthy of discussion; however, there are also some programs that appear to essentially pay mentors to "hang out" with identified kids. These undirected programs rely entirely on the good sense of their mentors. Although people willing to mentor youth with emotional and behavioral challenges are noble whether they are volunteers or paid employees, it is not a good idea to simply rely on their goodness as a program policy. A structured mentoring model that provides a framework for the nature, goals, and objectives of this work should be the program standard. This model should provide a framework for training new mentors and monitoring the efforts of all mentors working in the program.

An interesting model of mentoring that I have had the pleasure of studying is the Talks Mentoring Program based in Champaign, Illinois. Developed by Reverend Harold Davis and his wife Dr. Ollie Watts Davis, the Talks Mentoring Model is based on books written for mentoring boys (*Talks My Father Never Had With Me*, written by the Reverend Davis, 2000) and mentoring girls (*Talks My Mother Never Had With Me*, written by Dr. Davis, 2000). In these straightforward and well-written books, the mentoring approach is laid out for mentors to understand and easily adopt for use with children. For example, in *Talks My Mother Never Had With Me*, Dr. Davis lays out three simple facts about teachers:

1. They want to teach.
2. They want for you to learn.
3. They have a lot to offer you.

As a school-based program, these simple truths provide the mentor with a framework to communicate with youth about working through their relationships with their teachers. In an interesting innovation, the Talks Program operates by selecting three students for each mentor group. The teacher guides the selection of students so that the constellation of the group contains one excellent student, one average student, and one student who is experiencing difficulties. The mentor group is referred to as a "leadership group" to reduce any stigma that might be associated with being singled out for participation. With the mentor and two good to average students, the student struggling with emotional or behavioral problems is not placed with other youth with similar problems. Thus, the types of contagion effects discussed earlier may be avoided.

The decision support and outcomes associated with mentoring services are not well developed. It seems likely that the characteristics of a child or youth who could benefit from a mentoring relationship would involve either deficits in parental relations (e.g., an absent father) or limitations in interpersonal functioning (e.g., no friends). Social and relationship functioning would seem to be key outcomes.

Respite

Intensive community treatment plans often include respite services. Although little empirical research has been undertaken that demonstrates the effectiveness of this service, consumer satisfaction data and focus group results point to this service as a key to maintaining high-need, challenging children at home and in their communities.

There are two types of respite service—crisis and planned. Crisis respite involves short-term housing for youth so that they can ride out a crisis and return home. New Jersey has a crisis housing component in their Mobile Response Program. Early data suggests that youth who utilize this service have disruptive behavior problems, but are not necessarily engaging in a great deal of high-risk behavior. They often have caregivers who are struggling with their capacity to parent. Thus, the crisis respite service serves both the child and parent, but provides a safe separation so that problems can be worked out without requiring a long-term or permanent separation.

Planned respite is conceptually similar to baby-sitting, except that the respite worker has greater expectations placed on them because the needs of the child are generally greater than typical needs. However, planned respite represents a time in which parents of high-need children know that the child is safe and cared for appropriately. This gives the parent some free time away from taking care of his or her children to take care of personal business or just relax.

Use of respite likely does not require a decision support model, but should be managed within the framework of child–family team planning within intensive community treatment programs. In terms of outcomes monitoring, the primary outcomes may be satisfaction with the respite worker by both parent and child and duration of community tenure by the child.

Decision support and outcomes associated with the use of respite are not well developed. It would seem logical that respite would be indicated based more on caregiver needs or a combination of disruptive or difficult behavior problems and caregiver needs. The primary outcome would be sustaining the community placement, although this is a complicated outcome that would have other factors influencing it. Caregiver burden would be an outcome more closely tied to the respite intervention.

Summary

Despite the current problems, it is clear that assets exist in the current public mental health system that can be brought to bear on an evolving system committed to accessibility and effectiveness. In fact, all of the existing components serve important roles in such a system.

CHAPTER 7

CREATING SOLUTIONS ACROSS THE SYSTEM OF CARE

Total Clinical Outcomes Management (TCOM) only identifies the directions in which the children's system of care must move. This is a critical, but insufficient, part of the process of repairing our children's public mental health system. Getting change to occur is, of course, much more difficult than is simply knowing the right direction. The focus of this chapter is on strategies that can be used to generate system change.

Planned Incrementalism

Over the past 20 years of working in public sector service systems, I have become a firm believer in the concept of "planned incrementalism." The concept is that permanent change is extremely hard and best accomplished in small steps. Once you have a vision of the direction you want to go, the journey is best accomplished one step at a time. Sweeping changes have a certain popular, and, therefore, political appeal. Sadly the history of sweeping changes is often fraught with poor outcomes, untoward consequences, and significant chaos during the course of the change. Change in small steps is not very "sexy," and thus not very appealing within the short time frames of political cycles. However, if you can think of each step as a successful change, then you have far more positive experiences using this approach.

The main challenge with planned incrementalism is that not only do you have to establish a vision for the distant future, but you also have to establish a series of steps that must be accomplished in order to reach the vision. These steps must be feasible and take the system in the desired direction, setting the stage for the next step.

An example of planned incrementalism, mentioned briefly in chapter 5, has been the evolution of the use of decision support criteria in crisis assessments for child welfare in Illinois. The first step was to select a tool to support good crisis assessment. In Illinois, this program is called Screening and Support Services (SASS). We had developed the Childhood Severity of Psychiatric Illness (CSPI; Lyons, 1998) for a reform of the use of residential services, but felt that it would be a good predictor of appropriate decisions with regard to the use of psychiatric hospitalization. We tested the CSPI with a sample of SASS cases using a case review method (Lyons, Kisiel, Dulcan, Cohen, & Chesler, 1997). In this review, we established a relationship between CSPI scores and hospital versus deflection decisions. We shared these findings with agency and program leadership as a way of demonstrating the potential utility of the CSPI to gain "buy in" for implementing the tool.

In the next year, we had the 32 SASS agencies around the state complete the tool at the time of screening and send in the data. We did no quality control and did not even monitor the percentage of cases for which completed forms were sent in. However, using this first set of data, we tested a decision support algorithm to give crisis workers and their supervisors feedback on their decision making. This data replicated what we had found in the retrospective chart review. At this point, about 70 percent of hospital/deflection decisions were predicted by the key items of the CSPI.

Our next step was to begin to give feedback to crisis workers and programs with regard to their decision making. We did this in two ways. For crisis workers, we identified individual children who were either hospitalized when they were predicted to be deflected (low-risk admission) or deflected when they were predicted to be hospitalized (high-risk deflection). We asked them to get back to us to explain what the circumstances were in each identified case that led to their decision. For programs, we gave them their program rates of low-risk admissions and high-risk deflections.

The initial reaction to this feedback was what you might expect if you are cynical and have worked in the system for a long time. A number of workers made the conclusion that they needed to "fill out the form" differently. Therefore, the initial response to feedback was that they had to do a better job of "gaming" the paperwork so that they didn't get caught. This reaction, of course, is entirely at odds with the goal of the project, which was simply to ensure that children in state custody got the level of care they needed at times of crisis.

We addressed this problem in two ways. First, we reassured programs and workers that no sanctions would result from "wrong" decisions. We repeated that we were all just trying to learn together about how to best serve children. We also implemented an audit. Because we used the CSPI and it is an information integration tool, it could be completed using existing case records. Therefore, we randomly sampled cases from each agency and redid the CSPI based on medical records and compared that CSPI to the one turned in.

What we found was that, for the most part, people were quite reliable. The statewide average was about 0.70, which is good (Lyons, Rawal, Yeh, Leon, & Tracy, 2002). However, we found several agencies with horrible reliability. In fact, one agency scored a 0.00, which takes some doing, because the CSPI is pretty simple to use. What had happened in this case was that the agency had experienced more than 100 percent turnover of program leadership and staff. They had lost the manuals to the CSPI and were just filling out the forms and sending them in without even knowing what they were supposed to mean. The consequence for this agency was training. It turns out that training is a powerful disincentive for unreliability. At the next audit, this agency (and all other agencies) achieved adequate reliability.

We are now in the fifth year of the project; the fourth in which feedback has been given. As mentioned in chapter 5, the CSPI now reliably predicts about 80 percent of hospital/deflection decisions. The improvement in accuracy has resulted primarily in a reduction in the number of minorities (e.g., African American and Hispanic people) who were low-risk admission (Rawal, Romansky, & Lyons, 2003). Over the course of the feedback process, the proportion of hospital admissions that were low risk was reduced dramatically for minority children. Without ever telling anyone what to do on a given case, by focusing on the clinical characteristics that should inform decision making, other factors (e.g., race) that should not influence this decision, fade in importance.

Incremental Implementation of TCOM

With the implementation of outcomes measures, it is necessary to take an incremental, "go-slow" approach. I like to think of a three-phase model that can consist of multiple subphases. The first phase is the *Exposure Phase*. In this phase, the options for tools are presented and discussed, and partner buy-in is secured to the greatest extent possible. This is the phase in which everyone is given an opportunity to voice issues and concerns. Observations of prior experiences are noted. The planning process should be inclusive without becoming out of control, which takes strong but flexible leadership. Staying on course with an open process is a fairly difficult process to manage. People with primary data or evaluation skills are often not equipped with the interpersonal skills necessary to pull this off. It is essential to not appear imperial while still exercising some level of control. My strategy has been to get agreement on the basic structure of the tools immediately and allow the dialog to involve precisely which items should be included in the tools rather than which tools to choose, what method to use, or any more fundamental discussion. This strategy provides structure that can help to guarantee closure to the process while still maintaining an opportunity to demonstrate that partners' suggestions are heard. In addition, leeway can be given with regard to the specific strategies for implementation. Allowing flexibility with implementation is anathema to most research models of measurement. However, a robust, communications-based assessment process can be quite flexible in this regard, without suffering significant reliability or validity problems.

The second phase is the *Initial Use Phase*. In this phase, the tools are implemented, but the results of the tools are not immediately utilized for planning or decision-making processes. Partners in the system become familiar with the assessment tools and gain experiences that inform them of the value and potential local applications of the tools. In addition, because nothing immediately happens as the result of the findings on the tool, the rush to learning to "game" the tools is slowed. As mentioned in chapter 2, there is a long history in behavioral health of using clinical assessments to advocate for single cases (e.g., pick the diagnosis that is least stigmatizing and most likely to result in reimbursement). For TCOM to be successful, it is critical to eliminate this syndrome. Getting partners familiar with a tool without consequences helps in that process, at least initially.

The third phase is the *Full Use Phase*. This is the vision of TCOM as described in chapter 5. At this point, the outcomes tools are fully and reliably implemented. They matter in all aspects of the management of the system, from individual children and families to statewide systems administration and planning. They may be tied to performance contracting when appropriate.

Mark O'Donnel, the director of several Substance Abuse Mental Health Services Administration (SAMHSA) system-of-care projects in North Carolina, describes managing change as similar to orchestrating a jazz song. First, you have to establish a melody. You introduce each of the different musicians who play different instruments, but all follow the basic melody with slight deviations along the way. Periodically, you have somewhat unpredictable periods of wild improvisation, but you also try to return to the melody. The song lasts a very long time. In fact, Dr. O'Donnel and many other experts in this type of work describe system development as a 20- to 30-year commitment. It may take a decade before dramatic impact of change processes can be experienced and stabilized.

Enhancing Family Involvement

As discussed in chapter 4, one of the key visions for evolving the children's mental health system is to create an environment in which families are maximally involved in the system of care. Given the individuality and nuances of family involvement, there likely is no one model for how to involve families. However, Barbara Huff of the Federation of Families has identified the key principles of family involvement (Table 7.1). There are several overarching concepts to these principles. First, families define themselves; they are not defined by expert opinion. Second, families are full partners with professionals in the process of planning and delivering care. This is true at the level of the individual family, a program, and a system of care. Third, families must be supported in forming and maintaining advocacy organizations.

Probably the most difficult of these principles to implement is number 5—sharing power. At times, professionals are able to eloquently express the ideals of family involvement, but when it comes time for families to exercise some control over the service-planning process or policies and procedures, resistance arises. Power must be shared at each of the levels of the system—the individual family, the program/agency, and the system of care. Power at the individual family level is probably the easiest, because it primarily involves respecting the family's perspective and empowering each member to share responsibility for decisions and outcomes. Sharing power at the program/agency level requires family representatives to be integrated into the agency's

Table 7.1
Principles of Family Involvement

---

1. Families define themselves and their own culture.

2. Families have their basic needs met.

3. Families have access information and training.

4. Families identify priorities and concerns to drive policy and practice.

5. Families share decision-making authority and responsibility for outcomes.

6. Families and system partners know their individual strengths, limitations, and fears.

7. Families have their own independent organizations to speak with a collective voice for system change.

8. Families and their organizations get both respect and protection from their system partners.

Source: Adapted from Barbara Huff, Federation of Families, presented to the Louis de la Parte Florida Mental Health Institute annual research conference in 2002.

policy and planning functions. This takes a significant commitment from agency leadership and management. Sharing power at the system level requires addressing the seventh and eighth principles—only through a strong family organization can families effectively become involved in system-level planning, policy, and management.

There are some appealing approaches that have been used around the country to enhance family involvement. These approaches tend to address some, but not all, of the principles in Table 7.1. One approach that addresses at least the first four principles is the use of a parent liaison as the initial access person to community-based services. In this approach, a parent of a child with serious emotional or behavioral difficulties is trained to meet with the family initially. In some models, these trained parents complete the CANS with the new family in order to provide the family with an assessment that will give them access to the language and the approach that professionals will use in the assessment of their child. Thus, the parent liaison works to help the family understand what the processes of service receipt involve and prepare them for understanding the needs and strengths of their child in preparation for working with professionals to meet these needs. Parents in Allegheny County, Pennsylvania, worked with me to develop a family-friendly interview version of the CANS, which is available for free.

The Inside/Out to Outside/In Strategy

One strategy that can be used to generate change in these environments could be called an inside/out to outside/in approach. The basic idea is that rapid change is best accomplished outside of large bureaucracies, particularly those that have a large number of staff who are resisting change. Smaller "outside" organizations can be staffed with eager-adopter types, who can work quickly and effectively to design and implement a vision (inside/out). However, the types of people and organizations who can do this rapid response and implementation are not ideally suited for sustaining a change over a long period of time—a function that is, in fact, the expertise of the permanent bureaucracy. Thus, once the change has been "institutionalized" in a system, managing that new process can be returned to the bureaucracy (outside/in). The basic strategy, therefore, is to design and implement the strategy outside of the organization and then over time move the implementation of the strategy back into the organization.

Some Rules of Engagement

The Howard Rule—Accept the Fact that There Will Always Be Problems with Any Solution

Ken Howard was one of the pioneers of outcomes management in psychotherapy. He also was an interesting thinker. Just before he died, he claimed that he had invented a new therapy—soros distribution therapy. The idea behind his approach was that we all have our worries and anxiety (thus "soros," which roughly translated from Yiddish would be "sorrows"). Problems, in Ken's theory, would occur when all of your worries get focused on a single thing. Soros distribution therapy would attempt to spread these worries across all life domains. Therefore, if someone came into therapy worried about their relationship with their spouse, the soros distributive therapist would say "What? Your job is going all that well? What about your kids? Wasn't your son recently arrested?" The theory behind this therapy is that you cannot worry as much about your marriage if you've got problems at work and with your kids. You've only got so many worries to go around.

The same phenomenon can happen in change processes. All the energy of individuals or even organizations can get tied up into one crisis. This focus can slow, sabotage, or even derail a change process. There will always be problems; therefore you need to focus on the things you can do and not get paralyzed by the things you cannot do.

The Shallcross Rule: Process Can Be As Important As Product

A friend and colleague, Harry Shallcross, is a master at managing process. This is an unusual, and often unappreciated, art. Most people focus rather exclusively on products. Unfortunately, a failure to recognize the importance of process can impede the creation of products. Learning to pay attention to process is a critical skill, because changing organizations and systems is more of a process than a product. There are products along the way, but they only make sense within the context of the change process.

The Sudekom Rule: Don't Do Anything Part Way—Do It All the Way or Don't Do It at All

I have a friend who is a lawyer and a fitness aficionado. At our Christmas party, we were discussing a variety of things, including his penchant for cycling and investment strategies during recent stock market woes. My friend, Rick Sudekom (hence the name of the rule) said that it was his belief that it was not a very good idea to do anything unless you were going to do it "all out—fully and completely." In other words, he would not consider "dabbling in the stock market"—either learn it and stay on top of it, or don't even go there. He has the same belief about cycling—take it seriously or don't do it; doing it halfway just risks that you'll get injured.

I'm not sure whether I've personally followed the Sudekom Rule, but it seems like a profoundly good idea. It's implications for the children's mental health service system are far reaching. States come up with the new best thing nearly every year and put out requests for proposals from providers who are interested in providing these new services. Agencies that respond with proposals to provide the latest, best new thing likely do themselves and the children they serve a disservice if they do not fully embrace and engage the new service. If the agency is simply seeking to expand their services by capturing whatever new money is available, it may not be particularly effective in delivering the new service.

This will not be a particularly popular rule with large community agencies that have strong grant application-writing abilities. They survive, and sometimes prosper, off of effectively capturing new service dollars whenever available. However, if our focus is on the effectiveness of the system and its component services, it is an exceptionally good idea to ensure that whomever is funded to deliver new services is fully invested in learning the philosophy and strategies involved in their full and effective implementation. This is particularly timely with our interest in evidence-based practices (EBPs). It is not likely to be effective to simply fund agencies to provide these EBPs without a strong emphasis on initial and ongoing training to ensure that all parties can implement the practice and ongoing monitoring of the fidelity with which the practice is implemented.

The Accountability Matrix

A key principle of outcomes management is accountability. However, traditional notions of accountability tend to be linear and unidirectional. For example, a provider is accountable to the third-party payor. This linear thinking is somewhat naive in the complex public system of care for children. There is no hierarchy to the system; thus, hierarchical thinking creates some of the syndromes described in chapter 2 (e.g., the Imperialism Syndrome)

Within the concept of total clinical outcomes management, accountability should be thought of as nonlinear and multidirectional. In the children's system of care, accountability is a matrix of interlocking relationships in which the actions of one party impact the reactions of multiple other parties simultaneously. Thus, all partners are accountable to all other partners, but in complex and interlocking ways. For example, at minimum, the following accountability relationships exist:

> The provider is accountable to the recipient and his or her family to be respectful, thorough, offer informed choices, and provide high-quality treatment with the best opportunity for success.

> The recipient and his or her family is accountable to the provider to be honest and open to the fullest degree possible and to follow through on attending agreed-on scheduled meetings and treatment sessions.

> The provider is accountable to the third-party payer to provide timely and effective treatment at a reasonable cost.

> The third-party payer is accountable to the provider to pay for treatment in a timely fashion at a reasonable rate.

As you consider the relational complexity of the system of care, the range of accountability broadens.

> Schools are accountable to parents and children to identify behavioral health problems when they occur, and either address them directly or refer the child and family to appropriate services.
>
> Parents and children are accountable to the schools to address identified behavioral health problems by following through on referrals or supporting direct interventions.
>
> Schools are accountable to behavioral health providers to supply relevant information about the child's school-related needs and to participate in any consensually determined interventions that involve in-school behavior.
>
> Behavioral health providers are accountable to schools to maintain communication about the treatment of school-related behavior problems and collaborate in the planning of interventions that are intended to impact these behaviors.

The same patterns of accountability can be observed among juvenile justice and child welfare systems, children and families, and behavioral health providers.

> Probation officers are accountable to the courts to ensure that the youth is monitored to ensure compliance with court orders.
>
> The youth is accountable to the probation officers to participate in court-ordered activities.
>
> The probation officers are also accountable to behavioral health providers to support adherence to court-ordered treatments.
>
> Behavioral health care providers are accountable to the probation officers to also support adherence to court-ordered treatments.
>
> Providers are also accountable to the courts to provide timely and effective services.

Even the juvenile judges are accountable:

> Because the court does not generally pay for the services it mandates, the presiding judge is accountable to the payer not to order inappropriate services that are unlikely to benefit the youth.
>
> The court is accountable to the general public to maintain community safety.
>
> The court is accountable to the youth to understand each youth's circumstances and to order treatments that are consistent with the

youth's actual needs and likely to benefit either the youth or the community.

Rethinking accountability into a matrix of relationships has a number of positive effects. First, it makes clear that straightforward definitions of responsibility are necessary to manage complex systems. In fact, as a team-building process, it can be useful for system partners to clarify their accountability relationships together. Second, matrix accountability is another reason why it does not make sense for oversight authorities such as states and counties to engage in direct service provision. These dual roles weaken the accountability matrix. Third, this concept of accountability emphasizes the importance of all partners having equal voice in a system. A partner (e.g., families) with limited or no voice cannot manage the accountability in relationships. Voice is a necessary, although insufficient, requirement for leveraging a system. There is no opportunity to leverage a system without voice.

Leveraging System Evolution

There are essentially four mechanisms by which a system of care is managed. Financial mechanisms involve lining up the dollars to support the vision of the system. Regulatory mechanisms involve establishing the rule to encourage compliance to the vision. Charismatic mechanisms require the leadership of a strong personality who generates a following to lead the system partners into the vision. Lastly, moral mechanisms call system partners to the higher shared purpose of doing the right things for children and families. Of course, having all four of the mechanisms lined up to the same vision is the ideal. Realistically, however, any locale probably only has one or two of these mechanisms available at a given time.

Financial Mechanisms

Lenin said, "follow the money." Jenrette said, "money talks." Politicians for centuries have been aware of the power of money. We also know that funding mechanisms have significant impact on service access and use (LoSasso & Lyons, 2002; Taube, Kessler, & Burns, 1986). Therefore, one of the most powerful mechanisms of managing the public mental health service system is through the management of funding mechanisms. However, creative funding mechanisms can be fraught with the danger of untoward consequences. We recently experienced a classic example of this in an innovative program that was intended to link youth with psychiatric disorders who were in juvenile detention facilities to community mental health treatment—the Mental Health Juvenile Justice (MH-JJ) initiative described in chapter 5.

There are 16 programs in the state to correspond to each of the existing juvenile detention centers. However, the programs are based in community mental health agencies. In addition to funding for a liaison and supervisor, the program provides $50,000 per year in flexible funding. The program design intended for these funds to be used as needed to provide services or things to youth based on need that would otherwise not be possible for the youth to secure. For example, if a youth needed glasses, the agency could tap into flex dollars to pay for an eye examine and a pair of eyeglasses. The potential examples of possible good uses for these dollars are endless.

In the first two and one-half years of the program, only a very small amount of the flex dollars had been spent, less than 10 percent. This problem is a classic example of the law of untoward consequences. In Illinois, the state has worked to try to keep dollars that are committed to mental health in the mental health service system. Thus, funds not expended within the program lapse are returned to providers so that they do not end up in the general state fund. Because the annual contracting process often takes a good part of each year before dollars can actually change hands between the state and the funded agencies, it is sometimes hard to expend all the money on a designated contract. In other words, there is often a substantial amount of lapsed funds.

In the MH-JJ initiative with the flex dollars, if a liaison fails to spend these dollars on the youth in the program, the money reverts back to the agency for its own uses. This system, although well intended, places the liaison in a conflict-of-interest position between the needs of the youth and those of his or her own agencies. Although $1,000 per youth is budgeted for flex dollars, several liaisons have reported that their agencies have placed much lower caps on their spending—about $300 per youth. Therefore, the MH-JJ program model is compromised and youth do not get the resources that are designated for them.

Regulatory Mechanisms

There are thousands of pages of regulations that influence the delivery of children's mental health services. There are separate regulations involving reimbursement from Medicaid, funding from other state agencies, confidentiality of records, use of restraints, and accessibility of services, just to name a few. Medicaid is a good example. Funding from Medicaid comes from three sources—the federal government, a state match, and a local match. There are rules by which each of these three governmental entities participates in the match, there are rules by which any particular child may be eligible for Medicaid funding, and there are rules for every provider about what services provided within what context are reimbursable through Medicaid. In addition, all of these rules are changing every year.

There are two levels to thinking about regulatory mechanisms for system evolution. The first level is the law. Laws are passed by Congress, state legislatures, or local governments. Laws define the broad parameters for expected behaviors of citizens and organizations. Legislation is also used to fund particular types of programs and/or initiatives.

The second level of regulation involves how laws are implemented. Within the framework of existing laws and legislation are the rules established by the agencies with responsibility for executing laws. These rules are what most people think of when they consider regulations. However, it is critical to remember that regulatory change can occur either through new laws/legislation or through rule changes within existing laws/legislation. Equally important to remember is that change can be thwarted in either of these ways, as well.

Writing good law is difficult; wording is everything in order to ensure that the intent of the law can be implemented effectively. Good advocacy does not just mean convincing legislators to pass a law; it includes assisting them in drafting it.

Charismatic Mechanisms

In social services in general, and community mental health in particular, there is a history of charismatic leadership at the local level. As discussed in chapter 1, mental health services in the United States have evolved as a cottage industry, with many providers springing up in an unorganized fashion to address perceived needs of potential customers. It is not uncommon for the most successful of these agencies to have a founding director who is charismatic.

Webster's second definition of charisma is "a personal magic of leadership arousing special popular loyalty or enthusiasm for a public figure (as a political leader), a special magnetic charm or appeal." It is quite likely that charisma is a gift, not a skill (Popper, 2003). As such, it is probably not something that a potential leader can develop.

Although some charismatic communication training has been developed in business schools (e.g., Towler, 2003), in all likelihood, you cannot expect a continuing education workshop on "Developing Charisma" to be successful. You have either got charisma or you don't. Because this leadership style is a trait of an individual person and likely cannot be developed, if this is the only available mechanism for leveraging change in a system, a great deal of care must go into the selection of individuals for leadership positions.

On the other hand, I do think that there are a number of potentially charismatic individuals whose charisma is blocked by anxiety and a lack of self-confidence. Thus, although it is likely that you can't simply become charismatic, you can maximize the charisma that you have by being confident, relaxed, and enthusiastic.

Charismatic Approaches beyond Leadership

Charisma is a primary characteristic of leadership. Classically, to have charismatic change, it is necessary to have a charismatic leader. Ideally, this leader is able to generate a following within his or her organization and to generate support outside of the organization. However, there are other aspects of this form of leverage system change. Nonleadership approaches to charismatic change are really a matter of generating enthusiasm.

In order to think about how to generate enthusiasm for any system change, it is necessary to consider the characteristics of the organization (Glisson, 2002; Glisson & James, 2002). Four concepts from organizational development are important to consider: climate, culture, structure, and readiness to change.

Organizational climate describes the shared perceptions of employees about their work environment (Jones & James, 1979). An overall positive attitude among workers about the nature and impact of their work is a goal of healthy organizational development (Brown & Leigh, 1996; Glisson & James, 2002). Charismatic approaches within the ranks of employees can facilitate these positive attitudes. Feedback of successful outcomes and concomitant recognition for these efforts also can improve the organizational climate.

Organizational culture is a deeper construct that has been defined as the normative beliefs and shared behavior expectations of an organization or work unit. From these beliefs and expectations, a guiding framework is created that explicates the priorities of the organization (Cooke & Szumal, 1993). Creating an organizational culture in support of change is more difficult and it may be that ideological leadership, rather than charismatic leadership, is more likely to be effective in evolving organizational culture (Strange & Mumford, 2002).

The organizational structure is the formal design of relationships within an organization. This can have major impact on climate and culture. Clear lines of authority and responsibility are helpful. Delegation of responsibility throughout the organization facilitates involvement of employees. Organizational structures also can be used to place charismatic employees in positions of greater influence.

Finally, there has been recent interest in the concept of an organization's readiness to change (e.g., Berland, 2003; Simpson & Brown, 2002). Some organizations appear more adept at adapting to changing circumstances than do others. Characteristics associated with greater readiness to change are not well understood and it may be that this construct is mediated by the other three—climate, culture, and structure.

One of the major problems with the public mental health system is that with civil service regulations, job sanctions are difficult and dismissal is extremely rare. In my experience with large public agencies, it is often the case that a small number of competent individuals do the majority of the work. Over time, these individuals inherit more and more responsibility as the system responds to work around the less-competent (or at least less-motivated) employees who do not get work done. The hard-working employees become overwhelmed and burned out or leave public service for more rewarding work elsewhere. This can leave a permanent bureaucracy staffed primarily by less-motivated, less-competent staff. Large public agencies often have an overrepresentation of "resisters" in their ranks (Rosen & Weil, 1996). This makes change more difficult in these environments. Elsewhere, we have talked of the disadvantages of the political cycle on continuity; however, one of the great advantages of the political cycle is that it periodically forces an influx of new enthusiasm into state bureaucracies.

Moral Mechanisms

Change strategies that base their energy and leverage on "doing the right thing" can be considered moral mechanisms of change. There are at least three basic types of moral mechanisms for system evolution: crisis management, litigation, and outcomes management.

Crisis Management

Periodically, really bad things happen. When bad things happen to children, it is particularly tragic. The reactions to tragedy often mirror the stages of grieving. First, there is shock and horror. However, not far on the heals of the horror is a healthy dose of anger. Particularly in situations with substantial media coverage, this anger can be intense and powerful. Usually, it starts at the original source of the bad event, then it quickly moves to the people and institutions that are intended to protect children from bad things happening. Although it is the natural human response of people, agencies, and institutions who are caught in the "crosshairs" of intense public anger to protect themselves, this anger is actually a notable opportunity to leverage system change.

Below is the Chinese spelling of "crisis." The Chinese have an instructive conceptualization of crisis. Because the Chinese "alphabet" is actually a collection of symbols, each with their own meaning, complex concepts are generated with multiple symbols. For "crisis," the Chinese use the symbols for "danger" and "opportunity." Thus, when bad things happen, danger is involved; however, there also is an opportunity that arises from all such events.

危 机

Litigation

The United States is the most litigious society in the world. As the host used to say in the original courtroom series, "The People's Court," "When you feel like you've been wronged, don't take it in your own hands. Take it to court." In the United States, people take things to court in record numbers. The court plays an important role in the children's mental health service system as well.

The court has a rather interesting and complex role in children's services in general. Although many times state agencies do not want to be sued, there are times when state agencies are actually pleased to be sued and may even work behind the scenes to encourage advocacy groups to sue. The reason for this is that state agencies have complex relationships with the rest of state government. The governor's office dictates policy, and the legislature develops the budget. If you can obtain a consent decree from a judge that forces certain desirable actions, then regardless of large "P" (i.e., Democrat, Republican) and small "p" politics, it has to get done. As such, consent decrees and other judicial orders can create powerful leverage "to do the right thing" in state governments. One might be tempted to call this the B'rer Rabbit

Syndrome (i.e., "Please don't throw me in the briar patch"), except that it does not fit the criteria for a syndrome. Sometimes litigation is extremely helpful for pushing needed reforms through. It is, however, expensive and can have unintended consequences. A consent decree on the Illinois Department of Children and Family Services in the 1980s forced the rapid hiring of unqualified case managers. It was not until the late 1990s that this was rectified by developing a new regulation requiring all case managers to have at least a Master's degree.

Outcomes Management

As discussed in the previous chapter, the existing mental health and social service system for children and families has many strengths that can be elicited to help evolve a system of care. First among these strengths is that the vast majority of people in this field got into their work because they wanted to help children and families. Almost nobody goes into mental health or social service to make money. Comparison of salaries with nearly any other enterprise will quickly confirm this observation. There are many careers that pay much better than does public mental health. Even middle-management positions are well behind, relative to other careers. It may be only the chief executive officers of large agencies who garner wages that are competitive with peers in other fields, and even these salaries cannot compete with the chief executives of large corporations. Thus, people are often called to this work for other reasons. Sometimes people enter the field of mental health because of their own experiences as service recipients or because of their own needs relative to their relationships to other people. However, most people enter social service careers out of a noble goal of pubic service. They join in order to help.

The fact that there is a shared vision of helping children that is common to nearly everyone in the system provides a critical opportunity for leveraging system change. TCOM, in fact, is a moral mechanism for change. Any changes that are justified based on a clear benefit to children and families are far easier to implement across the board than are any other changes. Identifying the "right thing to do" is the moral mechanism for change.

Creating a Learning Organization Culture

Peter Senge (1990), in his seminal text on how to create an organizational cultural that can learn from its own experiences to become more effective and innovative, describes the Laws of the Fifth Discipline:

1. Today's problems come from yesterday's solutions.
2. The harder you push, the harder the system pushes back.
3. Behavior grows worse before it grows better.
4. The easy way out usually leads us back in.
5. The cure can be worse than the disease.
6. Faster is slower.
7. Cause and effect are not closely related in time and space.
8. Small changes can produce big results—but the areas of highest leverage are often the least obvious.
9. You can have your cake and eat it too—but not at once. (Think process.)
10. Dividing an elephant in half does not produce two small elephants.
11. There is no blame.

According to Senge (1990), in order to create the kind of environment that supports effective change, we need to change our mindset. We should not get too caught up in "snapshots" of the current status of things, but instead focus on the process that brought us to where we are and the processes that can move us forward. We should shift from linear notions of causality (this happened because of that) to circular notions of cause and effect—often the effect has a feedback effect to reinforce or alter a prior cause. Awareness of and sensitivity to points of leverage in an organization and a system is fundamental to the effective management of that organization or system. Most of all, we need information so that our thinking is informed by facts, not by opinions or anecdotes. Anecdotes are great for illustrating facts, but they can be very misleading for identifying them.

Positive social change is glacial. We establish a vision and set processes in place to move things to a better place. Often progress is measured in inches. In this regard, we all have a choice. We can each choose to be either the mountain or the ice. Be the ice.

Child and Adolescent Needs and Strengths

An Information Integration Tool for
Children and Adolescents with
Mental Health Challenges
CANS-MH
Manual
Copyright, 1999

The Copyright for the CANS-MH Information Integration Tool is held by the Buddin Praed Foundation to ensure that it remains an open domain tool, free for anyone to use. Information on guidelines for use and development can be obtained by contacting Melanie Buddin Lyons of the Foundation at 847-501-5113 or Mlyons405@aol.com or visit the Web site at www.buddinpraed.org

A large number of individuals have collaborated in the development of the CANS-MH. Along with the CANS versions for developmental disabilities, juvenile justice, and child welfare, this information integration tool is designed to support individual case planning and the planning and evaluation of service systems. The CANS-MH is an open domain tool for use in service delivery systems that address the mental health of children, adolescents and their families. The copyright is held by the Buddin Praed Foundation to ensure that it remains free to use. For specific permission to use please contact Melanie Lyons of the Foundation. For more information on the CANS-MH assessment tool contact:

John S. Lyons, Ph.D.
Mental Health Services and Policy Program
Northwestern University
710 N. Lakeshore Drive, Abbott 1206
Chicago, Illinois 60611
(312) 908-8972
Fax (312) 503-0425
JSL329@northwestern.edu

Eugene Griffin, Ph.D., JD
Illinois Department of Children and Family Services
100 W. Randolph Street, 6th Floor
Chicago, Illinois 60601
(312) 793-2030

Marcia Fazio
Bureau of Children and Families
New York Office of Mental Health
44 Holland Street
Albany, New York 12208
coevmf@omh.state.ny.us

Melanie Buddin Lyons
558 Willow Road
Winnetka, Illinois 60093
(847) 501-5113
Fax (847) 501-5291
Mlyons405@aol.com

Introduction and Method

As children and families seek assistance in addressing problems that arise, the first step of helping involves assessment. A good assessment provides information about service planning and communicates to the larger system of care about the needs and strengths of children and families. We have used a uniform methodological approach to develop assessment tools to guide service delivery for children and adolescents with mental, emotional and behavioral health needs, mental retardation/developmental disabilities, and juvenile justice involvement. The basic approach allows for a series of locally constructed decision support tools that we refer to as the Child & Adolescent Needs and Strengths (CANS-MH).

The background of the CANS comes from our prior work in modeling decision-making for psychiatric services. In order to assess appropriate use of psychiatric hospital and residential treatment services, we developed the Childhood Severity of Psychiatric Illness (CSPI). This measure was developed to assess those dimensions crucial to good clinical decision-making for expensive mental health service interventions. We have demonstrated its utility in reforming decision making for residential treatment (Lyons, Mintzer, Kisiel, & Shallcross, 1998) and for quality improvement in crisis assessment services (Lyons, Kisiel, Dulcan, Cohen, & Chesler, 1997; Leon, Lyons, Uziel-Miller, & Tracy, 1998). The strength of the measurement approach has been that it is face valid and easy-to-use, yet provides comprehensive information regarding the clinical status of the child or youth.

The CANS-MH builds on the methodological approach for the CSPI but expands the assessment to include a broader conceptualization of needs and the addition of an assessment of strengths. It is a tool developed to assist in the management and planning of services to children and adolescents and their families with the primary objectives of permanency, safety, and improved quality of life. The CANS is designed for use at two levels—for the individual child and family and for the system of care. The CANS provides a structured assessment of children along a set of dimensions relevant to service planning and decision-making. Also, the CANS provides information regarding the child and family's service needs for use during system planning and/or quality assurance monitoring. Due to its modular design the tool can be adapted for local applications without jeopardizing its psychometric properties.

The CANS-MH is designed to be used either as a *prospective* assessment tool for decision support during the process of planning services or as a *retrospective* assessment tool based on the review of existing information for use in the design of high quality systems of services. This flexibility allows for a variety of innovative applications.

As a *prospective* assessment tool, the CANS-MH provides a structured assessment of children with mental health challenges along a set of dimensions relevant to case service decision-making. The CANS-MH provides information regarding the service needs of the child and their family for use during the development of the individual plan of care. The assessment tool helps to structure the staffing process in *strengths-based* terms for the care manager and the family.

As *a retrospective* assessment tool, the CANS-MH provides an assessment of the children and adolescents currently in care and the functioning of the current system in relation to the needs and strengths of the child and family. It clearly points out "service gaps" in the current services system. This information can then be used to design and develop the community-based, family-focused system of services appropriate for the target population and the community. Retrospective review of prospectively completed CANS allows for a form of measurement audit to facilitate the reliability and accuracy of information (Lyons, Rawal, Yeh, Leon, & Tracy, 2002).

In addition, the CANS-MH assessment tool can be used by care coordinators and supervisors as a quality assurance/monitoring device. A review of the case record in light of the CANS-MH assessment tool will provide information as to the appropriateness of the individual plan of care and whether individual goals and outcomes are achieved.

The dimensions and objective anchors used in the CANS-MH were developed by focus groups with a variety of participants including families, family advocates, representatives of the provider community, mental health case workers and staff. The CANS measure is then seen predominantly as a communication strategy. Testing of the reliability of the CANS in its applications for developmental disabilities and mental health indicate that this measurement approach can be used reliably by trained professionals and family advocates.

Reliability

A number of reliability studies have been accomplished using the CANS-MH including studies with a variety of practitioners and researchers. A total sample of more than 300 subjects have been included in these reliability studies. When clinical vignettes are used as the source of ratings, the average reliability across studies is 0.74. When case records or current cases are used as the source of ratings, the average reliability across studies is 0.85. In a study in Iowa, the reliability of individual items was assessed between clinicians and researchers. The average reliability of individual items of the CANS-MH was 0.73 across 40 cases. A number of different types of individual have been trained to use the CANS-MH reliably including mental health providers, child welfare case workers, probation officers, and family advocates (parents of children with difficulties). A minimum of a bachelor's degree with some training or experience with mental health is needed to use the CANS-MH reliably after training.

Validity

The validity of the CANS-MH has been studied in a variety of ways. In a study in Allegheny County, Pennsylvania, the CANS was found to be significantly correlated with an independently assessed CAFAS (Rautkis & Hdalio, 2001). In this study, the Caregiver Needs & Strengths total was found to be correlated with an independent measure of burden. In a sample of more than 1700 cases in 15 different program types across the State of New York, the total scores on the dimensions of the CANS-MH (e.g. Problems, Risk Behaviors) reliably distinguished level of care. In a comparison of CANS-MH level of care guidelines to clinical judgment, staff at Multnomah County, Oregon found that the CANS-MH informed level of care criteria agreed with the expert panel decision 91% of the time. It has also been used to distinguish needs of children in rural and urban settings (Anderson & Estle, 2001).

Administration Overview

When the CANS-MH is administered, each of the dimensions is rated on its own 4-point scale after the initial intake interview, routine service contact or following the review of a case file. Even though each dimension has a numerical ranking, the CANS-MH assessment tool is designed to give a profile of the needs and strengths of the child and family. *It is* not *designed to require that you "add up" all of the "scores" of the dimensions for an overall score rating,* although such scoring is an option for evaluation applications. When used in a *retrospective* review of cases, it is designed to give an overall "profile" of the system of services and the gaps in the service system not an overall "score" of the current system. Used as a profile based assessment tool, it is reliable and gives the care coordinator, the family and the agency, valuable existing information for use in the development and/or review of the individual plan of care and case service decisions.

The basic design of the ratings is:

- 0 indicates no need for action
- 1 indicates *a need for watchful waiting* to see whether action is needed (i.e. flag it for later review to see if any circumstances change) or prevention planning

- 2 indicates *a need for action*
- 3 indicates the need for either immediate or intensive action

The rating of 'U' for unknown should be considered a flag for a need to find this information for a complete profile or picture of the needs and strengths of the child and their family. In order to maximize the ease of use and interpretation, please note that the last two categories of dimensions, Caregiver Capacity and Strengths, are rated in a reverse logical manner, i.e., a rating of '0' is seen as a *positive* strength.

Two items are exceptions to this response format. Situational Consistency ranges from a 0 reflecting problems in only one situation to a 3 reflecting a similar severity of problems across all situations. Temporal Consistency ranges from '0' which describes an adjustment reaction to '3' which is a persistent level of problems.

Following are a summary of the dimensions of the CANS-MH. Unless otherwise specified, each rating is based on the last 30 days. Each of the dimensions is rated on a 4-point scale after routine service contact or following review of case files. The basic design is that '0' reflects no evidence, a rating of '1' reflects a mild degree of the dimension, a rating of '2' reflects a moderate degree and a rating of '3' reflects a severe or profound degree of the dimension. Another way to conceptualize these ratings is that a '0' indicates no need for action, a '1' indicates a need for watchful waiting to see whether action is warranted, a '2' indicates a need for action, and a '3' indicates the need for either immediate or intensive action. In order to maximize the ease of use and interpretation, please note that the last two clusters of dimensions, Caregiver Capacity and Strengths, are rated in the opposite logical manner to maintain consistency across the measure. Thus, in all cases, a low rating is positive. The basic structure of the CANS-MH is:

A. Problem Presentation	Attachment
Psychosis	Situational Consistency of Problems
Attention Deficit/Impulse Control	Temporal Consistency of Problems
Depression/Anxiety	**B. Risk Behaviors**
Oppositional Behavior	Danger to Self
Antisocial Behavior	Danger to Others
Substance Abuse	Runaway
Adjustment to Trauma	Sexually Abusive Behavior

Social Behavior

Crime/Delinquency

C. Functioning

Intellectual/Developmental

Physical/Medical

School Achievement

School Behavior

School Attendance

Sexual Development

D. Care Intensity & Organization

Monitoring

Treatment

Transportation

Service Permanence

E. Family/Caregiver Needs and Strengths

Physical

Supervision

Involvement with Care

Knowledge

Organization

Residential Stability

Resources

Safety

F. Strengths

Family

Interpersonal

Relationship Permanence

Education

Vocational

Well-being

Spiritual/Religious

Talents/Interest

Inclusion

Coding Criteria

Problem Presentation

Psychotic Symptoms

This rating is used to describe symptoms of psychiatric disorders with a known neurological base. DSM-IV disorders included on this dimension are Schizophrenia and Psychotic Disorders (unipolar, bipolar, NOS). The common symptoms of these disorders include hallucinations, delusions, unusual thought processes, strange speech, and bizarre/idiosyncratic behavior.

0   This rating indicates a child with no evidence of thought disturbances. Both thought processes and content are within normal range.

1   This rating indicates a child with evidence of mild disruption in thought processes or content. The child may be somewhat tangential in speech or evidence somewhat illogical thinking (age inappropriate). This also includes children with a history of hallucinations but none currently. The category would be used for children who

are below the threshold for one of the DSM IV diagnoses listed above.

2 This rating indicates a child with evidence of moderate disturbance in thought process or content. The child may be somewhat delusional or have brief intermittent hallucinations. The child's speech may be at times quite tangential or illogical. This level would be used for children who meet the diagnostic criteria for one of the disorders listed above.

3 This rating indicates a child with a severe psychotic disorder. Symptoms are dangerous to the child or others.

Attention Deficit/Impulse Control

Symptoms of Attention Deficit and Hyperactivity Disorder and Impulse Control Disorder would be rated here. Inattention/distractibility not related to opposition would also be rated here.

0 This rating is used to indicate a child with no evidence of attention/hyperactivity problems.

1 This rating is used to indicate a child with evidence of mild problems attention/hyperactivity or impulse control problems. Child may have some difficulties staying on task for an age appropriate time period.

2 This rating is used to indicate a child with moderate attention/hyperactivity or impulse control problems. A child who meets DSM-IV diagnostic criteria for ADHD or an impulse control disorder would be rated here.

3 This rating is used to indicate a child with severe impairment of attention or impulse control. Frequent impulsive behavior is observed or noted that carries considerable safety risk (e.g. running into the street, dangerous driving, or bike riding). A child with profound symptoms of ADHD would be rated here.

Depression/Anxiety

Symptoms included in this dimension are depressed mood, social withdrawal, anxious mood, sleep disturbances, weight/eating disturbances, loss of motivation. This dimension can be used to rate symptoms of the following psychiatric disorders as specified in DSM-IV: Depression (unipolar, dysthymia, NOS), Bipolar, Generalized Anxiety, and Phobias.

0 This rating is given to a child with no emotional problems. No evidence of depression or anxiety.

1 This rating is given to a child with mild emotional problems. Brief duration of depression, irritability, or impairment of peer, family, or academic function that does not lead to gross avoidance behavior. This level is used to rate either a mild phobia or anxiety problem or a level of symptoms that is below the threshold for the other listed disorders.

2 This rating is given to a child with a moderate level of emotional disturbance. This could include major conversion symptoms, frequent anxiety attacks, obsessions, rituals, flashbacks, hypervigilance, depression, or school avoidance. This level is used to rate children who meet the criteria for an affective disorder listed above.

3 This rating is given to a child with a severe level of emotional disturbance. This would include a child who stays at home or in bed all day due to anxiety or depression or one whose emotional symptoms prevent any participation in school, friendship groups, or family life. More severe forms of anxiety or depressive diagnoses would be coded here. This level is used to indicate an extreme case of one of the disorders listed above.

Oppositional Behavior (compliance with authority)

This rating is intended to capture how the child relates to authority. Oppositional behavior is different from conduct disorder in that the emphasis of the behavior is on non-compliance to authority rather than on seriously breaking social rules, norms and laws.

0 This rating indicates that the child is generally compliant.

1 This rating indicates that the child has mild problems with compliance to some rules or adult instructions.

2 This rating indicates that the child has moderate problems with compliance to rules or adult instructions. A child who meets the criteria for Oppositional Defiant Disorder in DSM-IV would be rated here.

3 This rating indicates that the child has severe problems with compliance to rules and adult instructions. A child rated at this level would be a severe case of Oppositional Defiant Disorder. They would be virtually always disobedient.

Antisocial Behavior (Compliance with Society's Rules)

These symptoms include antisocial behaviors like shoplifting, lying, vandalism, cruelty to animals, and assault. This dimension would include the symptoms of Conduct Disorder as specified in DSM-IV.

0   This rating indicates a child with no evidence of behavior disorder.

1   This rating indicates a child with a mild level of conduct problems. Some antisocial behavior in school and/or home. Problems recognizable but not notably deviant for age and sex and community. This might include occasional truancy, lying, or petty theft from family.

2   This rating indicates a child with a moderate level of conduct disorder. This could include episodes of planned aggressive or other antisocial behavior. A child rated at this level should meet the criteria for a diagnosis of Conduct Disorder.

3   This rating indicates a child with a severe Conduct Disorder. This could include frequent episodes of unprovoked, planned aggressive or other anti-social behavior.

Substance Abuse

These symptoms include use of alcohol and illegal drugs, the misuse of prescription medications and the inhalation of any substance for recreational purposes. This rating is consistent with DSM-IV Substance-related Disorders.

0   This rating is for a child who has no substance use difficulties at the present time. If the person is in recovery for greater than 1 year, they should be coded here, although this is unlikely for a child or adolescent.

1   This rating is for a child with mild substance use problems that might occasionally present problems of living for the person (intoxication, loss of money, reduced school performance, parental concern). This rating would be used for someone early in recovery (less than 1 year) who is currently abstinent for at least 30 days.

2   This rating is for a child with a moderate substance abuse problem that both requires treatment and interacts with and exacerbates the psychiatric illness. Substance abuse problems consistently interfere with the ability to function optimally but do not completely preclude functioning in an unstructured setting.

3   This rating is for a child with a severe substance dependence condition that presents a significant complication to the coordination of care (e.g. need for detoxification) of the individual.

Adjustment to Trauma

This rating covers the reactions of children and adolescents to any of a variety of traumatic experiences from child abuse and neglect to forced separation from family. This dimension covers both adjustment disorders and post-traumatic stress disorder from DSM-IV.

0   Child has not experienced any trauma or has adjusted well to significant traumatic experiences. If the child is separated from parents, he/she has adjusted to this separation.

1   Child has some mild adjustment problems to separation from parent(s) or other caregivers or as a result of earlier abuse. Child may be somewhat distrustful or unwilling to talk about parent(s) or other caregivers.

2   Child has marked adjustment problems associated either with separation from parent(s) or other caregivers or with prior abuse. Child may have nightmares or other notable symptoms of adjustment difficulties.

3   Child has post-traumatic stress difficulties as a result of either separation from parent(s), multiple other caregivers, or prior abuse. Symptoms may include intrusive thoughts, hypervigilance, constant anxiety, and other common symptoms of Post-Traumatic Stress Disorder (PTSD).

Attachment (Use Only For Children Less Than 6 Years Old)

This dimension should be rated within the context of the child's significant parental relationships.

0   No evidence of attachment problems. Parent-child relationship is characterized by satisfaction of needs, child's development of a sense of security and trust.

1   Mild problems with attachment. This could involve either mild problems with separation or mild problems of detachment.

2   Moderate problems with attachment. Child is having problems with attachment that require intervention. A child who meets the criteria for an Attachment Disorder in DSM-IV would be rated here. Children with developmental delays may experience challenges with attachment and would be rated here.

3   Severe problems with attachment. A child who is unable to separate or a child who appears to have severe problems with forming or maintaining relationships with caregivers would be rated here.

Problem Modifiers

Situational Consistency of Problems

This rating captures the variation in problem presentation across different situations and environments in the child/youth's life (e.g., home and school)

0   Problems generally occur in only one environment and/or situation.

1   Problems occur in multiple settings and/or situations but tend to be most severe in a single setting.

2   Problems occur in many settings and/or situations but there is variability in the severity of the problems with the child/youth doing better in some circumstances than in others.

3   Problems occur consistently in all situations.

Temporal Consistency of Problems

This rating captures the duration of mental health problems experienced by the child or youth. Include both problems (i.e., symptoms) and risk behaviors in this rating.

0   Problems have begun in the past six months after the occurrence of a specific stressful event.

1   Problems began more than six months but less than two years ago or problems have begun in the past six months in the absence of any specific stressful event.

2   Problems began more than two years ago but individual has had at least one period of more than one month where he/she has been relatively symptom free.

3   Problems began more than two years ago and the individual has remained fairly consistently symptomatic over this period of time.

Risk Behaviors

Danger to Self

This rating describes both suicidal and significant self-injurious behavior. A rating of 2 or 3 would indicate the need for a safety plan.

0   Child has no evidence or history of suicidal or self-injurious behaviors.

1   History of suicidal or self-injurious behaviors but no self-injurious behavior during the past 30 days.

2   Recent, (last 30 days) but not acute (today) suicidal ideation or gesture. Self-injurious in the past 30 days (including today) without suicidal ideation or intent.

3   Current suicidal ideation and intent in the past 24 hours.

Danger to Others

This rating includes actual and threatened violence. Imagined violence, when extreme, may be rated here. A rating of 2 or 3 would indicate the need for a safety plan.

0 Child has no evidence or history of aggressive behaviors or significant verbal aggression towards others (including people and animals).

1 History of aggressive behavior or verbal aggression towards others but no aggression during the past 30 days. History of fire setting (not in past year) would be rated here.

2 Occasional or moderate level of aggression towards others including aggression during the past 30 days or more recent verbal aggression.

3 Frequent or dangerous (significant harm) level of aggression to others. Any fire setting within the past year would be rated here. Child or youth is an immediate risk to others.

Runaway

In general, to classify as a runaway or elopement, the child is gone overnight or very late into the night. Impulsive behavior that represents an immediate threat to personal safety would also be rated here.

0 This rating is for a child with no history of running away and no ideation involving escaping from the present living situation.

1 This rating is for a child with no recent history of running away but who has expressed ideation about escaping present living situation or treatment. Child may have threatened running away on one or more occasions or have a history (lifetime) of running away but not in the past year.

2 This rating is for a child who has run away from home once or run away from one treatment setting within the past year. Also rated here is a child who has run away to home (parental or relative) in the past year.

3 This rating is for a child who has (1) run away from home and/or treatment settings within the last 7 days or (2) run away from home and/or treatment setting twice or more overnight during the past 30 days. Destination is not a return to home of parent or relative.

Sexually Abusive Behavior

Sexually abusive behavior includes both aggressive sexual behavior and sexual behavior in which the child or adolescent takes advantage of a younger or less powerful child through seduction, coercion, or force.

0   No evidence of problems with sexual behavior in the past year.

1   Mild problems of sexually abusive behavior. For example, occasional inappropriate sexual behavior or language.

2   Moderate problems with sexually abusive behavior, For example, frequent inappropriate sexual behavior. Frequent disrobing would be rated here only if it was sexually provocative. Frequent inappropriate touching would be rated here.

3   Severe problems with sexually abusive behavior. This would include the rape or sexual abuse of another person involving sexual penetration.

Social Behavior

This rating refers to how a child behaves in public or social settings and should reflect problematic social behaviors (socially unacceptable behavior for the culture and community in which he/she lives) that put the child at some risk (e.g. not excessive shyness).

0   Child shows no evidence of problematic social behaviors.

1   Mild level of problematic social behaviors. This might include occasionally inappropriate social behavior. Infrequent inappropriate comments to strangers or unusual behavior in social settings might be included at this level.

2   Moderate level of problematic social behaviors. Frequent cursing in public would be rated at this level. Social behavior is causing problems in the child's life.

3   Severe level of problematic social behaviors. This would be indicated by frequent seriously inappropriate social behavior such as threatening strangers. Social behaviors are sufficiently severe that they place the child at risk.

Crime/Delinquency

This rating includes both criminal behavior and status offenses that may result from child or youth failing to follow required behavioral standards (e.g. truancy). Sexual offenses should be included as criminal behavior.

0   Child shows no evidence or has no history of criminal or delinquent behavior.

1 History of criminal or delinquent behavior but none in the past 30 days. Status offenses in the past 30 days would be rated here.

2 Moderate level of criminal activity including a high likelihood of crimes committed in the past 30 days. Examples would include vandalism, shoplifting, etc.

3 Serious level of criminal or delinquent activity in the past 30 days. Examples would include car theft, residential burglary, gang involvement, etc.

Functioning

Intellectual/Developmental

This rating describes the child's cognitive/intellectual functioning.

0 Child's intellectual functioning appears to be in normal range. There is no reason to believe that the child has any problems with intellectual functioning.

1 Low IQ or learning disability (IQ between 70 and 85) or mild developmental delay.

2 Mild to moderate mental retardation (IQ between 50 and 69) or significant developmental delay.

3 Severe or profound mental retardation (less than 50) or pervasive developmental delay.

Physical/Medical

This rating describes both health problems and chronic/acute physical conditions.

0 Child appears physically healthy. There is no reason to believe that the child has any medical or physical problems.

1 Mild or well-managed physical or medical problems. This might include well-managed chronic conditions like juvenile diabetes or asthma.

2 Chronic physical or moderate medical problems.

3 Severe, life threatening physical or medical problems.

Family Functioning

The definition of family should be from the perspective of the child or youth (i.e., who does the child consider to be family). The family can include all biological relatives with whom the child or youth remains in some contact with and individuals with relationship ties to these relatives. Family functioning should be rated independently of the problems experienced by the child.

0   Family appears to be functioning adequately. There is no evidence of problems in the family.

1   Mild to moderate level of family problems including marital difficulties, problems with siblings.

2   Significant level of family problems including frequent arguments, difficult separation and/or divorce or siblings with significant mental health, developmental or juvenile justice problems.

3   Profound level of family disruption including significant parental substance abuse, criminality, or domestic violence.

School Achievement

This rating describes the child or adolescent's academic performance in school.

0   Child is doing well in school.

1   Child is doing adequately in school, although some problem with achievement exists.

2   Child is having moderate problems with school achievement. He/she may be failing some subjects.

3   Child is having severe achievement problems. He/she may be failing most subjects or is more than one year behind same age peers in school achievement.

School Behavior

This item describes the behavior of the child or youth in school. A rating of 3 would indicate a child who is still having problems after special efforts have been made, i.e., problems in a special education class.

0   No evidence of behavior problems at school. Child is behaving well.

1   Mild problems with school behavioral problems.

2   Child is having moderate behavioral difficulties at school. He/she is disruptive and may receive sanctions including suspensions.

3   Child is having severe problems with behavior in school. He/she is frequently or severely disruptive. School placement may be in jeopardy due to behavior.

School Attendance

This item describes the child or adolescents pattern of coming to and remaining at school for each required school day.

0   No evidence of attendance problems. Child attends regularly.

1   Child has some problems attending school, although he/she generally goes to school. Or, he/she may have had moderate to severe problems in the past six months but has been attending school regularly in the past month.

2   Child is having problems with school attendance. He/she is missing at least one out of every 7 (14%) school days on average.

3   Child is generally truant or refusing to go to school.

Sexual Development

This rating describes issues around sexual development including developmentally inappropriate sexual behavior and problematic sexual behavior.

0   Child shows no evidence of problems with sexual behavior or development in the past year.

1   Mild problems of sexual development. For example, occasional inappropriate sexual behavior or language. Some mild forms of sexual behavior might be rated here.

2   Moderate to serious problems of sexual development. For example, frequent inappropriate sexual behavior, including public disrobing or multiple older sexual partners.

3   Severe problems of sexual development. Prostitution, sexual aggression, exhibitionism, voyeurism, or other severe problems would be rated here.

Care Intensity and Organization

Monitoring

This dimension describes the level of adult monitoring needed to address the safety and functioning need of the child or youth.

0   Child has minimal monitoring needs. For example, caregiver could leave the house to run an errand of at least 30 minutes.

1   Child has some monitoring needs. For example, a caregiver would need to check on the individual more than every 30 minutes or so during awake hours, but not during asleep hours.

2 Child has significant monitoring needs. For example, a caregiver would need to be in the same room or nearby most of the time during awake hours and nearby during asleep hours.

3 Child needs 24-hour awake monitoring.

Treatment

This rating describes the intensity of the treatment needed to address the problems, risk behaviors, and functioning of the child or youth.

0 Child has no behavioral/physical/medical treatment needs to be administered by the parent/primary caregiver.

1 Child requires weekly behavioral/physical/medical treatment by the parent/primary caregiver.

2 Child requires daily behavioral/physical/medical treatment by the parent/primary caregiver. This would include ensuring the child takes daily medication.

3 Child requires multiple and complex daily behavioral/physical/ medical treatments by the parent/primary caregiver (complicated treatment cases).

Transportation

This rating reflects the level of transportation required to ensure that the child or youth could effectively participate in his/her own treatment.

0 Child has no transportation needs.

1 Child has occasional transportation needs (e.g. appointments). These needs would be no more than weekly and not require a special vehicle. Child with a parent(s) who needs transportation assistance to visit a child would be rated here.

2 Child has occasional transportation needs that require a special vehicle or frequent transportation needs (e.g. daily to school) that do not require a special vehicle.

3 Child requires frequent (e.g. daily to school) transportation in a special vehicle.

Service Permanence

This dimension describes the stability of the service providers who have worked with the child and/or family.

0 Service providers have been consistent for more than the past two years. This level is also used to rate a child/family who is initiating

services for the first time or re-initiating services after an absence from services of at least one year.

1 Service providers have been consistent for at least one year, but changes occurred during the prior year.

2 Service providers have been changed recently after a period of consistency.

3 Service providers have changed multiple times during the past year.

Family/Caregiver Needs and Strengths

Caregiver refers to parent(s) or other adult with primary care-taking responsibilities for the child.

Physical/Behavioral Health

Physical and behavioral health includes medical, physical, mental health, and substance abuse challenges faced by the caregiver(s).

0 Caregiver(s) has no physical or behavioral health limitations that impact assistance or attendant care.

1 Caregiver(s) has some physical or behavioral health limitations that interfere with provision of assistance or attendant care.

2 Caregiver(s) has significant physical or behavioral health limitations that prevent them from being able to provide some of needed parenting and caregiving or make attendant care difficult.

3 Caregiver(s) is physically unable to provide any needed assistance or attendant care.

Supervision

This rating is used to determine the caregiver's capacity to provide the level of monitoring and discipline needed by the child/youth.

0 This rating is used to indicate a caregiver circumstance in which supervision and monitoring is appropriate and well functioning.

1 This level indicates a caregiver circumstance in which supervision is generally adequate but inconsistent. This may include a placement in which one member is capable of appropriate monitoring and supervision but others are not capable or not consistently available.

2 This level indicates a caregiver circumstance in which supervision and monitoring are very inconsistent and frequently absent.

3 This level indicates a caregiver circumstance in which appropriate supervision and monitoring are nearly always absent or inappropriate.

Involvement

This rating should be based on the level of involvement the caregiver(s) has in planning and provision of mental health and related services.

0   This level indicates a caregiver(s) who is actively involved in the planning and/or implementation of services and is able to be an effective advocate on behalf of the child or adolescent.

1   This level indicates a caregiver(s) who is consistently involved in the planning and/or implementation of services for the child or adolescent.

2   This level indicates a caregiver(s) who is only somewhat involved in the care of the child or adolescent. Caregiver may consistently visit individual when in out-of-home placement, but does not become involved in service planning and implementation.

3   This level indicates a caregiver(s) who is uninvolved with the care of the child or adolescent. Caregiver likely wants individual out of home or fails to visit individual when in residential treatment.

Knowledge

This rating should be based on caregiver's knowledge of the specific strengths of the child and any problems experienced by the child and their ability to understand the rationale for the treatment or management of these problems.

0   This level indicates that the present caregiver is fully knowledgeable about the child's psychological strengths, weaknesses, talents, and limitations.

1   This level indicates that the present caregiver, while being generally knowledgeable about the child, has some mild deficits in knowledge or understanding of either the child's psychological condition or his/her talents, skills, and assets.

2   This level indicates that the caregiver does not know or understand the child well and that notable deficits exist in the caregiver's ability to relate to the child's problems and strengths.

3   This level indicates that the present caregiver has a significant problem in understanding the child's current condition. The placement is unable to cope with the child, given his/her status at the time, not because of the needs of the child but because the caregiver does not understand or accept the situation.

Organization

This rating should be based on the ability of the caregiver to participate in or direct the organization of the household, services, and related activities.

0 Caregiver(s) is well organized and efficient.

1 Caregiver(s) has some difficulties with organizing or maintaining household to support needed services. For example, may be forgetful about appointments or occasionally fails to call back case manager.

2 Caregiver(s) has significant difficulty organizing or maintaining household to support needed services.

3 Caregiver(s) is unable to organize household to support needed services.

Resources

This rating refers to the financial and social assets (extended family) and resources that the caregiver(s) can bring to bear in addressing the multiple needs of the child and family.

0 Caregiver(s) has sufficient resources so that there are few limitations on what can be provided for the child.

1 Caregiver(s) has the necessary resources to help address the child's basic needs and are helpful in the care and treatment of the child.

2 Caregiver(s) has limited financial and other resources (e.g. grandmother living in same town who is sometimes available to watch child).

3 Caregiver has severely limited resources that are available to assist in the care and treatment of the child.

Residential Stability

This dimension rates the caregivers' current and likely future housing circumstances.

0 Caregiver(s) has stable housing for the foreseeable future.

1 Caregiver(s) has relatively stable housing but has either moved in the past three months or there are indications that housing problems could arise at some point within the next three months.

2 Caregiver(s) has moved multiple times in the past year. Housing is unstable.

3 Caregiver(s) has experienced periods of homelessness in the past six months.

Safety

This rating refers to the safety of the assessed child. It does not refer to the safety of other family or household members based on any danger presented by the assessed child.

0   This level indicates that the present placement is as safe or safer for the child (in his or her present condition) as could be reasonably expected.

1   This level indicates that the present placement environment presents some mild risk of neglect, exposure to undesirable environments (e.g. drug use, gangs, etc.) but that no immediate risk is present.

2   This level indicates that the present placement environment presents a moderate level of risk to the child including such things as the risk of neglect or abuse or exposure to individuals who could harm the child.

3   This level indicates that the present placement environment presents a significant risk to the well-being of the child. Risk of neglect or abuse is eminent and immediate. Individuals in the environment offer the potential of significantly harming the child.

Strengths

Family

Family refers to all biological or adoptive relatives with whom the child or youth remains in contact along with other individuals in relationships with these relatives.

0   Significant family strengths. This level indicates a family with much love and mutual respect for each other. Family members are central in each other's lives. Child is fully included in family activities.

1   Moderate level of family strengths. This level indicates a loving family with generally good communication and ability to enjoy each other's company. There may be some problems between family members. Child is generally included.

2   Mild level of family strengths. Family is able to communicate and participate in each other's lives; however, family members may not be able to provide significant emotional or concrete support for each other. Child is often not included in family activities.

3   This level indicates a child with no known family strengths. Child is not included in normal family activities.

Interpersonal

This rating refers to the interpersonal skills of the child or youth both with peers and adults.

0   Significant interpersonal strengths. Child is seen as well liked by others and has significant ability to form and maintain positive relationships with both peers and adults. Individual has multiple close friends and is friendly with others.

1   Moderate level of interpersonal strengths. Child has formed positive interpersonal relationships with peers and/or other non-caregivers. Child may have one friend.

2   Mild level of interpersonal strengths. Child has some social skills that facilitate positive relationships with peers and adults but may not have any current relationships, but has a history of making and maintaining healthy friendships with others.

3   This level indicates a child with no known interpersonal strengths. Child currently does not have any friends nor has he/she had any friends in the past. Child does not have positive relationships with adults.

Relationship Permanence

This rating refers to the stability of significant relationships in the child or youth's life. This likely includes family members but may also include other individuals.

0   This level indicates a child who has very stable relationships. Family members, friends, and community have been stable for most of his/her life and are likely to remain so in the foreseeable future. Child is involved with both parents.

1   This level indicates a child who has had stable relationships but there is some concern about instability in the near future (one year) due to transitions, illness, or age. A child who has a stable relationship with only one parent may be rated here.

2   This level indicates a child who has had at least one stable relationship over his/her lifetime but has experienced other instability through factors such as divorce, moving, removal from home, and death.

3   This level indicates a child who does not have any stability in relationships.

Educational

This rating refers to the strengths of the school system and may or may not reflect any specific educational skills possessed by the child or youth.

0 This level indicates a child who is in school and is involved with an educational plan that appears to exceed expectations. School works exceptionally well with family and caregivers to create a special learning environment. A child in a mainstream educational system who does not require an individual plan would be rated here.

1 This level indicates a child who is in school and has a plan that appears to be effective. School works fairly well with family and caregivers to ensure appropriate educational development.

2 This level indicates a child who is in school but has a plan that does not appear to be effective.

3 This level indicates a child who is either not in school or is in a school setting that does not further his/her education.

Vocational

Generally this rating is reserved for adolescents and is not applicable for children 12 years and under. Computer skills would be rated here.

0 This level indicates an adolescent with vocational skills who is currently working in a natural environment.

1 This level indicates an adolescent with pre-vocational and some vocational skills but limited work experience.

2 This level indicates an adolescent with some pre-vocational skills. This also may indicate a child or youth with a clear vocational preference.

3 This level indicates an adolescent with no known or identifiable vocational or pre-vocational skills and no expression of any future vocational preferences.

Well-Being

This rating should be based on the psychological strengths that the child or adolescent might have developed including both the ability to enjoy positive life experiences and manage negative life experiences. This should be rated independent of the child's current level of distress.

0   This level indicates a child with exceptional psychological strengths. Both coping and savoring skills are well developed.

1   This level indicates a child with good psychological strengths. The person has solid coping skills for managing distress or solid savoring skills for enjoying pleasurable events.

2   This level indicates a child with limited psychological strengths. For example, a person with very low self-esteem would be rated here.

3   This level indicates a child with no known or identifiable psychological strengths. This may be due to intellectual impairment or serious psychiatric disorders.

Optimism

This rating should be based on the child or adolescent's sense of him/herself in his/her own future. This is intended to rate the child's positive future orientation.

0   Child has a strong and stable optimistic outlook on his/her life. Child is future oriented.

1   Child is generally optimistic. Child is likely able to articulate some positive future vision.

2   Child has difficulties maintaining a positive view of him/herself and his/her life. Child may vary from overly optimistic to overly pessimistic.

3   Child has difficulties seeing any positives about him/herself or his/her life.

Spiritual/Religious

This rating should be based on the child or adolescent's and their family's involvement in spiritual or religious beliefs and activities.

0   This level indicates a child with strong moral and spiritual strengths. Child may be very involved in a religious community or may have strongly held spiritual or religious beliefs that can sustain or comfort him/her in difficult times.

1   This level indicates a child with some moral and spiritual strengths. Child may be involved in a religious community.

2   This level indicates a child with few spiritual or religious strengths. Child may have little contact with religious institutions.

3   This level indicates a child with no known spiritual or religious involvement.

Talent/Interests

This rating should be based broadly on any talent, creative or artistic skill a child or adolescent may have including art, theatre, music, athletics, etc.

0   This level indicates a child with significant creative/artistic strengths. A child/youth who receives a significant amount of personal benefit from activities surrounding a talent would be rated here.

1   This level indicates a child with a notable talent. For example, a youth who is involved in athletics or plays a musical instrument, etc. would be rated here.

2   This level indicates a child who has expressed interest in developing a specific talent or talents even if they have not developed that talent to date.

3   This level indicates a child with no known talents, interests, or hobbies.

Inclusion

This rating should be based on the child or adolescent's level of involvement in the cultural aspects of life in his/her community.

0   This level indicates a child with extensive and substantial, long-term ties with the community. For example, individual may be a member of a community group (e.g. Girl or Boy Scout etc.) for more than one year, may be widely accepted by neighbors, or involved in other community activities, informal networks, etc.

1   This level indicates a child with significant community ties although they may be relatively short term (e.g. past year).

2   This level indicates a child with limited ties and/or supports from the community.

3   This level indicates a child with no known ties or supports from the community.

References

Anderson, R.L., Estle, G. (2001). Predicting level of mental health care among children served in a rural delivery system. *Journal of Rural Health 17*, 259–265.

Anderson, R.L., Lyons, J.S., Giles, D.M., Price, J.A., Estes, G. (2002). Examining the reliability of the Child and Adolescent Needs and Strengths-Mental Health (CANS-MH) Scale from two perspectives: A comparison of clinician and researcher ratings. *Journal of Child and Family Studies 12*, 279–289.

Leon, S. C., Lyons, J. S., Uziel-Miller, N. D., Tracy, P. (1999). Psychiatric hospital utilization of children and adolescents in state custody. *Journal of the American Academy of Child and Adolescent Psychiatry, 38*, 305–310.

Lyons, J. S. (1997). The evolving role of outcomes in managed mental health care. *Journal of Child and Family Studies, 6*, 1–8.

Lyons, J. S. (1998). *Severity and acuity of psychiatric illness manual. Child and adolescent version.* San Antonio: The Psychological Corporation, Harcourt Brace Jovanovich.

Lyons, J. S., Chesler, P., Shallcross, H. M. (1996). Using a measure of children's mental health needs to inform system changes. *Family Matters,* a national newsletter published by the Mental Health Services Program for Youth, a national program of the Robert Wood Johnson Foundation, 2nd Special Edition, May 1996, 1–8.

Lyons, J. S., Howard, K. I., O'Mahoney, M. T., Lish, J. (1997). *The measurement and management of clinical outcomes in mental health.* New York: John Wiley & Sons.

Lyons, J. S., Kisiel, C. L., Dulcan, M., Cohen, R., Chesler, P. (1997). Crisis assessment and psychiatric hospitalization of children and adolescents in state custody. *Journal of Child and Family Studies, 6*, 311–320.

Lyons, J. S., Kisiel, C., West, C. (1997). Child and adolescent strengths assessment: A pilot study. *Family Matters,* a national newsletter published by the Mental Health Services Program for Youth, a national program of the Robert Wood Johnson Foundation, Fall 1997, 30–32.

Lyons, J. S., Mintzer, L. L., Kisiel, C. L., Shallcross, H. (1998). Understanding the mental health needs of children and adolescents in residential treatment. *Professional Psychology: Research and Practice, 29*, 582–587.

Lyons, J. S., Rawal, P., Yeh, I., Leon, S. C., Tracy, P. (2002). Use of measurement audit in outcomes management. *Journal of Behavioral Healthcare Services & Research, 29*, 75–80.

Lyons, J. S., Shallcross, H. M., Sokol, P. T. (1998). *Using outcomes management for systems planning and reform, the complete guide to managed behavioral healthcare, chapter K,* Chris E. Stout, Editor. New York: John Wiley & Sons.

Lyons, J. S., Uziel-Miller, N. D., Reyes, F., Sokol, P. T. (2000). The strengths of children and adolescents in residential settings: Prevalence and associations with psychopathology and discharge placement. *Journal of the Academy of Child and Adolescent Psychiatry, 39*, 176–181.

Rautkis, M. B., Hdalio, J. (2001). *The validity of the Child and Adolescent Needs and Strengths.* Presented to the Louis del Parte Florida Mental Health Institute Annual Convention, Tampa, FL.

Rawal, P., Lyons, J. S., MacIntyre, J., Hunter, J. C. (2004). Regional variations and clinical indicators of antipsychotic use in residential treatment: A four state comparison. *Journal of Behavioral Health Services & Research 31*, 178–189.

BIBLIOGRAPHY

Abramovitz, R., & Bloom, S.L. (2003). Creating sanctuary in residential treatment for youth: From the "well ordered asylum" to a "living-learning environment." *Psychiatric Quarterly, 74,* 119–135.

Agency for Healthcare and Policy Research (AHCPR). (1993). *Using clinical practice guidelines to evaluate quality of care. 2. Methods* (AHCPR Publication No. 940046). Rockville, MD: Author.

Akerloff, G. A. (1970). The market for "lemons": Uncertainty and the market mechanism." *Quarterly Journal of Economics, 84* (3), 488–500.

American Institute for Research. (1994). The natural agenda for achieving better results for children and youth with serious emotional disturbance (SED). Report to the U.S. Department of Education, Washington, DC. Available: http://www.air.dc.org.

American Psychiatric Association. (1994). *Diagnostic and statistical manual of mental disorders* (4th ed.). Washington, DC: Author.

American Psychiatric Association. (2000). Supportive residential services to reunite homeless mentally ill single parents with their children. *Psychiatric Services, 51,* 1433–1435.

Anastasi, A. (1968). *Psychological testing* (3rd ed.). Toronto: The Macmillan Company.

Anderson, R. L., Lyons, J. S., Giles, D. M., Price, J. A., & Estle, G. (2002). Examining the reliability of the Child and Adolescent Needs and Strengths-Mental Health (CANS-MH) Scale. *Journal of Child and Family Studies, 12,* 279–289.

Andrade, A.R., Lambert, E.W., & Bickman, L. (2000). Dose effect in child psychotherapy: Outcomes associated with negligible treatment. *Journal of the American Academy of Child and Adolescent Psychiatry, 39,* 161–168.

Apgar, V. (1966). The newborn (Apgar) scoring system. Reflections and advice. *Pediatric Clinics of North America, 13,* 645–650.

Astrachan, B.M., Flynn, H.R., Geller, J.D., & Harvey, H.H. (1971). Systems approach to day hospitalization. *Current Psychiatric Therapies, 2,* 175–182.

Barker P. (1998). The future of residential treatment for children. In C. Schaefer & A. Swanson (Eds.), *Children in residential care: Critical issues in treatment* (pp. 1–16). New York: Van Nostrand Reinhold.

Bassuk, E.L., Buckner, J.C., Weinreb, L.F., Browne, A., Bassuck, S.S., Dawson, R., & Perloff, J.N. (1997). Homelessness in female-headed families: Childhood and adult risk factors and protective factors. *American Journal of Public Health, 87,* 241–248.

Bates, B.C., English, D.F., & Kouidou-Giles, S. (1997). Residential treatment and its alternatives: A review of the literature. *Child and Youth Care Forum, 26,* 7–51.

Bechtel, G.G., Ofir, C., & Ventura, J.A. (1990). Combining perceptual and economic variables in the demand functions. *Journal of Economic Psychology, 11,* 209–225.

Beers, C. (1908). *A mind that found itself.* Pittsburgh, PA: University of Pittsburgh Press.

Berland, A. (2003). Modernizing mental health services: Mission impossible? *Administration & Policy in Mental Health, 30,* 219–229.

Bickman, L. (1996). Implications of a children's mental health managed care demonstration evaluation. *Journal of Mental Health Administration, 23,* 107–117.

Bickman, L., Lambert, E.W., Andrade, A.R., & Penaloza, R.V. (2000). The Fort Bragg Continuum of Care for Children and Adolescents: Mental health outcomes over 5 years. *Journal of Consulting and Clinical Psychology, 68,* 710–716.

Bickman, L., Noser, K., & Summerfelt, W.T. (1999). Long-term effects of a system of care on children and adolescents. *Journal of Behavioral Health Services & Research, 26,* 185–202.

Blader, S.L., & Tyler, T.R. (2003). A four-component model of procedural justice: Defining the meaning of a "fair" process. *Personality and Social Psychology Bulletin, 29,* 747–758.

Blodgett, C., & Molinari, C. (2001). Trends in psychiatric inpatient rates from 1991–1995 in the State of Washington: The effect of insurance type on utilization. *Administration & Policy in Mental Health, 28* (5): 393–405.

Bloem, R.B., Beckley, D.J., van Hilten, B.J., & Roos, R.A. (1998). Clinimetrics of postural instability in Parkinson's disease. *Journal of Neurology, 245,* 669–673.

Blumberg, S. H. (2002). Crisis intervention program: An alternative to inpatient psychiatric treatment for children. *Mental Health Services Research, 4*, 1–6.

Boring, E. G. (1950). *A history of experimental psychology.* 2nd ed. New York: Appleton-Century-Crofts.

Bourduin, C. M., & Schaeffer, C. M. (2001). Multisystemic treatment of juvenile sexual offenders: A progress report. *Journal of Psychology & Human Sexuality, 13*, 25–42.

Bowlby, J. (1951). Maternal care and mental health. *Bulletin of the World Health Organization, 3*, 355–533.

Brown, S. P., & Leigh, T. V. (1996). A new look at psychological climate and its relationship to job involvement, effort, and performance. *Journal of Applied Psychology, 81*, 125–137.

Burchard, J. D., Bruns, E. J., & Burchard, S. N. (2002). The wraparound approach. In B. J. Burns & K. Hoagwood (Eds.), *Community treatment for youth* (pp. 125–154). Oxford: Oxford University Press.

Burchard, J. D., Burchard, S. N., Sewell, R., & VanDenBerg, J. (1993). *One kid at a time: Evaluative case studies and description of the Alaska Youth Initiative Demonstration Project.* Juneau: State of Alaska, Division of Mental Health and Mental Retardation.

Burg, M. A. (1994). Health problems of sheltered homeless women and their dependent children. *Health & Social Work, 19*, 125–131.

Burke, M. R. (2002). School-based substance abuse prevention: Political finger pointing does not work. *Federal Probation, 66*, 66–71.

Burns, B. J. (1991). Mental health service use by adolescents in the 1970s and 1980s. *Journal of the American Academy of Child and Adolescent Psychiatry, 30* (1), 144–150.

Burns, B. J., Compton, S. N., Egger, H. L., Farmer, E. M. Z., & Robertson, E. B. (2002). In B. J. Burns & K. Hoagwood (Eds.), *Community treatment for youth* (pp. 96–124). Oxford: Oxford University Press.

Burns, B. J., & Friedman, R. M. (1990). Examining the research base for children's mental health services and policy. *Journal of Mental Health Administration, 17*, 87–98.

Burns, B. J., & Hoagwood, K. (Eds.). (2002). *Community treatment for youth.* Oxford: Oxford University Press.

Burns, B. J., Hoagwood, K., & Mrazek, P. J. (1999). Effective treatment for mental disorders in children and adolescents. *Clinical and Family Psychology Review, 2* (4), 199–254.

Butcher, J. N., Dahlstrom, W. G., Graham, J. R., Tellegen, A., & Kaemmer, B. (1989). *MMPI-2: Manual for administration & scoring.* Minneapolis: University of Minnesota Press.

Carr, E. G., Dunlap, G., Horner, R. H., Koegel, R. L., Turnbull, A. P., & Sailor, W. (2002). Positive behavior support: Evolution of an applied science. *Journal of Positive Behavior Interventions, 4*, 4–16.

Casarino, J., Wilner, M., & Maxey, J. (1982). American Association for Partial Hospitalization (AAPH) standards and guidelines for partial hospitalization. *International Journal of Partial Hospitalization, 1*, 5–21.

Cervero, R. (1989). Jobs-housing balancing and regional mobility. *Journal of the American Planning Association, 55*, 136–150.

Cervero, R. (1996). Jobs-housing balance revisited. *Journal of the American Planning Association, 62*, 492–511.

Clark, G. B., Schyve, P. M., Lepoff, R. B., & Ruess, D. T. (1994). Will quality management paradigms of the 1990s survive into the next century? *Clinical Laboratory Management Review, 8*, 426–428, 430–434.

Clements, R. (2002). Psychometric properties of the Substance Abuse Subtle Screening Inventory-3. *Journal of Substance Abuse Treatment, 23* (4), 419–423.

Cohen, J. A., Mannarino, A. P., & Deblinger, E. (2002). *Child and parent trauma-focused cognitive behavior therapy treatment manual.* Pittsburgh: Allegheny General Hospital Center for Traumatic Stress in Children.

Cooke, R. A., & Szumal, J. L. (1993). Measuring normative beliefs and shared behavioral expectations in organizations: The reliability and validity of the Organizational Culture Inventory. *Psychological Reports, 72*, 1299–1330.

Costello, E. J., Angold, A., Burns, B. J., Erkanli, A., Stangl, D. K., & Tweed, D. (1996). The Great Smoky Mountain Study of Youth: Functional impairment and serious emotional disturbance. *Archives of General Psychiatry, 53*, 1137–1143.

Cowal, K., Shinn, M., Weitzman, B. C., Stojanovic, D., & Labay, L. (2002). Mother-child separation among homeless and housed families receiving public assistance in New York City. *American Journal of Community Psychology, 30*, 711–730.

Davis, H. (2000). *Talks my father never had with me* (Vol. 1). Champaign: KJAC Publishing.

Davis, O. W. (2000). *Talks my mother never had with me* (Vol. 1). Champaign: KJAC Publishing.

Dilley, J. (2003, August). *A comparison of the child and adolescent needs and strengths to the CAFAS.* Paper presented at the annual meeting of the American Psychological Association, Toronto.

Dishion, T. J., Bullock, B. M., & Granic, I. (2002). Pragmatism in modeling peer influence: Dynamics, outcomes, and change processes. *Development & Psychopathology, 14*, 969–981.

Drake, R. (2002, November). *Psychiatric rehabilitation and evidence-based medicine.* Carl Taube Award Lecture presented at the meeting of the American Public Health Association, Philadelphia.

Drasgow, F., & Schmitt, N. (Eds.). (2002). *Measuring and analyzing behavior in organizations: Advances in measurement and data analysis.* San Francisco: Jossey-Bass.

Duchnowski, A.J. (1994). Innovative service models: Education. *Journal of Clinical Child Psychology, 23*, 13–18.

Durr, M., Lyons, T.S., & Lichtenstein, G.A. (2000). Identifying the unique needs of urban entrepreneurs: African American skill set development. *Race & Society, 3*, 75–90.

Dwyer, K.P. (2002). Mental health in schools. *Journal of Child and Family Studies, 11* (1), 101–111.

Epstein, M.H., Ryser, G., & Pearson, N. (2002). Standardization of the Behavioral and Emotional Rating Scale: Factor structure, reliability, and criterion validity. *Journal of Behavioral Health Services & Research, 29*, 208–216.

Feinstein, A.R. (1999). Multi-item "instruments" vs. Virginia Apgar's principles of clinimetrics. *Archives of Internal Medicine, 159*, 125–128.

Folk, K.F., & Yi, Y. (1994). Piecing together child care with multiple arrangements: Crazy quilt or preferred pattern for employed parents of preschool children? *Journal of Marriage & the Family, 56*, 669–680.

Frensch, K.M., & Cameron, G. (2002). Treatment of choice or a last resort? A review of residential mental health placements for children and youth. *Child & Family Youth Care Forum, 31* (5), 307–339.

Freud, S. (1938). Three contributions to the theory of sex. In A.A. Britt (Ed.), *The basic writing of Sigmund Freud* (pp. 553–632). New York: Random House.

Friedland, L.A. (2001). Communication, community, and democracy: Toward a theory of communicatively integrated community. *Communication Research, 28*, 358–391.

Gates, G.A. (2000). Clinimetrics of Meniere's disease. *Laryngoscope, 110*, 8–11.

Geller, B. (1991). Psychopharmacology of children and adolescents: Pharmacokinetics and relationships of plasma/serum levels to response. *Psychopharmacology Bulletin, 27*, 401–409.

Glisson, C. (2002). The organizational context of children's mental health services. *Clinical Child and Family Psychology Review, 5*, 233–253.

Glisson, C., & James, L.R. (2002). The cross-level effects of culture and climate in human services teams. *Journal of Organizational Behavior, 23*, 1–28.

Gober, P., McHugh, K.E., & LeClerc, D. (1993). Job-rich but housing-poor. *Professional Geographer, 45* (1), 12–20.

Goffman, E. (1961). *Asylums: Essays on the social situation of mental patients and other inmates.* Cambridge: Harvard University Press.

Goldman, S.K., & Faw, L. (1999). Three wraparound models as promising approaches. In B.J. Burns & S.K. Goldman (Eds.), *Promising practices in wraparound for children with severe emotional disturbance and their families. Systems of care: Promising practices in children's mental health* (1998 Series

Vol. IV, pp. 17–59). Washington, DC: Center for Effective Collaboration and Practice, American Institutes of Research.

Graham-Bermann, S. A., Coupet, S., Egler, L., Mattis, J., & Banyard, V. (1996). Interpersonal relationships and adjustment of children in homeless and economically distressed families. *Journal of Clinical Child Psychology, 25,* 250–261.

Green, R. J., & Framo, J. L. (Eds.). (1981). *Family therapy. Major contributions.* New York: International Universities Press.

Grizenko, N. (1997). Outcome of a multimodal day treatment for children with severe behavior problems: A five-year follow-up. *Journal of the American Academy of Child and Adolescent Psychiatry, 36* (7), 989–997.

Grossman, D. (2001). On killing. II. The psychological cost of learning to kill. *International Journal of Emergency Mental Health, 3,* 137–144.

Habermas, J., & Seidman, S. (1989). *Juergen Habermas on society and politics: A reader.* Frankfort: University of Frankfort.

Hall, G. S. (1883). *The contents of children's minds.*

Harris, T. E. (2002). *Applied organizational communication: Principles and pragmatics for future practice.* Mahwah, NJ: Lawrence Erlbaum Associates.

Hembree, E. A., & Foa, E. B. (2003). Interventions for trauma-related emotional disturbances in adult victims of crime. *Journal of Traumatic Stress, 16,* 187–199.

Henggeler, S. W., Rowland, M. D., Pickrel, S. G., Miller, S. L., Cunningham, P. B., Santos, A. B., Schoenwald, S. K., Randall, J., & Edwards, J. E. (1997). Investigating family-based alternatives to institution-based mental health services for youth: Lessons learned from the pilot study of a randomized field trial. *Journal of Clinical Child Psychology, 26,* 226–233.

Herz, M. J., Ferman, J., & Cohen, M. (1985). Increasing utilization of day hospitals. *Psychiatric Quarterly, 57* (3 & 4), 187–192.

HEW Task Force. (1978). Report of the HEW Task Force on implementation of the report to the president from the President's Commission on Mental Health (DHEW Publication No. [ADM] 79-848). Rockville, MD: Alcohol, Drug Abuse, and Mental Health Administration.

Hoagwood, K., Burns, B. J., Kiser, L., Ringeisen, H., & Schoenwald, S. K. (2001). Evidence-based practice in child and adolescent mental health services. *Psychiatric Services, 52,* 1179–1189.

Hodges, K., & Wotring, J. (2000). Client typology based on functioning across domains using the CAFAS: Implications for service planning. *Journal of Behavioral Health Services & Research, 27,* 257–270.

Hoff, J. I., van Hilten, B. J., & Roos, R. A. (1999). A review of the assessment of dyskinesias. *Movement Disorders, 14,* 737–743.

Hoffman, D., & Rosenheck, R. (2001). Homeless mothers with severe mental illness and their children: Predictors of family reunification. *Psychiatric Rehabilitation Journal, 25,* 163–169.

Howard, K. I., Kopta, M., Krause, M. S., & Orlinsky, D. E. (1986). The dose-effect relationship in psychotherapy. *American Psychologist, 41*, 159–164.

Howard, K. I., Moras, K., Brill, P. L., Martinovich, Z., & Lutz, W. (1996). Evaluation of psychotherapy. Efficacy, effectiveness, and patient progress. *American Psychologist, 51*, 1059–1064.

Hussey, D. L., & Guo, S. (2002). Profile characteristics and behavioral change trajectories of young residential children. *Journal of Child & Family Studies, 11* (4), 401–410.

James, B. (1989). *Treating traumatized children: New insights and creative interventions.* New York: Free Press.

Jensen, P. S. (1998). Ethical and pragmatic issues in the use of psychotropic agents in young children. *Canadian Journal of Psychiatry—Reveu Canadienne de Psychiatrie, 43*, 585–588.

Joint Commission on the Mental Health of Children. (1969). *Action for Mental Health for Children.* New York: Basic Books.

Jones, A. P., & James, L. R. (1979). Psychological climate: Dimensions of individual and aggregated work environment perceptions. *Organizational Behavior and Human Performance, 23*, 201–250.

Kanner, L. *Child psychiatry.* Springfield, IL: Thomas.

Kazdin, A. E., & Weisz, J. R. (1998). Identifying and developing empirically supported child and adolescent treatments. *Journal of Consulting and Clinical Psychology, 66*, 19–36,

Kihlstroem, A., & Israel, J. (2002). Communicative or strategic action—an examination of fundamental issues in the theory of communicative action. *International Journal of Social Welfare, 11*, 210–218.

Knitzer, J. (1982). *Unclaimed children: The failure of public responsibility to children and adolescents in need of mental health services.* Washington, DC: Child Defense League.

Koike, A. K., Unutzer, J., & Wells, K. B. (2002). Improving the care for depression in patients with comorbid medical illness. *American Journal of Psychiatry, 158*, 1738–1745.

Krulish, L. H. (2002). A basic and practical overview of the six steps of outcome-based quality improvement: Part 2. *Home Healthcare Nurse, 20*, 585–586.

Kuhn, T. S. (1962). *The structure of scientific revolution.* Chicago: University of Chicago Press.

Lambert, E. W., Brannan, A. M., Breda, C., Heflinger, C. A., & Bickman, L. (1998). Common patterns of service use in children's mental health. *Evaluation and Program Planning, 21*, 47–57.

Lambert, M. J., Ogles, B. M., & Masters, K. S. (2000). Choosing outcome assessment devices: An organizational and conceptual scheme. *Journal of Counseling & Development, 70*, 527–532.

LeCroy, C. W., & Ashford, J. B. (1992). Children's mental health: Current findings and research directions. *Social Work Research & Abstracts, 28*, 13–30.

Leon, S.C., Uziel-Miller, N.D., Lyons, J.S., & Tracy, P. (1999). Psychiatric hospital utilization of children and adolescents in state custody. *Journal of the American Academy of Child and Adolescent Psychiatry, 38,* 305–310.

Leon, S.C., Lyons, J.S., Uziel-Miller, N.D. (2000). Variations in clinical presentations of children and adolescents across eight psychiatric hospitals. *Psychiatric Services, 51,* 786–790.

Leon, S.C., Lyons, J.S., Uziel-Miller, N.D., Rawal, P., Tracy, P., Williams, J. (2001). Evaluating the use of psychiatric hospitalization by residential treatment. *Journal of American Academy of Child and Adolescent Psychiatry, 39,* 1496–1501.

Lichtenstein, G.A., & Lyons, T.S. (1996). *Incubating new enterprises. A guide to successful practice.* Washington, DC: The Aspen Institute Rural Economic Policy Program.

Lichtenstein, G.A., & Lyons, T.S. (2001). The Entrepreneurial Development System: Transforming business talent and community economies. *Economic Development Quarterly, 15,* 3–20.

Lichtman, D.M., & Appleman, K.A. (1995). Measures of effectiveness: A methodology of integrating planning, measurement, and continuous improvement. *Military Medicine, 160,* 189–193.

LoSasso, A.T., & Lyons, J.S. (2002). The effects of copayments on substance abuse treatment expenditures and treatment reoccurrence. *Psychiatric Services, 53,* 1605–1611.

Lueger, R.J., Howard, K.I., Martinovich, Z., Lutz, W., Anderson, E.E., & Grissom, G. (2001). Assessing treatment progress of individual patients using expected treatment response models. *Journal of Consulting and Clinical Psychology, 69,* 150–158.

Lyman, R.D., & Campbell, N.R. (1996). Treating children and adolescents in residential and inpatient settings. *Developmental Clinical Psychology and Psychiatry, 36,* 1–149.

Lyons, J.S. (1998). *The Severity and Acuity of Psychiatric Illness. Child and Adolescent Version.* San Antonio, TX: The Psychological Corporation.

Lyons, J.S., Baerger, D.R., Quigley, P., Erlich, J., & Griffin, G. (2001). Mental health service needs of juvenile offenders: A comparison of detention, incarceration, and treatment settings. *Children's Services: Social Policy, Research, & Practice, 4,* 69–85.

Lyons, J.S., Griffin, G., Jenuwine, M., Shasha, M., & Quintenz, S. (2003). The mental health juvenile justice initiative: Clinical and forensic outcomes for a state-wide program. *Psychiatric Services, 54,* 1629–1634.

Lyons, J.S., Howard, K.I., O'Mahoney, M.T., & Lish, J. (1997). *The measurement and management of clinical outcomes in mental health.* New York: John Wiley & Sons.

Lyons, J.S., Kisiel, C.L., Dulcan, M., Cohen, R., & Chesler, P. (1997). Crisis assessment and psychiatric hospitalization of children and adolescents in state custody. *Journal of Child and Family Studies, 6,* 311–320.

Lyons, J.S., MacIntyre, J.C., Lee, M.E., Carpinello, S., Zuber, M.P., & Fazio, M.L. (2004). Psychotropic medication prescription patterns for children and adolescents in New York: Public mental health system. *Community Mental Health*, 40, 101–118.

Lyons, J.S., Mintzer, L.L., Kisiel, C.L., & Shallcross, H. (1998). Understanding the mental health needs of children and adolescents in residential treatment. *Professional Psychology: Research and Practice*, 29, 582–587.

Lyons, J.S., Rawal, P., Yeh, I., Leon, S., & Tracy, P. (2002). Use of measurement audit in outcomes management. *Journal of Behavioral Health Services & Research*, 29, 75–80.

Lyons, J.S., & Shallcross, H. (2000). *The needs and strengths of children and adolescents served by the public mental health system in New York State. Report to the New York Office of Mental Health* [On-line]. Winnetka, IL: Buddin Praed Foundation. Available: www.buddinpraed.org

Lyons, J.S., Stutesman, J., Neme, J., Vessey, J.T., O'Mahoney, M.T., & Camper, H.J. (1997). Predicting psychiatric emergency admissions and hospital outcomes. *Medical Care*, 35, 792–800.

Lyons, J.S., Terry, P., Martinovich, Z., Petersen, J., & Bouska, B. (2001). Outcome trajectories for adolescents in residential treatment: A statewide evaluation. *Journal of Child and Family Studies*, 10, 333–345.

Lyons, J.S., Uziel-Miller, N.D., Reyes, F., & Sokol, P.T. (2000). The strengths of children and adolescents in residential settings: Prevalence and associations with psychopathology and discharge placement. *Journal of the Academy of Child and Adolescent Psychiatry*, 39, 176–181.

Manderscheid, R.W., Henderson, M.J., Witkin, M.J., & Atay, J.E. (2000). The U.S. mental health system of the 1990s: The challenges of managed care. *International Journal of Law & Psychiatry*, 23, 245–259.

Manning, W.G., Jr., Wells, K.B., & Benjamin, B. (1987). Use of outpatient mental health services over time in a health maintenance organization and fee-for-service plan. *American Journal of Psychiatry*, 144, 283–287.

Marx, R.G., Bombardier, C., Hogg-Johnson, S., & Wright, J.G. (2000). Clinimetric and psychometric strategies for development of a health measurement scale. *Journal of Clinical Epidemiology*, 52, 105–111.

Maxey, J.T. (1979). Partial hospitalization: A review of growth and development in the United States. *Community Mental Health Review*, 4 (4), 1–8.

McFarland B.H., Khorramzadeh S., Millius R., & Mahler, J. (2002). Psychiatric hospital length of stay for Medicaid clients before and after managed care. *Administration & Policy in Mental Health*, 29 (3), 191–199.

McKnight, J.L., & Kretzmann, J.P. (1993). *Building communities from the inside out: A path towards finding and mobilizing a community's assets.* Evanston, IL: Northwestern University, Institute for Policy Research.

Mosier, J., Burlingame, G.M., Wells, M.G., Ferre, R., Latkowski, M., Johansen, J., Peterson, G., & Walton, E. (2001). In-home, family-centered psychiatric treatment for high-risk children and youth. *Children's Services: Social Policy, Research, & Practice, 4,* 51–68.

Musso, D. F. (2002). History of child psychiatry. In M. Lewis (Ed.), *Child and adolescent psychiatry* (pp. 1446–1449). Philadelphia: Lippincott Williams, & Wilkins.

Narrow, W. E., Reiger, D. A., Goodman, S. H., Rae, D. S., Roper, M. T., Bourdon, K. H., Hoven, C., & Moor, R. (1998). A comparison of federal definitions of severe mental illness among children and adolescents in four communities. *Psychiatric Services, 49,* 1601–1608.

National Center on Family Homelessness. (1999). *Homeless children: America's new outcasts.* Newton, MA: National Center on Homelessness.

National Institute of Mental Health, Survey and Reports Branch, Division of Biometry. (1974). *Alcohol, drug abuse, and mental health administration, state and regional data, federally funded community health centers.* Bethesda, MD: Author.

National Institutes of Research. (1994). *Volume III: The role of education in a system of care: Effectively serving children with emotional or behavioral disorders* [On-line]. Available: http://cecp.air.org/resources/ntlagend.html

National Institutes of Research. (1998). *National agenda for achieving better results for children and youth with serious emotional disturbance* [On-line]. Available: http://cecp.air.org/promisingpractices/1998monographs/execsumvol3.htm

New Freedom Commission on Mental Health. (2003). *Achieving the promise: Transforming mental health care in America* (SMA 03-3832). Rockville, MD: Substance Abuse and Mental Health Services Administration.

Nierman, P., & Lyons, J. (2001). State mental health policy: Shifting resources to the community: Closing the Illinois State Psychiatric Hospital for Children in Chicago. *Psychiatric Services, 52* (9), 1157–1159.

Nordness, P. D., & Epstein, M. H. (2003). Reliability of the Wraparound Observation Form—second version: An instrument designed to assess the fidelity of the wraparound approach. *Mental Health Services Research, 5,* 89–96.

Nunnally, J. (1976). *Psychometric theory.* New York: John Wiley & Sons.

Nurcombe, B., & Gallagher, R. M. (1986). *The clinical process in psychiatry: Diagnosis and management planning.* London: Cambridge University Press.

Ogles, B. M., Lambert, M. J., & Masters, K. S. (1996). *Assessing outcome in clinical practice.* Needham Heights, MA: Ally & Bacon, Inc.

Oswald, D. P., Cohen, R., Best, A. M., Jensen, C. E., & Lyons, J. S. (2001). Child strengths and level of care for children with emotional and behavioral disorders. *Journal of Emotional and Behavioral Disorders, 9,* 192–199.

Popper, M. (2003). Narcissism and attachment patterns of personalized and socialized charismatic leaders. *Journal of Social & Personal Relationships, 19,* 797–809.

Rawal, P., Lyons, J.S., MacIntyre, J., & Hunter, J.C. (2004). Regional variations and clinical indicators of antipsychotic use in residential treatment: A four state comparison. *Journal of Behavioral Health Services and Research, 31*, 178–189.

Rawal, P., Romansky, J., & Lyons, J.S. (2003, June). *Reducing racial disparities in psychiatric hospital admissions of children.* Paper presented at the American Health Services Association, Nashville, TN.

Reeder, T., Locascio, E., Tucker, J., Czaplijski, T., Benson, N., & Meggs, W. (2002). ED utilization: The effect of changing demographics from 1992 to 2000. *American Journal of Emergency Medicine, 20* (7), 583–587.

Reiger, D.A., & Burke, J.D. (1987). Psychiatric disorders in the community: The Epidemiological Catchment Area study. R.E. Hales & A.J. Frances (Eds.). *American Psychiatric Association Annual Review, 6,* 610–624.

Rautkis, M., & Sliefert, D. (2002). *The treatment of fidelity index for the child and adolscent needs and strengths.* Paper presented to the Louis de la Parte Florida Mental Health Institute, Tampa, March.

Robertson, M.J. (1991). Homeless women with children. *American Psychologist, 46,* 1198–1204.

Rones, M., & Hoagwood, K. (2000). School-based mental health services: A research review. *Clinical Child and Family Psychology Review, 3,* 233–241.

Rosen, L.D., & Weil, M.M. (1996). Easing the transition from paper to computer-based system. In T. Trabin (Ed.), *The computerization of behavioral healthcare. How to enhance clinical practice, management, and communications* (pp. 87–107). San Francisco: Jossey-Bass.

Rosenberg, M. (1965). *Society and the adolescent self-image.* Princeton, NJ: Princeton University Press.

Rosenblatt, A. (1993). In home, in school, and out of trouble. *Journal of Child and Family Studies. 2,* 275–282.

Rost, J., & Langeheine, R. (1997). *Applications of latent train and latent class models in the social sciences.* New York: Waxmann Publishing Co.

Saunders, B.E., Berliner, L., & Hanson, R.F. (Eds.). (2003). *Child physical and sexual abuse: Guidelines for treatment (Final report: 1/15/2003)* [On-line]. Charleston, SC: National Crime Victims Research and Treatment Center. Available: www.musc.edu/cvc/

Sawicki, D.S., & Moody, M. (2000). Developing transportation alternatives for welfare recipients moving to work. *Journal of the American Planning Association, 66* (3), 306–318.

Scarr, S., Phillips, D., & McCartney, K., (1991). Working mothers and their families. In M.E.S. Chess & Hertzig (Eds.), *Annual progress in child psychiatry and child development* (pp. 261–278). Philadelphia: Brunner/Magel.

Schiff, G.D., & Goldfield, N.I. (1994). Deming meets Braverman: Toward a progressive analysis of the continuous quality improvement paradigm. *International Journal of Health Services, 24,* 655–673.

Scott, T.M., & Eber, L. (2003). Functional assessment and wraparound as systemic school processes: Primary, secondary, and tertiary systems examples. *Journal of Positive Behavior Interventions, 5,* 131–143.

Senge, P.M. (1990). *The fifth discipline: The art and practice of the learning organization.* New York: Doubleday.

Shaften, D., Gould, M.S., Brasie, J., Ambrosini, P., Fisher, P., Bird, H., & Aluwahlia, S. (1983). A children's global assessment scale (CGAS). *Archives of General Psychiatry, 40,* 1228–1231.

Shen, Q. (2001). A spatial analysis of job openings and access in a U.S. metropolitan area. *Journal of the American Planning Association, 67* (1), 53–68.

Sherman, L., Gottfredson, D., Mackenzie, D.L., Eck, J., Reuter, P., & Bushway, S.D. (1998). *Preventing crime: What works, what doesn't, what's promising. A report to the United States Congress for the National Institute of Justice.* Washington, DC: National Institute of Justice.

Simpson, D.D., & Brown, B.S. (2002). Transferring research to practice. *Journal of Substance Abuse Treatment, 22,* 171–182.

Sokol, A. (1989). Early mental health intervention in combat situations: The USS Stark. *Military Medicine, 154,* 407–409.

Sondheimer, D., Schoenwald, S.K., & Rowland, M. (1994). Alternatives to hospitalization of youth with serious emotional disturbance. *Journal of Clinical Child Psychology, 23,* 7–12.

Sondheimer, J.M. (1994). Gastroesophageal reflux in children. Clinical presentation and diagnostic evaluation. *Gastrointestinal Endoscopy Clinics in North America, 4,* 55–74.

Spence, M.A. (1973). Market signaling. *Quarterly Journal of Economics, 87* (3), 355–374.

Steinwachs, D.M., Flynn, L.M., Norquist, G., & Skinner, E.A. (Eds.). (1996). *Using client outcomes information to improve mental health and substance abuse treatment.* San Francisco: Jossey-Bass.

Stone, M., Salonen, D., Lax, M., Payne, U., Lapp, V., & Inman, R. (2001). Clinical and imaging correlates of response to treatment with infliximab in patients with ankylosing spondylitis. *Journal of Rheumatology, 28,* 1605–1614.

Stone, W.E. (1997). Residential treatment centers for youth. In R.K. Schreter & S.S. Shartskin (Eds.), *Managing care, not dollars: The continuum of mental health services* (pp. 139–150). Washington, DC: American Psychiatric Press.

Stovell, K. (Ed.). (1999). *Prevention programs for youth: A guide to outcomes evaluation, successful funding.* Providence, RI: Manisses Communications Group.

Strange, J.M., & Mumford, M.D. (2002). The origins of vision: Charismatic versus ideological leadership. *Leadership Quarterly, 13,* 343–377.

Stroul, B. A. (1993). *Systems of care for children and adolescents with severe emotional disturbances: What are the results?* Washington, DC: Georgetown University Child Development Center.

Stroul, B. A., & Friedman, R. M. (1986). *A system of care for severely emotionally disturbed children and youth.* Washington, DC: Georgetown University Child Development Center.

Szasz, T. S. (1974). *The myth of mental illness. Foundations of a theory of personal conduct.* New York: Harper & Row.

Taube, C. A., Kessler, L. G., & Burns, B. J. (1986). Estimating the probability and level of ambulatory mental health service use. *Health Services Research, 21*, 321–340.

Timmer, S. G., & Urquiza, A. J. (1996). Parent-child interaction therapy: An intensive dyadic intervention for physically abusive families. *Child Maltreatment, 1* (2), 132–141.

Towler, A. J. (2003). Effects of charismatic influence training on attitudes, behavior, and performance. *Personnel Psychology, 56*, 363–381.

Tyler, T., Rasinski, K. A., & Spodick, N. (1985). Influence of voice on satisfaction with leaders: Exploring the meaning of process control. *Journal of Personality and Social Psychology, 48*, 72–81.

U.S. Surgeon General. (1999). *Mental health: A report to the Surgeon General.* Washington, DC: Department of Health and Human Services.

U.S. Surgeon General. (2001a). *Mental health: Culture, race, and ethnicity supplement.* Washington, DC: Department of Health and Human Services.

U.S. Surgeon General. (2001b) *Report of the United States Surgeon General's Conference on Children's Mental Health: A national action agenda.* Washington, DC: Department of Health and Human Services.

VanDenBerg, J., & Grealish, E. M. (1998). *The wraparound process* [Training manual]. Pittsburgh: Author.

Vernberg, E. M., Roberts, M. C., & Nyre, J. E. (2002). School-based intensive mental health treatment. In D. Marsh & M. Fristad (Eds.), *Handbook of serious emotional disturbance in children and adolescents* (pp. 412–427). New York: John Wiley & Sons.

Vessey, J. T., Howard, K. I., Lueger, R. J., & Kaechele, H. (1994). The clinician's illusion and the psychotherapy practice: An application of stochastic modeling. *Journal of Consulting and Clinical Psychology, 62*, 679–685.

Vitiello, B., & Jensen, P. S. (1995). Developmental perspectives in pediatric psychopharmacology. *Psychopharmacology Bulletin, 31*, 75–81.

Webster-Stratton, C., Hollinsworth, T., & Kolpacoff, M. (1989). The long-term effectiveness and clinical significance of three cost-effective training programs for families with conduct-problem children. *Journal of Consulting and Clinical Psychology, 57*, 550–553.

Webster-Stratton, C., Kolpacoff, M., & Hollinsworth, T. (1988). Self-administered videotaped therapy for families with conduct-problem children: Comparison with two cost effective treatments and a control group. *Journal of Consulting and Clinical Psychology, 56,* 558–566.

Wells, K. (1991). Placement of emotionally disturbed children in residential treatment: A review of placement criteria. *American Journal of Orthopsychiatry, 61,* 339–347.

Weintraub, P., Pynoos, R.S., & Hall, H.L. (2001). Columbine High School shootings: Community response. In M. Shafii & S.L. Shaffi (Eds.), *School violence: Assessment, management, and prevention.* Washington, DC: American Psychiatric Press.

Weiss, B., Catron, T., Harris, V., & Phung, T.M. (1999). The effectiveness of traditional child psychotherapy. *Journal of Consulting and Clinical Psychology, 67,* 82–94.

Weisz, J.R., & Jensen, P.S. (1999). Efficacy and effectiveness of child and adolescent psychotherapy and pharmacotherapy. *Mental Health Services Research, 1* (3), 125–157.

White, W.J. (2001). A communication model of conceptual innovation in science. *Communication Theory, 11,* 290–314.

Whitelaw, C.A., & Perez, E.L. (1987). Partial hospitalization programs: A current perspective. *Administration in Mental Health, 15* (2), 62–72.

Whittaker, J.K. (2000). Reinventing residential child care: An agenda for research and practice. *Residential Treatment for Children and Youth, 17,* 13–30.

Williams, J.B.W., Karls, J.M., & Wandrei, K. (1989). The person-in-environment (PIE) system for describing problems of social functioning. *Hospital and Community Psychiatry, 40,* 1125–1127.

Wolmer, L., Laor, N., & Yazgan, Y. (2003). School reactivation programs after disaster: Could teachers serve as clinical mediators? *Child and Adolescent Psychiatric Clinics of North America, 12,* 363–381.

Yehuda, R. (Ed.). (2002). *Treating trauma survivors with PTSD.* Washington, DC: American Psychiatric Press.

Zimet, S.G., & Farley, G.K. (1985). Day treatment for children in the United States. *Journal of the American Academy of Child Psychiatry, 24,* 732–738.

Zito, J.M., Safer, D.J., DosReis, S., Gardner, J.F., Boles, M., & Lynch, F. (2000). Trends in the prescribing of psychotropic medications to preschoolers. *Journal of the American Medical Association, 283* (8), 1025–1030.

Zito, J.M., Safer, D.J., DosReis, S., Gardner, J.F., Magder, L., Soeken, K., Boles, M., Lynch, F., & Riddle, M.A. (2003). Psychotropic practice patterns for youth: A 10 year perspective. *Archives of Pediatric Adolescent Medicine, 157,* 17–25.

Zyzanski, S.J., & Perloff, E. (1999). Clinimetrics and psychometrics work hand in hand. *Archives of Internal Medicine, 159,* 1816–1817.

INDEX

About the Series Editor
and Advisory Board

CHRIS E. STOUT, Psy.D., M.B.A., holds a joint governmental and academic appointment at Northwestern University Medical School, and serves as Illinois's first chief of Psychological Services. He served as a nongovernment special representative to the United Nations, was appointed by the U.S. Department of Commerce as a Baldridge examiner, and served as an advisor to the White House for both political parties. Dr. Stout was appointed to the World Economic Forum's Global Leaders of Tomorrow. He has published and presented more than 300 papers and 29 books, and his works have been translated into six languages. Dr. Stout has lectured across the nation and internationally in 16 countries, visiting more than 60 nations. He has been on missions around the world and has summated three of the World's Seven Summits.

BRUCE E. BONECUTTER, Ph.D., is director of Behavioral Services at the Elgin Community Mental Health Center, the Illinois Department of Human Services state hospital that serves adults in greater Chicago. He is also a clinical assistant professor of Psychology at the University of Illinois at Chicago. A clinical psychologist specializing in health, consulting, and forensic psychology, Dr. Bonecutter is also a longtime member of the American Psychological Association Taskforce on Children & the Family.

JOSEPH FLAHERTY, M.D., is chief of Psychiatry at the University of Illinois Hospital, a professor of Psychiatry at the University of Illinois College of Medicine, and a professor of Community Health Science at the University of Illinois at Chicago College of Public Health. He is a founding member of the Society for the Study of Culture and Psychiatry. Dr. Flaherty has been a consultant to the World Health Organization, the National Institutes of Mental Health, and the Falk Institute in Jerusalem.

MICHAEL HOROWITZ, Ph.D., is president and professor of Clinical Psychology at the Chicago School of Professional Psychology, one of the nation's leading not-for-profit graduate schools of psychology. Earlier, he served as dean and professor of the Arizona School of Professional Psychology. A clinical psychologist practicing independently since 1987, his work has focused on psychoanalysis, intensive individual therapy, and couples therapy. Dr. Horowitz has provided Disaster Mental Health Services to the American Red Cross. His special interests include the study of fatherhood.

SHELDON I. MILLER, M.D., is a professor of Psychiatry at Northwestern University, and director of the Stone Institute of Psychiatry at Northwestern Memorial Hospital. He is also director of the American Board of Psychiatry and Neurology, director of the American Board of Emergency Medicine, and director of the Accreditation Council for Graduate Medical Education. Dr. Miller is also an examiner for the American Board of Psychiatry and Neurology. He is founding editor of the *American Journal of Addictions*, and founding chairman of the American Psychiatric Association's Committee on Alcoholism.

DENNIS P. MORRISON, Ph.D., is chief executive officer at the Center for Behavioral Health in Indiana, the first behavioral health company ever to win the JCAHO Codman Award for excellence in the use of outcomes management to achieve health care quality improvement. He is president of the Board of Directors for the Community Healthcare Foundation in Bloomington, and has been a member of the Board of Directors for the American College of Sports Psychology. Dr. Morrison has served as a consultant to agencies including the Ohio Department of Mental Health, Tennessee Association of Mental Health Organizations, Oklahoma Psychological Association, the

North Carolina Council of Community Mental Health Centers, and the National Center for Health Promotion in Michigan.

WILLIAM H. REID, M.D., M.P.H., is a clinical and forensic psychiatrist, and consultant to attorneys and courts throughout the United States. He is a clinical professor of Psychiatry at the University of Texas Health Science Center. Dr. Reid is also an adjunct professor of Psychiatry at Texas A&M College of Medicine and Texas Tech University School of Medicine, as well as a clinical faculty member at the Austin Psychiatry Residency Program. He is chairman of the Scientific Advisory Board and medical advisor to the Texas Depressive & Manic-Depressive Association, as well as an examiner for the American Board of Psychiatry & Neurology. Dr. Reid has served as president of the American Academy of Psychiatry and the Law, as chairman of the Research Section for an international conference on the Psychiatric Aspects of Terrorism, and as medical director for the Texas Department of Mental Health and Mental Retardation.About the Series Editor and Advisory Board.

About the Author

JOHN S. LYONS is professor of Psychiatry and Community Medicine at Northwestern University's Feinberg School of Medicine, and director of the University's Mental Health Services and Policy Program.